THE ENGLISH
FLOWER GARDEN

THE ENGLISH
FLOWER GARDEN
AND HOME GROUNDS

Design and Arrangement shown by existing
examples of Gardens in Great Britain and Ireland
by W. ROBINSON

Author of *The Wild Garden*

Edited with an Introduction by Peter King

BLOOMSBURY

BLOOMSBURY GARDENING CLASSICS

Editorial Advisory Board

This edition first published in Great Britain 1996
Bloomsbury Publishing Plc, 38 Soho Square, London W1V 5DF

copyright © William Robinson

The moral right of the author has been asserted

First published 1883

A CIP catalogue record for this book is available
from the British Library

ISBN 0 7475 3008 4

10 9 8 7 6 5 4 3 2 1

Typeset by Hewer Text Composition Services, Edinburgh
Printed by Clays Limited, St Ives plc

CONTENTS

FOREWORDS TO NEW EDITION

This book is the muster of various once forlorn hopes and skirmishing parties now united with better arms and larger aims, and its beginnings may have an interest for others. I came to London just when the Royal Horticultural Society's garden at Kensington was being laid out, a series of elaborate patterns set at different levels, and the Crystal Palace, in its glory, was described by the Press of the day to be the most wonderful instance of modern gardening—water-temples, water-paths, vast stone basins and all the theatrical gardening of Versailles reproduced in Surrey.

There was little or no reason admitted into garden design: the same poor imitation of the Italian garden being set down in all sorts of positions. If the place did not suit the style, the ground had to be bolstered up in some way so that the plan might be carried out—a costly way to get an often ridiculous result. The great writers of the past had laughed the carpenter's rule out of the parks of England, and pictures arose where they were once impossible; but the ugliness of the garden about the house was assumed to be an essential part of the thing itself, removing that for ever from the sympathies of artistic people.

The flower garden planting was made up of a few kinds of flowers which people were proud to put out in thousands and tens of thousands, and with these, patterns, more or less elaborate, were carried out in every garden save the very poorest cottage garden. It was not easy to get away from all this false and hideous "art," but I was then in the Botanic Gardens, Regent's Park, where there was at that time a small garden of British plants, which had to be kept up, and this led me into the varied country round London, from the orchid-flecked meadows of

Bucks to the tumbled down undercliffs on the Essex coast, untroubled by the plough; and so I began to get an idea (which should be taught to every boy at school) that there was (for gardens even) much beauty in our native flowers and trees, and then came the thought that if there was so much in our own island flora, what might we not look for from the hills and valleys of the countries of the northern and temperate world?

From thoughts of this kind if I turned to actual things, I saw the flower-gardener meanly trying to rival the tile or wallpaper men, and throwing aside with contempt all the lovely things that through their height or form did not conform to this idea (so stupid as to life), and this too the rule, not only in the villa garden, but in our great public and private gardens. There was, happily, always the beauty of the woods and lanes and the lovely cottage gardens in the country round London, and here and there, though rare, a quiet garden with things as the great mother made them and grouped them. And so I began to see clearly that the common way was a great error and the greatest obstacle to true gardening or artistic effects of any kind in the flower-garden or home landscape, and then, made up my mind to fight the thing out in any way open to me.

The English Flower Garden deals with the question of design—the aim being to make the garden a reflex of the beauty of the great garden of the world itself, and to prove that the true way to happiest design is not to have any stereotyped style for all flower gardens, but that the best kind of garden should arise out of its site and conditions as happily as a primrose out of a cool bank.

This is not a botanical book, as should be clear from its title; but some may expect in the book technical terms which I wish to keep out of it. Although the debt of the gardener to Botany is great, the subordination of the garden to Botany has been fruitful of the greatest evil to artistic gardening. The way of arranging a garden like a book, and a very ugly book, as in the French botanic gardens (Caen, Angers, Rouen), in which one sees a sea of showy labels, where one might look for the life and peace of a garden, is a blinding obstacle to beautiful gardening, and the Garden of Plants, in Paris, may be cited as one having had for ages a disastrous effect in the gardening of France. It is the spirit of natural beauty we should seek to win into the garden, and so get away from the set patterns on the one hand, and labelled "dots" on the other.

English names are given where possible—as it is best to speak of things growing about our doors in our own tongue, and the practice of using in conversation long Latin names, a growth of our own century, has done infinite harm to gardening in shutting out people who have a heart for a garden, but none for the Latin of the gardener. There is no more need to speak of the plants in our gardens by their Latin names than to speak of the dove or the rabbit by Latin names, and where we introduce plants that have no good English names we must make them as well as we may. Old English books like Gerard were rich in English names, and we should follow their ways and be ashamed to use for things in the garden a strange tongue—dog Latin, or as it may be. Every plant grown in gardens should have an English name, among the many reasons for this being the frequent changes that Latin names undergo in the breaking down of the characters which are supposed to separate genera. For instance, Azalea and Rhododendron are now one genus; such changes are even more troublesome when they occur in less well-known plants; and one of the most beautiful plants of our gardens, the Irish Heath (Dabœcia, now Boretta), will not be found now by its hitherto recorded name in the London Catalogue of British Plants. But if we have a good English name, these ceaseless botanical changes are of less consequence. It is impossible for gardeners and nurserymen to keep up with such changes, not always indeed accepted even by botanists themselves. The fact that in speaking of plants we use English names does not in the least prevent us from using the Latin name in its right place, when we have need to do so. The systematic nomenclature followed is that of the Kew list, wherever use does not compel us to adhere to old names like Azalea.

PREFACE TO NEW EDITION

The first editions of this book were burdened with much about the ways of flower-gardening current at the time; many thousands of plants set out in May or early June in formal and geometrical array, the result a bad carpet. Experience has taught me to throw overboard all tender plants and devote the book to hardy things only, that may be planted in the open air on every fine day in the fall or winter.

Tropical weeds that give a little showy colour for a few months and plants that do not flower in cold districts if at all; coarse herbs that rob the ground and give little return in beauty; palms never at home in look in our clime. This is not a theory but a record of what took place in my garden for many years past.

As this book is now to be given to hardy trees and flowers, we begin at once with the work and with the home landscape. As the use of hardy flowers only is urged, an example is given of my flower garden planted that way every fall.

One of the first things the lover of flower gardening should do is to get a clear idea of the distinction between gardening and botany. Gardening is an inexhaustible art; botany is a world science, and the great mistake is to consider gardening from the point of view of the botanist. To the botanist every plant, weed or poisonous herb is of equal value, which is right from his point of view, but the gardener must be very careful not to take that view. Numbers of plants which have lately come to us from China are useless for the garden, though, along with them, there are beautiful garden plants. The old botanic gardens of Europe were often planned as though the garden were a sort of book, and we see the results of this in many gardens abroad. It is neither artistic nor natural. Where garden space is often limited and labour scarce, the garden should only be given to plants of garden value. It is impossible to get the world's flora represented in it, and a garden made by a collector is rarely beautiful. Colour, stature and form should come before any botanical consideration. Even beautiful plants like the Clematis, Honeysuckle, etc., may be found after trial to be, many of them, not worthy of a place in the garden compared with others. The gardener is very much indebted to the botanist for his own work, that is the naming of plants, and also for discovering new species of plants. Botany teaches us the native habitats of some of our most beautiful garden plants, also about the flora of many countries, and can teach us many lessons which can be learnt with great pleasure, but there cannot be any proper system of teaching young men gardening unless they are taught the plants of their own country. When it comes to design and landscape gardening one may learn more in some of the back valleys of the Tyrol and parts of Switzerland than from any book, though books on the flora of countries like our own as to climate may tell us what we want to know about the habitats of the plants and trees we wish to know.

"Lumping" is a term sometimes used for botanists throwing things together that are distinct in life or cultivation. Botanists often work in herbaria so that things come together that in cultivation in the living state are really different. An example of this is placing the Austrian and Corsican pines under one species, whereas in Nature and in cultivation they are clearly distinct in form and stature. In botanical books we frequently find changes of genera made often without much reason. This shows the need for an English name. Not only is it difficult to follow the changes in Latin names in many cases, but these names are also very ugly and awkward, as, for example, *pseudo-tsuga* applied to one of the greatest of trees.

Botanical books are often empty as regards the garden value of plants. Great works, like those of Don and Miller, afford us no guidance for the garden value. The objection does not apply to the floras of countries which may be rich in plants and trees of value.

So many things are coming from strange countries to our gardens that one is often led to plant shrubs that have but little chance of doing well. I thought myself very careful not to plant what I did not know to be quite hardy, and so came my mistakes with even hardy plants that did not flower well. The Rose of Sharon, which is beautiful in France and also in our country, I planted a large group of. It grew well for many years, but never flowered, and seeing it was hopeless, I gave it to a friend in the Thames Valley, where it grew and flowered well. In the southern part of Sussex it flowers admirably. The Winter's Bark, of the Straits of Magellan grew and flowered well for a few years and then was suddenly cut to the ground by a hard frost. Clianthus, which does very well near the coast-line of Ireland and the West Country, died after trials, and several Mutisias, too, which Mr Beamish, in Cork, grows so well, and no doubt many others in Devonshire, died without much loss of time.

What is the good of risking such things when there are many plants of N. America and other lands which are really hardy? It is not only the difference between Aberdeen and Worthing one has to think of; it is the much wider one of things in the same county. Some plants that failed with me do thrive below the Downs. The soil is a thing to be reckoned with, and no doubt my soil on a cool hill was against the Rose of Sharon, which, perhaps, a hundred miles further north, on a free soil, would be quite happy.

EVILS OF GRAFTING IN ENGLISH AND AMERICAN GARDENS

Disastrous for all lands, to me the art of grafting is most so in England, as ours is the country of the Rose in continuous bloom.

In New England, or in Italy, Canada and other countries, where the Rose bloom is burnt up in the summer heat, in our cool land she goes on in her beauty all the summer. In my garden we have Roses in all their beauty from June until well into October. One gets this only when the Rose is growing on its natural root.

This prolonged bloom is the greatest gain. One evil of grafting is a short life. On their natural root they will live as long as men do now, but on the grafted stock the life is a short one. Some Roses never show their beauty in a grafted state. I never knew what a fine Rose Madame Hoste was until I saw it growing in the station yard where there was no clay near. Pharisaer, a beautiful Rose, was deformed on the briar and had to be thrown away in a few years. On its natural root it is a lovely and stately Rose for many years.

In cold and mountain districts which might be thought more difficult for the Rose, the best way is to grow the Rose on its natural root. In warm countries there is the greater need for the natural root. Various stocks have been tried: Japanese and one or two others. The Manetti paralyses the Rose worked upon it. None of these stocks are in value equal to the natural root.

The first thing to do is to get rid of some delusions, the first being that the Dog Briar is the best stock to graft on. It is in very general use, and it is quite useless to fight against the trade practice. The true way for the Rose lover is to put Rose cuttings in in September, or, where the soil is warm, a little later even. Where nurserymen care for the propagation of the Rose they could do it in glass houses in the winter. Very many stocks have been tried, but growth and maturance are never the same as on the natural root.

The next delusion to get rid of is the mulching of manure on the surface of the Rose bed. The only reason for this heavy mulching is that the Dog Rose has to be fed. In my own garden I never use this at all. It is a most unpleasant practice in sight of the house, so in place of it I use living plants: Viola, Mignonette, Shamrock Pea, and some of the beautiful annuals of California, which, if they escape the slugs in the winter, give us very beautiful results.

The next delusion is that the plants must be pruned late in the spring, April, say, so that they are left all the winter to be knocked about by storms and frosts. This habit is given as law in every Rose book, but it is a much better practice to prune all our Roses before Christmas, if possible, and set them to work to make roots.

Our own native Thorn is known to all as a beautiful tree, but in the great tree lands of America there are many other kinds. These are easily raised from seed, which is the right way, but the habit of grafting has got such a deep hold on nurseries that it is often practised on our native Thorn.

I planted a large group of Thorns—Asian and European as well as American kinds—on a bank above the Moat Cottage, but in the end, after many years, they began to die one by one, and nearly all were lost. They are very handsome trees for park planting and deserving of a long life, and should be raised from seed.

A North American tree which William Cobbett praised. Robinia or False Acacia is a hardy tree which varies very much from seed, and some beautiful forms I brought from France grafted on the wild tree, planted them in the best soil we had, but the wild parent tree seemed to take a pleasure in killing them rapidly. The only way with these is to keep the seedling on its own roots. A friend from Orleans sent me a few rooted cuttings and they are living and have formed graceful bushes.

For long years the Lilac has been grafted on Privet and this had meant certain death. In the squares of London one may see the result of the stock having its own way. It is a very beautiful thing in flower, is the Lilac. It is generally much better grown in France, and is, as here, pruned close after flowering, in the spring bearing great wreaths of flowers. It deserves good free soil. A friend in Hungary says it is the home of the nightingale.

INTRODUCTION BY PETER KING

This is "the most widely-read and influential gardening book even written", and its author, the Irishman William Robinson, used its pages to bring about the most fundamental revolution in the history of British horticulture. Bold claims, and though made by his biographer, most historians would endorse them as accurate.

One of the difficulties about presenting this book to the public today is that over the 50 years since its first publication in 1883 Robinson personally supervised 15 new editions and nine reprints, so which of these is the definitive text? It seemed to me that the last printing he supervised, in 1934 (a few months before his death the following year), ought to be the one to serve as model. However, he made so many changes as time went by—some for the sake of novelty alone—that I have also included some chapters which appeared only in earlier editions. For those readers who want to know more about the various editions, an appendix to the text gives brief details.

Robinson himself described this as a "handbook", and nearly two thirds of his text was taken up with an illustrated alphabetical catalogue of plants and shrubs, each described in detail, that was added to as revised editions came along to reflect the spate of horticultural introductions during the half-century after initial publication. The author's aim was, of course, to keep the book continually in print, which he virtually achieved except for a gap during World War I. But following his death the "handbook" element had become so outdated that I felt it best to eliminate it altogether. One effect of this is to considerably reduce the length of the book, which in the 1934 printing reached 720 closely-set pages instead of the 427 pages with which Robinson had begun 50 years before. His final printing of Part I, reproduced here with additions, totalled only 286 pages.

When the book was first published, Robinson was already 45 years old and an established authority, mainly through his writing. Later, he admitted that "the first editions of this book were burdened with much about the ways of flower gardening at the time; many thousands of plants set out in May or early June in formal and geometrical array, the result a bad carpet. Experience has taught me to throw overboard all tender plants and devote the book to hardy plants only that may be planted in the open air on every fine day in the fall or winter."

This was the nub of Robinsonianism—a dislike of the "carpet" bedding-out so beloved of Victorians, and the substitution of plants and shrubs that were natural—a thesis that he had proved not by theory but by "what took place in my garden for many years past".

Robinson had been a practical gardener since he was a boy, and in 1885, just after the *Flower Garden* was published, he had invested his considerable wealth in a 700-acre Sussex estate, Gravetye Manor. This became the place where his views would be put to the test. However, the inspiration for these views came not only from the gardens where he worked but also from those he saw on his travels, particularly what he called the English Cottage Garden. In his youth in Ireland, and for the formative years in Victorian England, the social unit in Europe was the village with its nucleus of cottages. The naturalness of their gardens (even those which were of a later development than the lowly cottage set alongside them) were often quoted by Robinson as the epitome of the English style – just as they were, too, for his friend Gertrude Jekyll. For example, he tells how, during one autumn in the Weald of Kent, "we stopped to look over a low garden wall [and] were asked in to see the pretty old house and to stroll about the small garden, little more than a cottage garden. No pretentious plants to consider [he says] only the yellow sunflowers of the season, massed in their own way . . . and by their profusion giving a unity."

Robinson loved "profusion", hating the regimentation of plants like soldiers on a parade ground almost as much as he hated topiary. Thus he became a proponent of The Wild Garden, The Rock Garden, the Alpine and—most of all—the Herbaceous Border. These were his positive achievements, though his contemporaries must have thought of him as more like a preacher on the attack, or a revolutionary "fulminating against formalism", as Hugh Johnson puts it. Another writer who may have met him, Edward Hyams, describes Robinson as "rude, noisy, impatient, extravagant and arrogant". This may have been true when he attacked Paxtonism (he was particularly rude about the Crystal Palace Gardens in the 1850s) or inveighed against what he called "pastry-work gardening". Yet remember that this was also a man whom most of the great horticultural figures of the day (like Jekyll) revered as a fine editor, a man whose star-studded cast of contributors included John Ruskin, James Russell Lowell and such luminaries as Dean Hole.

My own theory about his antagonisms—a theory for which there is no specific evidence or authority—is as follows. His background was not initially one of rural poverty as many writers suggest. His father was land-agent to a local aristocrat but when William was 10 years old the father deserted his wife and children and eloped to America with the wife of his employer, Lady St George. Abandonment by his father would have created such a deep sense of guilt and suppressed rage in the boy (so my theory goes) that he would have been capable of almost any violent reaction against authority. Later, aged 35, he went to the United States on a business trip and is said to have searched for his father in San Francisco; but Robinson never afterwards mentioned his name.

The classic anecdote about Robinson's rebellious nature is that in his mid-twenties he was employed in a grand garden at Ballykilkavern during a winter (1860 or 1861—the historians differ) which was the coldest on record. He was bored and, having decided to leave his employer, he did so one night, having first put out the greenhouse fires and opened the windows.

Despite such a beginning, his old chief at Glasnevin, Dublin, recommended him to the Royal Botanic Society's garden in Regent's Park, London. Robinson became an authority on British wild flowers, and was given a grant to tour the country's other botanic gardens—a tour he wrote up in the press. This fed his passion for publicity. In 1865 he travelled to France for nearly a year, acting both as agent to Veitch, the leading nurseryman of the time, and as horticultural writer to *The Times*. He was able, on his return, to buy a house in a smart area of Kensington and publish books based on his continental experience: *Gleanings from French Gardens* and *The Palaces and Gardens of Paris*. He showed amazing prolixity, combining horticultural editorship of *The Field* with authorship of a best-seller still in print today, *The Wild Garden* (1870).

Such a man needed his own medium, and after 1871 the plan he had formulated for five years or more came to maturity—he founded *The Garden* magazine. The historian Miles Hadfield believes it is significant that the first issue of this journal was dedicated to J.C. Loudon who, together with his wife Jane, was an early nineteenth century proponent of the "natural" garden, thus establishing that the origins of the Robinsonian manner go back much further than his own time. Robinson's theories evolved through his long life (he lived to be nearly 100) as the various editions of his books amply illustrate. In the late 1870s he became immersed in colour and from 1876 each issue of his *The Garden* contained a colour plate. Three years later a new journal *Gardening Illustrated*, priced at only one penny, appeared, and it achieved such a massive circulation among the less affluent that by 1881 he had sold one and a half million copies in six months. More magazines followed from his offices in 37 Southampton Street, off the Strand, where he also established a mail-order house.

A clever businessman, Robinson invested the proceeds of his publishing ventures in property in London, and in 1885 he used the money to purchase the Lordship of the Manor of Gravetye which had a 700-acre estate that he quickly expanded. When he died, Robinson left his house and garden to the nation, though in fact it found a commercial buyer and is today a hotel, with its garden embodying Robinsonian principles. All around us, today, are gardens deploying these same principles, in particular the border. In *The Wild Garden* (1870) he suggests that "every garden should have a mixed border, but except in little cottage gardens, gardens dependent on it are quite out of the question". By 1883 he had developed this concept to a wider, grander form, one to which so many gardeners aspire today—the herbaceous border. "What ought to be aimed at," he wrote, "is not sameness but variety; instead of the beds being as nearly as possible the same throughout the season, the aim should be to produce the variety of Nature." Of course Robinson never succeeded in totally overcoming the fashion for formalism of some kind or other, but he lived to see his views become not revolutionary but respectable. Indeed, he was offered a place on the Honours List, but he declined, preferring, he said, to leave life as he entered it.

The art of "Natural" gardening is "a purely English one", Robinson believed. "We were the first to depart from the builder's and decorator's way with a garden" (the latter being two of his particular *bêtes-noirs* along with the fountain-mongers and landscape architects). Thus it is that not only the gardens around us but many in other countries too adhere to Robinsonian principles with their wide, sweeping lawns, the shrubs and roses in their shapely beds, and the herbaceous borders. It is true that the triumph of these principles owed as much to prevailing social trends as to Robinson's passsionate proselytising—the shortage of labour and hence the requirement for low-maintenance, the introduction of machinery and widely-available chemicals, the imports of more and more foreign plants. Nevertheless, Robinson's greatness, if it can never be entirely explained, was directly responsible for the wide acceptance of what Hyams calls "the English dream garden, the paradise as improved by man."

Peter King
Oxfordshire 1996

CHAPTER I

Landscape Mistakes near the Country House

It may not be clear to all that gardeners have to do with the landscape, but this they have to do to a great extent, if the comfort of all who live near is to be thought of. And it is not a question of "formalities or informalities," to use a term now often misused, but of the earth itself, and has no reference to plans.

In diversified land, roads are not so easy to make as in the plain, but in all cases they should have every care we may give. I went once to see the home of a poet of repute, and to get in was met by five different roads to find my way to the house. Where farm lands are in the same estate there may be reason for a separate entrance, the rule in this, as in all cases, always being not to make a yard more road than is needed for the work of the place. Grass walks help much, and may lessen the need and cost of the gravel walk, especially in wood or pleasure ground. The line of road is very important, taking the easiest grades, not always the shortest. Often the shortest way is the worst. The way in should show as much of the beauty of the land as possible. For centuries the way in to Gravetye from Turner's Hill was through the smugglers' lane, from which no view of the country near could be seen. Some land near gave place to a new road, airy, easy of grade, and with good views of the country near. Where needless roads are formed, an evil is cutting up the ground and destroying all repose. Too many roads and walks are enemies to good landscape views as well as to economy.

Much of the land in the home counties is injured in effect by iron-bound clumps of trees, costly to form and giving no shelter to man or beast, and breaking up the repose of the scene. The right way is to study the ground carefully, fix as far as may be the planting to do, what trees may best serve in sheltering house and grounds from the north or east, and after due care as to the quality of the ground, planting the poorest as a wood. Even the same space given to harmful clumps planted as a wood, which might do the work of a wood in giving much needed shelter, often give a home to birds, with shady walks through, affording a pleasure the clump never does.

Loss of grouping is a most serious defect: the loss is seen in many places where planting is done. The work is often done without control by labourers who plant to a face a mixture of trees or shrubs. Not many years pass before these discordant elements begin a struggle, which ends in ugliness or disease. The trees of New Zealand may be seen with those of Oregon with "filling up" of Privet or Cherry Laurel. The whole as it gets old is a sad comment on our way of planting. If a collection of trees or shrubs is planted that way, the result is no better. Half a dozen kinds of trees grouped in a natural way may be a picture, even if it were of our native trees only; say Ash on a Down farm, or the Cedar of Lebanon as a group, or our native Yew massed in a covert. This way leads to pictures in the home landscape; the mixed muddle spoils all.

The worst of all dangerous and ill-placed trees is the Field Elm, not a native tree, with suckers all around, and so facile of increase that it soon took place everywhere. A poor, short-rooted tree, that in gales is often blown down wholesale, and with the fault that it may kill us on a fine summer day. In a village called Stoke, were once planted this Elm along all the roads near, and after a gale all were blown down in field and road. Desolation is a weak word to use to tell of it. The tree has not the dignity and fine form of our Oak, Ash or Beech, and should not be planted near a house or any path. And apart from this tree, no forest tree should ever be planted near a house of any sort. Neglect of this rule leads to serious accidents, as this from the *Times* will show:—

> WORCESTER.—At Bromsgrove Isolation Hospital, three large trees were blown down and fell across the Tuberculosis Pavilion, smashing the roof of the women's ward, where there were eleven patients. Branches came through into the cubicles, but the patients were removed without injury. As this work was proceeding, a large chimney-stack over the servants' quarters fell and crashed through the roof into a bedroom. Another chimney on the administrative block also came down. The country-side is littered with uprooted trees.

Such accidents often arise from careless planting without thought of the stature of the trees. Forest trees are often overplanted by roads; time flies, and soon the trees are a danger, and have to be boughed—often dangerous work. Mistakes, too, are often seen as to the place of trees; Lombardy Poplars, a tree of the waterside, in dry ground; noble Cypress-like trees of N.W. America almost jammed against the house; Weeping Willows in dry fields.

The most frequent of garden delusions is the sunk garden. That is to say a garden sunk like a big grave and for no good reason. The difference of level leads to much increase to the labour of all seasons. To those who have to move in chairs it is an effective way to prevent them seeing the charms of the flowers. No one who had a garden in his head could have thought of the plan—more likely the work of an office clerk busy with his pencil. Shelter? Better begin on the natural ground and not seek it in digging a hole. And in the garden in any general sense the more we keep on high ground the better.

The clayed books of our day on Italian gardens lead some on a false pursuit of the Italian garden—a failure in our clime and the result often absurd. In Ireland too, once the land of saints, a man attempted it in an Isle, in the vain hope of making it into a Borromean pleasance—the result a failure. The statues have to be wrapped up in winter or they might dissolve. In Eastern America the statues are carried indoors for the winter, and that sort of gardening tends to conceal the truth that a garden is a thing of life and beauty that does not arise from any stone-work.

The carpet garden.—This parody on the true garden is still rife in France and Belgium. To make a flower-bed to imitate a bad carpet, and by throwing aside all grace of form and loveliness of bloom, was indeed a dismal mistake. There was a comic element seen in its doing—a plank supported by two large pots in the bed and two men on the plank pinching some hapless plant to get it carpet depth. The same hapless idea has sometimes been attempted with dwarf Box, and in one case near London hundreds of hapless Yews cut down to the heart to form a green carpet a few inches high.

Gardens of one colour are against natural law in all ways. For a true flower garden one must have freedom to select from every source of beauty among hardy things. To confine the planter to one colour cuts off many beautiful things and robs the scene of variety, a main source of beauty. Throw the very idea aside and think of the only rule worth an aim—the exclusion of all ugly things of any form. Also those that rob by their vigour, robbers of the good soil and give little back;

plants that one dislikes, why, one may not always explain; and, lastly, plants that hate our soil and refuse to thrive in our flower garden.

Styles.—There are only the good and the bad. If taken to see a Dutch garden, we may find it very like an English one: and the first effect of our gardens is to be English: formal, informal Dutch, Italian names, best thrown aside, are often misleading.

The Panel garden in origin was born of the attempt to oust the gardener from the garden. The designers had no thought of the needs and constant work of the garden, and so used drawings meant for flat surfaces on ground which might be alive with beauty. The result is a garden as bare of life as a piece of oilcloth. Many of the show gardens of Victorian days were designed in this deadly way and may still be seen. What is the right way in a garden site with every advantage as to position? Why, to make it a place for a real flower garden, with simple beds, which allow a good gardener to do his best work.

CHAPTER II

Some Evils of Bedding and Carpet Gardening

Cost of building, repairs and care of hot-houses to protect plants not
so beautiful as the flowers hardy in our clime. Two movements of earth
every year: to pursue this was false, better to follow the lasting way.
Useless, planting out in midsummer, when half the flower charms of
the year are past; misuse of glass-houses which might grow welcome
food in the spring; keeping up the race of "housemen"; often useless
in the open air. A roomy shed facing south is all that is needed for
the flower-garden work in winter.

Getting rid of the flower garden itself, a frequent thing about
country houses, the owners finding the cost and ugliness of the
system not worth having, and so they turn the old flower garden
into turf, of which there is usually plenty to be seen near. The old
English and French (Fleuriste) way of a garden within view of the
house was the right way, and we must go back for the true garden.
The worst of the evil is the expelling of the more precious flowers,
not allowed in the spectacular show, has passed for a garden in our
day—Lily, Rose, Virgin's Bower—all the fine hardy plants, from the
lovely Pasque flower of the spring to the splendid Cardinal flower of
the fall, and the annual flowers of California and Australia, including
some of the fairest flowers known. Getting rid of the pleasant work
of the fall in the true flower garden, where every fine day is precious
in all ways. Every year brings need of change: tried Roses to be
planted, failures thrown away, bulbs of value planted, surface plants
changed—these being shallow rooting are better for a change—turned
out ready for Carnations and other hopes of the coming year. The
permanent plants, like Clematis or Rose, should not be disturbed
for years. Good edgings in the garden are precious and need much

improvement in our day. Some Alpine flowers thrive if well planted. Some of the prettiest rock plants may be used as edgings, and all these good features were driven away from the flower gardens by the bad ways in vogue.

CHAPTER III

Misuse of the Yew Tree in Gardens

The Yew tree in its natural form is of good colour at various seasons; bronzy on some soils in winter, the flowering time, the fruiting time and, in the Fall, full of fieldfares seeking food when driven from the North. It is only in old trees that we see its varied charm, always showing the stem so fine in colour; but as most of the gardens of our day only show, in the Yew, hard, dark lines, to give backgrounds, hence many miles of this forest tree in every home county, offering us hard, dark lines, where all should be free and graceful. And in this, the land of our noble native Cedar, it is cut into absurd forms, seats and, worst of all, cut into covered ways, in poor imitation of the Pergola, but mostly without the grace of the Pergola when laden with the nobler climbing plants. In our day the trained gardener may give us the fruits of the earth, and its many flowers, also the fresh food and salads of the spring, and what a waste of his precious time, clipping trees into hideous forms—in some cases months of time given to the ignoble work. And the effect of these ugly trees when seen in the approach to a house, hiding the beauty of any native trees that happen to be near. As to the Yew tree, the best way with it is in the copse or wood, there to take its beautiful form. They are usually able to do so, but even when in the wood take care to fence them from straying cow or horse. When large enough, all the lower branches should be cut off to 12 feet or more, to show the colour of the stem. Old Yews may be safely left alone, but never with any drooping branches within reach of any straying animal.

Among the monstrosities through misuse of the Yew tree is the forming of the maze, with hundreds of young trees crowded together, in the end killing each other.

It is well to note that all clipped lines of Yew, and of the Cherry and Portugal Laurels are *dead* lines, and cannot carry any beauty of flower. On the other hand, the best dividing lines may be fountains of beauty, walls well planted, often gardens of delight in growing things that need more warmth than the open air may give; covered ways with Oak trellising overhead; sides carrying Clematis, Honeysuckle, Vine, and climbing Rose. And among our native evergreens the Holly and Box form better dividing lines and need not be clipped. The trouble with the Yew is, being a hungry forest tree and tall beyond garden stature, it comes under the shears.

The late Mark Fisher, best landscape painter of our day, was painting my garden, seated under the old Yews at the west end, and he said to me: "Why do you give me a hard line, ugly there, instead of a free and beautiful one?" The lesson was not lost on me. The black and hard line was of small Yews, found on the place when I came, and there being a difference of level between the little front garden and the west garden, I, being a little under the vogue of the day, gave way to a small line of clipped young Yews, so as soon as I heard the painter's view I carted them away to plant as a group in an old "shaw," where they throve apace in cold soil.

Clipped Yew hedges rob a garden, never shelter it. If shelter from north or east is needed, plant the natural tree at a safe distance from the house. No forest tree should ever be planted near a house.

The source of much of this deforming comes to us from the Dutch, who import their trees, issue circulars and little cuts to advertise them. And now an aid comes from *Country Life* of pages of some of the worst forms of this distortion of our forest evergreen tree. So, feeling these illustrations might mislead some country gentlemen to ask their gardeners to waste their time on such abortions, I wrote these pages to *Country Life* to neutralise the ill effect of this prostitution of gardeners' time. On the plea of no room, my paper was returned. So now for the book, "*Garden Craftmanship in Yew and Box*: By Nathaniel Lloyd, Officer of the most excellent Order of the British Empire."

It is the poorest book that so far has disgraced the garden. In looking at the distortions, the first feeling was of vexation, but it soon turned to pity that an artist in any shape should call his work, as shown in his book, art. The only things to compare with his pictures are the golliwogs that children are given at Christmas, and the witless distortion of the human face and frame which the editors of some daily journals offer their readers! Would some good lady take the author into the woods and the downs, where the Box tree in its natural form is, on Sussex or Surrey hills, far more beautiful than anything ever seen in a garden, and show what true form is?

The illustrations are all on the miscalled "art" paper of the day, not enduring paper, but on a clayed surface, not pleasant to the eyes in some lights, and books on it heavy as stone. Among the pictures is a topiary garden at Earlshall, a hideous distortion of the Yew tree—all over a lawn that might have been a living garden of varied life. It is not pleasant to see a maze at Hatfield, the maze once part of the old tea-garden distraction—the meanest use we may make of our native Cedar. There are examples of the Box, fencing all the beds in a parterre in the same place, a misuse of our native Box. A boy in a garden might tell him that little else would grow in the beds.

CHAPTER IV

*A Flower Garden of Hardy Plants
as finished December 1922*

The object was to get rid of the cost, labour and bad effect of the system of bedding, carpet gardening, etc., in vogue for several generations, because it—

1. Excludes the presence of the most admired plants—Rose, Lily, Clematis.
2. Encourages growth of tender plants of the tropical weeds which must not be planted until early summer.
3. Leaves the garden desolate and ugly in winter.
4. Drives the flower-garden work into a very short period at a season when other work presses, and prevents good work being done at all seasons.

A flower garden without Roses seemed to me something like a body without a heart. One of my first tasks was to get the Rose back to the flower garden. For several generations past the rule in these islands was to put the Rose garden away from the flower garden and house. How this came about it is not easy to say; it was in part owing to the short bloom-time of the old summer Rose. In any case, and even to the present day, landscape gardeners have practised this exclusion.

I began with all the best kinds of Rose—several thousand plants in all, and planted for the most part in bold groups, so as to test the value and endurance of each. Broadly, the result of that trial was that quite one-half of the plants died back on the Brier upon which they were invariably grafted. It being impossible to buy own-root plants in our country, the best one can do is to put up with plants as they come in, and scrape the stems above and around the graft, so as to encourage the plant to emit its own roots. The best Roses I have had—such as Marie van Houtte—were so treated. We strike the Roses on their own roots every September, and usually with good results, putting them in the open in ordinary soil, and as far as we could, on the highest ground. The only excuse for grafting on the Dog Brier is that it is easy to handle the stock; the plant on its natural root is more fragile than on the Dog Brier. That being so, it is a wise plan to put the cuttings where we want the plant to grow. For example, if we want the plant of a favourite Rose, such as Mme Léon Paine or Bouquet d'Or, we put the cuttings in at the foot of a wall on the north, or other side, and it will grow and keep in perfect health for a life-time.

Grafting the Tea Rose is a purblind and fatal practice if our aim is the endurance of the plants. We have here the hardiest China Rose known to Europe—Fellenberg. It has bloomed over thirty years in the same place in perfect health in cool soil. If it had been a grafted plant the Roses must have died four times over, and we should have had infinite trouble with the suckers in the meantime.

There is variety in the way Roses behave when grafted on the Brier. Of two such Roses planted in the same bed, one will perish in a few years' time, and another will linger on apparently happy for several more years.

The beds were dug in a cool shaly soil to a depth of 3 feet. They were not manured. With 3 feet of good soil below, the Roses were safe as regards food. Instead of mulching we covered the ground beneath the plants with rock and other small plants, feeling that to cover the surface of the beds was not against the Rose—and so it proved. These are some of the plants used for the surface:—

Evening Primrose	Silvery Rockfoils	Our native Geranium	Dwarf Toadflax
Mignonette	Anagallis—blue	Sand Pinks (Iunica)	(L. pallida)
Pansies—tufted	Hairbells—dwarf	Dwarf Thyme (Micans)	Gypsophila—Silvery
Silvery Speedwell	Rock Scabious	The Greek Viola	The Blue Bindweed
Baby Blue Eyes	Phacelia	(Gracilis)	The Shamrock Pea

Being of a fragile nature the surfacing flowers are in need of frequent attention; they have to be transplanted and the surface refreshed while the Roses and Clematis and other permanents are never disturbed for years. The Roses are not packed close together, but to allow of better growth, set a yard apart.

The laws of the Medes and Persians were not so strict as those that are laid down in the books as to pruning. So, feeling that I could not set myself against these rules without some proof of the futility of the practice, I let my Roses be dashed about in the storm and frost—all the winter until April. When the plants could gain nothing but injury in this way I gave it up. Now all my Roses are put to bed before Christmas to do their true work of making roots. In this way the plants escape all the effects of inclement weather, winter and early spring. The idea was that if you pruned before the spring the bushes started too early. This, after many years' trial, we have found not to be the case.

As regards manure, which for generations now has been spread over the surface of every Rose garden in Britain, it occurred to me that the excreta of animals of various kinds spread under the windows of a house was not a good way. I felt that the depth and texture of the soil was of more importance than any benefit to be got by the addition of animal and other manures.

Apart from the scarcity of stable manure, there is also the great danger of one of the most dreaded diseases (Tetanus) arising. It is known to arise frequently in heavily manured earth.

In deep and open soil of almost any formation, certainly not excluding chalk or sand, if made deep enough, Roses of the Tea and China sorts thrive on their own roots from cuttings

Clematis.—These splendid climbing plants—the larger ones which come to us from China and Japan—have been shut out of the gardens of Europe and, owing to the purblind practice of grafting them in nurseries on a native of our own hills, a plant upon which they never thrive. After many years of struggle with these we have at last succeeded with layers. Then all sign of disease was seen no more. And so we get the most graceful climber of the northern world in perfect health. We layer the plants in March and have good strong plants in September. We grow them on Oak trellis. Also, we find a good way is to let them climb up shrubs and low trees like Magnolia, in which way, and without any pruning or other care, they thrive.

To get the full beauty of the flower garden in our northern summer it is essential that we should reject certain plants, showy but poor in colour value and all-devouring as to soil. Of such are the North American hardy sunflowers—all well in their right place, which is the copse or the wild garden; Asters best apart; Cannas that seldom attain their true beauty in our country; standard Roses always ungraceful and, in our country, killed in hard winters. Of late years, tiring of plants like Heliotrope and other tender plants, and feeling sure that a garden ought to be in full beauty long before June, I resolved to give them up. It is a gain to exclude any flower which for any reason one does not enjoy in close view of the house. My garden is for summer flowers only, and the spring flowers are given to the fields around. The only spring flowers in the flower garden are the Crocus and Snow Glory, and these are planted 8 in., so that they may be followed by annual or other plants that flower in summer.

As there are thousands of spring flowers in the meadows and woods near, we reserve the beds for the summer flowers—Lily, Clematis, Rose, Pansy, Evening Primrose, Mignonette and hardy Ferns.

HARDY FLOWERS ONLY
AT GRAVETYE, DECEMBER 1922

No. 1. Border against house—left of porch—A large colony of Scabiosa Caucasica, purple and white forms, edging of Linaria pallida. On wall—Clematis Rose Lamarque and Paul's Scarlet, Vitis Wilsoni and also Rose, Climbing.

No. 2. Bed to right of porch—Rose Marie van Houtte both in bed and on wall, ten years in same place; also on wall, Rose, Mermaid and Clematis. Undergrowth, Missouri Evening Primrose, hardy here. Edging, Blue Windflower.

No. 3. Below and in front of Pergola and with 4-feet retaining wall of sandstone blocks in rear, the latter filled with Californian Fuchsia (Zauschneria), Shamrock Pea, Blue Bindweed, Alpine Phlox and Linarias. The bed contains Old Pink China Rose across one end carpeted with the Horned Violet (V. Cornuta) and at the opposite end is a group of Gen. MacArthur Roses, and in the centre of the bed, Blue Sweet Peas. Edging, Sedum Ewersii and planted deeply beneath Crocus Sir Walter Scott. The Water Lily Tank separates this and No. 4 bed, and is surrounded by water-loving Iris.

No. 4. Contains groups of Rose, Frances Gaunt and Joseph Hill, carpeted with Tufted Pansies, clumps of Red and Pink Sweet Peas, there being a large mass of Lobelia Fulgens at one end. Edging of purple Crocus beneath Campanula Muralis.

No. 5. is a long border with Hugh Dickson Roses at one end, and a mass of the Feather Fern (Struthiopteris) and Henry's

Lily at the other. The centre containing a variety of large flowered Delphiniums, edging consists of a broad belt of The Siberian Squill planted beneath Gypsophila.

No. 6. Zepherin Drouhin Roses, Lilium Regale and Narcissus, with a carpet of Hungarian Hepaticas (H. Angulosa) and mixed Rock plants.

No. 7. Collection of large-flowered Snowdrops, Crocus, Iris and Pasque Flowers. These are succeeded by Nemophila Insignis and Rhodanthe.

No. 8. Mixed bed of bronze-leaved Roses on own roots and Gladiolus Primulinus. Edging, Crocus beneath encrusted Rock Foils.

No. 9. has Trellis background with large-flowered Clematis, Romneya Trichocalyx, carpeted with Aquilegia Glandulosa.

No. 10. Rose Renee Wilmart Urban; underneath, encrusted Rock Foils. Edging, Gypsophila Dubia.

No. 11. Convolvulus Tenuissimus. Border, Carnations. Edging, Alpine Scabious.

No. 12. Incarvilleas in var. Carnations and Violet Cress (Ionopsidium). Edging Lady Knox Pansies. Trellis in rear covered with Roses and Clematis.

No. 13. Rose Theresa, carpeted with Collinsia Grandiflora.

No. 14. Mme Hector Leuillot and Nita Weldon Roses. Edging, Geranium Lancastriense.

No. 15. Rose Mme Ravary and Pansy True Blue.

No. 16. Royal Velours Clematis on rough Yew support, with undergrowth of encrusted Rock Foils and Greek Violet (V. Gracilis).

No. 17. Background of Roses and Clematis on Oak Trellis. In bed, Lady Hillingdon Roses, with undergrowth of encrusted Rock Foils and Horned Pansies (Viola Cornuta).

No. 18. La Tosca and Belladora Roses, edged with White Swan Pansies. Beneath the Roses, Mauve Queen and Lady Knox Pansies.

No. 19. Rose Pharisaer and Anna Olivier with undergrowth of young plants of the Prairie Primrose (Œnothera). Edging Campanula Muralis.

No. 20. Clematis on rough Yew stakes with Rose C. Louis Breslau, J. C. N. Forestier. Undergrowth of Pansy Mosely Perfection. Edging Blue Bindwood (C. Mauritanicus).

No. 21. Rose, Souv. de Stella Gray, Covent Garden, K. of K. Under-growth of Blue Flax. Edging, Geranium Lancastriense.

No. 22. Delphinium Belladonna with a background of Clematis and Roses. Edging, Gypsophila Muralis.

No. 23. China Roses in variety. Edging, a broad belt of Purple Crocus.

No. 24. Collection of large-flowered Clematis on rough Yew stakes and a group of Hugh Dickson Roses at one end with an undergrowth of Hardy Ferns, mostly evergreen, and the Great Chilian Evening Primrose (Œnothera Acaulis). Edging consists of a broad band of Snow Glories (Chionodoxa) which are followed in Summer by some light Annual, such as Swan River Daisy.

No. 25. Rose Mme Herriot. Undergrowth of Councillor Waters, Pansy.

No. 26. Rose Mrs David M'Kee and Louis Leroy. Scarlet Turk's Cap Lily and the Narbon Flax as an undergrowth to the whole.

No. 27. Rose Zepherin Drouhin planted a yard apart, with White Phlox. Tapis Blanc between. Edging, the pale blue Trebizond Muscari.

No. 28. Rose Mme Lambard. Undergrowth Phacelia Campanularia.

No. 29. Rose Irish Elegance, carpeted with Shamrock Pea (Paro-chetus). Edging consists of Corydalis Cheilanthifolia.

No. 30. Bright coloured Phlox in var. Edging, Thymus Micans with Crocus beneath.

No. 31. Rose, Mme Léon Pain. Undergrowth of Inchmery Pinks. Edging of Gypsophila over Margot Crocus.

No. 32. Golden Tea Roses in variety, with undergrowth of Silver-leaved Speedwell (Veronica Incana), and Horned Violet.

No. 33. Collection of Tea Roses including Joseph Hill, Le Progrès, also a group of Irish Fireflame, with undergrowth of Chinese Meadow Rue (Thalictrum Dipterocarpum). Edging, Gypsophilas.

No. 34. Clematis and Monkshood, with undergrowth of Pentste-mon Heterophyllus. Edging of Coronation Pinks.

No. 35. Rose, Mdlle de Kejegu, carpeted with Scabiosa Graminifolia. Edging, Campanula Muralis.

No. 36. Rose, Christine. Undergrowth, True Blue Pansy. Edging, Tunica Saxifraga.

No. 37. Rose, Mrs Aaron Ward, with an edging of Pinks.

No. 38. Clematis Nellie Moser on rough stake, undergrowth consisting of Linum Lewisii and Nemophila Insignis. Edging, Mosely Perfection Pansy.

No. 39. Convolvulus Althæiodes, Chinese Meadow Rue (T. Dipterocarpum), with edging of Helichrysum Bellidioides.

No. 40. Sun Roses mixed; Grey-leaved Senecio. Rose K. of K., Lillium Szovitzianum and Perowskia Atriplicifolia.

No. 41. On rough Yew stakes, Rose Billiard et Barre, and in bed a mass of Marie van Houtte and Mme Abel Chatenay, planted between the roses, Delphinium Bella Donna. Edging, G. Wermig Violet.

No. 42. Collection of Lavender interspersed with a variety of Sword Lillies (Gladiolus). Edging of white-flowered Thrift.

No. 43. Large flowered Clematis on rough supports. Undergrowth of Œnothera speciosa and Delphiniums.

No. 44. Rose, Grand Duke de Luxembourg with an undergrowth of Pinks in variety.

No. 45. Large flowering Clematis with undergrowth of Columbine species.

No. 46. A collection of large flowering Clematis on rough Yew supports, undergrowth of hardy Agapanthus (A. Mooreanus Minor) and Tulips. Edging of white-flowered Thrift.

SOUTH GARDEN

No. 1. Roses Mme Léon Pain, La Tosca and Golden Emblem, also Chelone Barbata, the whole having a carpet of Tropæolum Polyphyllum. Edging, Campanula Muralis and Gypsophila Muralis used alternately. The background to this bed consists of Lonicera Sempervirens, Clematis Coccinia and Trachelospermum Jasminoides.

No. 2. Contains Souvd. d. Gustave Pratt Roses with an undergrowth of Carnations. Edging of mixed Crocus beneath Rock Scabious.

No. 3. Princess d. Sagan Rose, undergrowth Swan River Daisy (Brachycombe). Edging, Crocus.

No. 4. Rose G. Nabonnaud, Gladiolus primulinus. Edging of Blue Bindwood (Convolvulus Mauritanicus).

No. 5. Roses. Lady Waterlow on rough stake, and President

Carnot with an undergrowth of mixed varieties of Pinks. The background to this bed consists of Clematis Lanuginosa, C. Comtesse de Bouchard, Japanese Wistaria and Horse Brier (Smilax Rotundifolia).

No. 6. Rose Ophelia. Undergrowth of Platycodon grandiflorum var. Mariesii.

No. 7. Red-letter Day Roses, Perowskia Atriplicifolia, with an edging of encrusted Saxifrage.

No. 8. Rose Prince de Bulgarie, Lilium Speciosum Magnificum, carpeted with tufted Pansies, Councillor Waters and White Swan.

No. 9. Madonna Lilies in groups. Late Red Dutch Honeysuckles; ground work of Pentstemon Heterophyllus. Edging, purple Crocus, beneath white-flowered Thrift.

No. 10. Border right of porch. Small collection of Iris, Bella Donna Lilies, sweet Verbena and China Roses. Undergrowth Campanula Muralis. Edging Carpathian Snowflakes and Rock Foils. On wall in rear of border is Abutilon Vitifolium, Clematis, Rose and Jalap plant.

No. 11. Long narrow border, left of porch, contains white Caucasian Scabious at one end edged with pink, Princess Mary, also Campanula Muralis, Sternbergia Lutea, Kaffir Lily, Amicia, Nerine Bowdeni, Bella Donna Lilies, Iris Tingitana, Iris Stylosa and Sweet Violets. Trained to wall behind is the Japanese Wistaria, Rosa Sinica Anemone, Rose Lemarque and L. Ideal, Magnolia Grandiflora, Solanum Jasminoides, Phygelius Capensis, Pomegranate and Lonicera Sempervirens.

No. 12. Rosemary in variety carpeted with Lady Knox Violas.

No. 13. Contains Tritoma Excelsa and Madonna Lily with an edging of Blue Bindweed.

CHAPTER V

Art in Relation to Flower-Gardening and Garden Design

There is no reason why we should not have true art in the garden, but much why we should have it, and no reason why a garden should be ugly, bare, or conventional. The word "art" being used in its highest sense here, it may perhaps be well to justify its use, and as good a definition of the word as any perhaps is "power to see and give form to beautiful things," which we see shown in some of its finest forms in Greek sculpture and in the works of the great masters of painting.

But art is of many kinds, and owing to the loose, "critical" talk of the day, it is not easy to see that true art is based on clear-eyed study of and love for Nature, rather than invention and the bringing of the "personality" of the artist into the work, of which we hear so much. The work of the artist is always marked by its fidelity to Nature, and proof of this may be seen in the greatest art galleries now open to all, so that there is little to hide evidence as to what is said here about art in its highest expression. But as a number of people write much about art in the magazines and papers, while blind as bats to its simple law, there is infinite confusion in many minds about it, and we may read essay after essay about art without being brought a bit nearer to the simple truth, but on the other hand get the false idea that it is not by observing, but by inventing and supplementing, that good work is done. The strong man must be there, but his work is to see the whole beauty of the subject, and to help us to see it, not to distort it in any way for the sake of making it "original." This is often a way to popularity, but in the end it means bad work. It may be the fashion for a season, owing to some one quality: but it is soon found out, and we have to return to the great masters of all ages, who are always distinguished for truth to Nature, and who show their strength by getting nearer to her.

The actual beauty of a thing in all its fulness and subtlety is almost the whole of the question, but the critics of the day will not take the trouble to see this, and write essays on art in which many long words occur, but in which we do not once meet with the word *truth*. "Realism" and "idealism" are words freely used and bad pictures are shown us as examples of "realism," which leave out all the refinement, subtlety, truth of tone, and perhaps even the very light and shade in which all the real things we see are set.

There are men so blind to the beauty of the things set before their eyes in sky, sea, or earth, that they would seek to idealise the eyes of a beautiful child or the clouds of heaven; while all who see natural beauty in landscape know that no imagining can come near to the beauty of things seen, art being often powerless to seize their full beauty, and the artist has often to let the brush fall in despair. There are more pictures round the year in many a parish in England than all the landscape painters of Europe could paint in a century. Only a little, indeed, of the beauty that concerns us most—that of the landscape—can be seized for us except by the very greatest masters. Of things visible—flower, tree, landscape, sky, or sea—to see the full and ever-varied beauty is to be saved for ever from any will-o'-the-wisp of the imaginary.

But many people do not judge pictures by Nature, but by pictures, and therefore they miss her subtleties and delicate realities on which all true work depends. Some sneer at those who "copy Nature," but the answer to such critics is for ever there in the work of the great men, be they Greeks, Dutchmen, Italians, French, or English.

It is part of the work of the artist to select beautiful or memorable things, not the first that comes in his way. The Venus of Milo is from a noble type of woman—not a mean Greek. The horses of the Parthenon show the best of Eastern breed, full of life and beauty. Great landscape painters like Crome, Corot, and Turner seek not things only because they are natural, but also beautiful; selecting views and waiting for the light that suits the chosen subject best, they give us pictures, working always from faithful study of Nature and from stores of knowledge gathered from her, and that, too, is the only true path for the gardener.

Why say so much here about art? Because when we see the meaning of true "art" we cannot endure what is ugly and false in art, and we cannot have the foregrounds of beautiful English scenery daubed with flower gardens like coloured advertisements. Many see the right way from their own sense being true, but others may wish for proof of what is urged here as to the true source of lasting work in art in the work of the great artists of all time. And we may be as true artists in the garden and home landscape as anywhere else.

There is no good picture which does not image for us the beauty of natural things, and why not begin with these and be artists in their growth and grouping?—for one reason among others that we are privileged to have the living things about us, and not merely representations of them.

So far we have spoken of the work of the true artist, which is always marked by respect for Nature and by keen study of her. But apart from this we have a great many men who do what is called "decorative" work, useful, but still not art in the sense of delight in, and study of, things as they are—the whole class of decorators, who make our carpets, tiles, curtains, and who adapt conventional or geometric forms mostly to flat surfaces. Skill in this way may be considerable without any attention whatever being paid to the greater art that is concerned with life in all its fulness.

This it is well to see clearly; as for the flower gardener it matters much on which side he stands. Unhappily, our gardeners for ages have suffered at the hands of the decorative artist when applying his "designs" to the garden, and designs which may be quite right on a surface like a carpet or panel have been applied a thousand times to the surface of the reluctant earth. It is this adapting of absurd "knots" and patterns from old books to any surface where a flower garden has to be made that leads to bad and frivolous design—wrong in plan and hopeless for the life of plants. It is so easy for anyone asked for a plan to furnish one of this sort without the slightest knowledge of the life of a garden.

For ages the flower garden has been marred by absurdities of this kind of work as regards plan, though the flowers were in simple and natural ways. But in our own time the same "decorative" idea has come to be carried out in the planting of the flowers under the name of "bedding out," "carpet bedding," or "mosaic culture." In this the beautiful forms of flowers are degraded to crude colour without reference to the natural forms or beauty of the plants, clipping being freely done to get the carpets level. When these tracery gardens were made, often by people without any knowledge of the plants of a garden, they were found to be difficult to plant; hence attempts to do without the gardener altogether, and get colour by the use of broken brick, white sand, and painted stone. All such work is wrong and degrading to art, and in its extreme expressions is ridiculous.

As I use the word "artistic" in a book on the flower garden, it may be well to say that as it is used it means right and true in relation to all the conditions of the case, and the necessary limitations of our art and all other human arts. A lovely Greek coin, a bit of canvas painted by Corot with the morning light on it, a block of stone hewn into the shape of the dying gladiator, the white mountain rocks built into a Parthenon—these are all examples of human art, every one of which can be only fairly judged in due regard to what is possible in the material of each. Often a garden may be wrong in various ways, as shown by the starving pines in front of many a house—ugly in form and not in harmony with our native or best garden vegetation; mountain trees set out on dry plains; so that the word inartistic may help us to describe many errors. And again, if we are happy enough to find a garden so true and right in its results as to form a picture that an artist would be charmed to study, we may call it an artistic garden, as a short way of saying that it is about as good as it may be, taking everything into account.

There are few pictures of gardens, because the garden beautiful is rare. Gardens around country houses, instead of forming, as they might, graceful foregrounds to the good landscape views, disfigure all, and drive the artist away in despair. Yet there may be real pictures in gardens; it is not a mere question of patterns of a very poor sort, but one of light and shade, beauty of form, and colour. In times when gardens were made by men who did not know one tree from another, the matter was settled by the shears—it was a question of green walls only. Now we are beginning to see that there is a wholly different and higher order of beauty to be found in gardens, and we are at the beginning of a period when we may hope to get much more pleasure and instruction out of this art than ever before.

CHAPTER VI

Garden Design and Recent Writings Upon it

Of all the things made by man for his pleasure a flower garden has the business to be ugly, barren, or stereotyped, because in it we may have the fairest of the earth's children in a living, ever-changeful state, and not, as in other arts, mere representations of them. And yet we find in nearly every country place, pattern plans, conventional design, and the garden robbed of all life and grace by setting out flowers in geometric ways. A recent writer on garden design tells us that the gardener's knowledge is of no account, and that gardens—

> Should never have been allowed to fall into the hands of the gardener or out of those of the architect; that it is an architectural matter, and should have been schemed at the same time and by the same hand as the house itself.

The chief error he makes is in saying that people, whom he calls "landscapists," destroyed all the formal gardens in England, and that they had their ruthless way until his coming. An extravagant statement, as must be clear to anyone who takes the trouble to look into the thing itself, which many of these writers will not do or regard the elementary facts of what they write about. Many of the most formal gardens in England have been made within the past century, when this writer says all his ideal gardens were cleared away, *e.g.*, the Crystal Palace, the Royal Horticultural Society's at Kensington, and Witley Court, Castle Howard, Mentmore, Drayton, Crewe Hall. During the whole of that period there was hardly a country seat laid out that was not marred by the idea of a garden as a conventional and patterned thing. With Castle Howards, Trenthams, and Chatsworths staring at him, it is ludicrous to see a young architect weeping over their loss. Even if there is no money to waste in gigantic water-squirts, the idea of the terrace is still carried out often in level plains. There are hundreds of such gardens about the country, and the ugliest gardens ever made in England have been made in Victorian days.

It cannot be too clearly remembered that geometrical gardens of a deplorable type are things of our own time, and it is only in our own time the common idea that there is only one way of making a garden was spread. Hence, in all the newer houses we see the stereotyped garden often made in spite of all the needs of the ground, whereas in really old times it was not so. Berkeley is not the same as Sutton, and Sutton is quite different from Haddon.

Moreover, on top of all this formality of design of our own day were grafted the most formal and inartistic ways of arranging flowers that ever came into the head of man, ways that were happily unknown to the Italians or the makers of the earliest terraced gardens. The true Italian gardens were often beautiful with trees in their natural forms, as in the Giusti gardens at Verona; but "bedding out," or marshalling the flowers in geometrical patterns, is a thing of our own precious time, and "carpet" gardening is simply a further remove in ugliness. The painted gravel gardens of Nesfield and Barry and other broken-brick gardens were also an attempt to get rid of the flowers and get rigid patterns instead. Part of the garden architect's scheme was to forbid the growth of plants on walls, as at Shrubland, where, for many years, there were strict orders that the walls were not to have a flower or a creeper of any kind upon them. As these pattern gardens were made by persons often ignorant of gardening, and if planted in any human way with flowers would all "go to pieces," hence the idea of setting them out as they appeared on the drawing-board, some of the beds not more than a foot in diameter, blue and yellow paints being used where the broken brick and stone did not give the desired colour!

Side by side with the adoption in most large and show places of the patterned garden, both in design and planting, disappeared almost everywhere the old English garden, that is, one with a variety of form of shrub and flower and even low trees; so that now we only find this kind of garden here and there in Cornwall, Ireland, and Scotland, and on the outskirts of country towns. All true plant form was banished because it did not fit into the bad carpet pattern! I am only speaking of what every one must know who cares the least about the subject, and of what can be seen to-day in all the public gardens round London and Paris. But we shall never see beautiful flower gardens again until natural ways of grouping flowers and variety of true form come back to us in the flower garden.

After the central error above shown there comes a common one of these writers, of supposing that those who seek natural form and beauty in the garden and home landscape are opposed to the necessary level and even formal spaces about a house. I wrote the *Wild Garden* to save, not to destroy, the flower garden; to show that we could have all the joy of spring in orchard, meadow, or wood, lawn or grove, and so save *the true flower garden near the house* from being torn up twice a year to effect what is called spring and summer "bedding." The idea could be made clear to a child, and it is carried out in many places easy to see. Yet there is hardly a cobbler who rushes from his last to write a book on garden design who does not think that I want to bring the wilderness in at the windows, I who have given all my days to save the flower garden from the ridiculous. A young lady who has been reading one of these bad books, seeing the square beds in my little south garden, says: "Oh! why, *you* have a formal garden!" It is a small square embraced by walls, and I could not have used any other form to get the best use of the space. They are just the kind of beds made in like spaces by the gardeners of Nebuchadnezzar, judging by what evidence remains to us. And he no more than I mistook stones for bushes or bad carpets for flowers, but enjoyed vine and fig and flower as Heaven sent them.

The real flower garden near the house is for the ceaseless care and culture of many and diverse things often tender and in need of protection in varied soils, staking, cleaning, trials of novelties, study of colour effects, sowings and plantings at all seasons. The wild garden, on the other hand, is for things that take care of themselves in the soil of the place, things which will endure for generations if we suit the plants to the soil, like Narcissus on a rich orchard bottom, or blue Anemone in a grove on the limestone soil as in much of Ireland. This garden is a precious aid to the other, inasmuch as it allows of our letting the flower garden do its best work because relieved of the intolerable need of the bedding system in digging up the garden twice a year.

Very often now terms of gardening are misapplied, confusing the mind of the student, and the air is full of a new term, the "formal" garden. For ages gardens of simple form have been common without anyone calling them "formal" until our own time of too many words confusing thoughts. Seeing an announcement that there was a paper in the *Studio* on the "Formal Garden in Scotland," I looked in it, seeking light,and found only plans of the usual approaches necessary for a country house, for kitchen, hall door, or carriage-way. And we gardeners of another sort do not get in like the bats through the roof, but have also ways usually level, to our doors, but we do not call them "formal gardens." There are gardens to which the term "formal" might with some reason be applied. Here are a few words about such by one Percy Bysshe Shelley, whose clear eyes saw beauty if there was any to be seen in earth or sky:

> We saw the palace and gardens of Versailles full of statues, vases, fountains, and colonnades. *In all that belongs essentially to a garden they are extraordinarily deficient.*

A few more by Victor Hugo:

> There fountains gush from the petrified gods, only to stagnate; trees are forced to submit to the grotesque caprices of the shears and line. Natural beauty is everywhere contradicted, inverted, upset, destroyed.

And Robert Southey tells us of one

> where the walks were sometimes of lighter or darker gravel, red or yellow sand, and, when such materials were at hand, pulverised coal and shells. The garden itself was a scroll-work cut very narrow, and the interstices filled with sand of different colours to imitate embroidery.

It is only where the plants of a garden are rigidly set out in geometrical design, as in carpet-gardening and bedding-out, that the term "formal" is rightly applied.

We live in a time when men write about garden design unmeaning words or absolute nonsense; these, as any one may see, are men who have had no actual contact with the work. They think garden design is a question that can be settled on a drawing-board, and have not the least idea that in any true sense the art is not possible without knowledge of many beautiful living things, and that the right planting of a country place is of far greater importance than the ground-plan about the house.

In many books on garden design the authors misuse words and confuse ideas. Many, not satisfied with the good word, "landscape gardener," used by Loudon, Repton, and many other men, call themselves "landscape architects"—a stupid term of French origin implying the union of two distinct studies, one dealing with varied life in a thousand different kinds and the natural beauty of the earth, and the other with stones and bricks and their putting together. The training for either of these arts is wide apart from the training demanded for the other, and the earnest practice of one leaves no time, even if there were the genius, for the other.

The term *landscape planting* is often scoffed at by these writers, yet it is a good one with a clear meaning, which is the grouping and growth of trees in natural forms as opposed to the universal aligning, clipping, and shearing of the Dutch; the natural incidence of light and shade and breadth as the true guide in all artistic planting. The term landscape gardening is a true and, in the fullest sense, a good English one, with a clear and even beautiful meaning, namely, the study of the forms of the earth, and frank acceptance of them as the best of all for purposes of beauty or use of planter or gardener.

We accept the varied slopes of the river bank and the path of the river as not only better than those of a Dutch canal, but a hundred times better; and not only for their beauty, but for the story they tell of the earth herself in ages past. We gratefully take the lessons of Nature in her most beautiful aspects of vegetation as to breadth, airy spaces, massing and grouping of the woods that fringe the valleys or garland the mountain rocks as better beyond all that words can express than anything men can invent or ever have invented.

We love and prefer the divinely-settled form of the tree or shrub or flower beyond any possible expression of man's misguided efforts with shears, such as we see illustrated in old Dutch books where every living thing is clipped to conform to an idea of "design" that arose in the minds of men to whom all trees were green things to be cut into ugly walls. We repudiate as false and ridiculous the common idea of the pattern-monger's book, that these aspirations of ours are in any way "styles," the inventions of certain men, because we know that they are based on eternal truths of Nature, free as the clouds to anyone who climbs the hills and has eyes to see.

The fact that ignorant men who have never had the chance of learning these lessons, make pudding-like clumps in a vain attempt to diversify the surface of the ground, and other foolish things, does not in the least turn us aside from following the true and only ways to get the best expression possible of beauty from any given morsel of the earth's surface we have to plant. We sympathise with the landscape-painter's work as reflecting for us, though often in a faint degree, the wondrously varied beauty of the earth, and in the case of the great master-painters full of truth and beauty. We hold that the only true test of our efforts in planting or gardening is the picture. Do we frighten the artist away, or do we bring him to see a garden so free from ugly patterns and ugly colours that, seen in a beautiful light, it would be worth painting? There is not, and there never can be, any other true test.

Even if our aim be right, the direction, as it is in other matters, may be vitiated by stupidity, as in gardens where false lines and curves abound, as in the Champs Elysée in Paris. It is quite right to see the faults of this and to laugh at them; but how about those who plant in true and artistic ways? In the case we mention there is ceaseless and inartistic and vain throwing up of the ground, and sharp and ugly slopes, which are often against the cultivation of the things planted.

The rejection of clipped forms and book patterns of trees set out like lamp-posts, costly walls where none are wanted, and of all the too facile labours of the drawing-board "artist" in gardens, first affected in England in what we call pleasure-ground and park, is set down by these writers on garden design as the wicked invention of certain men. No account has been taken of the eternally beautiful lessons of Nature or even the simple facts which should be known to all who write about such things. Thus in *The Art and Craft of Garden Making* we read:

> So far as the roads were concerned Brown built up a theory that, as Nature abhorred a straight line, it was necessary to make roads curl about. Serpentine lines are said to be the lines of Nature, and therefore beyond question the only proper lines.

But nothing is said of the fact that in making paths or roads in diversified country it is absolutely necessary to follow the line of easiest gradation, and this cannot always be a straight line, and is, indeed, often a beautiful bent line. In many cases we are not twenty paces from the level space around a house before we have to think of the lie of the ground in making walks, roads, or paths. We are soon face to face with the fact that the worst thing we can attempt is a straight line. If anyone for any reason persists in the attempt the result is ugliness, and, in the case of drives, danger. Ages before Brown was born the roads of England often followed beautiful lines, and it would be just as true to attribute to "Brownites" the invention of the forms of trees, hills, or clouds themselves as to say that they invented the waved line for path or drive. The statement is of a piece with the other, that the natural and picturesque view of garden design and planting is the mischievous invention of certain men, and not the outcome of the most precious of all gifts, of Nature herself, and of the actual facts of tree and landscape beauty. All who have seen the pictures by the roadsides of many parts of Britain and the paths over the hills, and, still more so, those who have to form roads or walks in diversified country, will best know how absurd such statements are.

The very statement that there is but one way of making a garden, is its own refutation; as with this formula before us what becomes of the wondrous variety of the earth and its forms, and of the advantages and needs of change that soil, site, climate, air, and view give us—plains, river valleys, old beach levels, mountains and gentle hills, chalk downs and rich loamy fields, forest and open country?

What is the use of Essex going into Dorset merely to see the same thing done in the home landscape or the garden? But if Essex were to study his own ground and do the best he could from his own knowledge of the spot, his neighbour might be glad to see his garden. We have too much of the stereotyped style already; in nine cases out of ten we can tell beforehand what we are going to see in a country place in the way of conventional garden design and planting; and clearly that is not art in any right sense of the word and never can be.

As we go about our country the most depressing sign for all garden lovers (and this often in districts of great natural beauty) is the stereotyped gardens, probably made by the "young man in the drawing-office." There is a harmful belief in the virtue of paper plans which is misleading and only suits the wants of professionalism in its worst form, and prevents the study of the ground itself, which is the only right way to get the best result.

To the good gardener all kinds of design are good if not against the site, soil, climate, or labours of his garden—a very important point the last. We frequently see beds a foot in diameter and many other frivolities of paper plans which prevent the labours of a garden being done with economy or simplicity. In many places where these tracery gardens are carried out, they are soon seen to be so absurd that the owners quietly turf the spot over, and hence we see only grass where there ought to be a real flower garden. The good gardener is happy adorning old walls or necessary terraces, as at Haddon, as he knows walls are good friends in every way both as backgrounds and shelters but he is as happy in a lawn garden, in a rich valley soil, or on the banks of a river, or on those gentle hill-slopes that ask for no terraces or in the hundreds of gardens in and near towns and cities of Europe that are enclosed by walls and where there is no room for landscape effect (many of them distinctly beautiful too, as in Mr Fox's garden at Falmouth); as much at home in a border-castle garden as in the lovely Penjerrick, like a glimpse of a valley in some Pacific isle, or Mount Usher, cooled by mountain streams.

The architect writer turns on the waterworks as his chief solace:

But of all the fascinating sources of effect in garden-making the most fascinating are waterworks. An expensive luxury as a rule, but they well repay the expense.

Well, there is some evidence of the sort of design these afford; some instances terrible in their ugliness (one hideous at Bayreuth).

And with all the care that a rich State may take of them, can we say that the effect at Versailles is artistic or delightful? Water tumbling into the blazing streets of Roman cities and nobly designed fountains supplying the people with water was right; but in our cool land artificial fountains are very different in effect, and often hideous extravagance. Of their ugliness there is evidence in nearly every city in Europe, including our own Trafalgar Square, and that fine work at the head of the Serpentine. We have also our Crystal Palace and Chatsworth, designed as they might be by a theatrical super who had suddenly inherited a millionaire's fortune. So far as our island countries go, nothing asks for more care and modest art than the introduction into the garden or home landscape of artificial water. Happily our countries are rich in the charms of natural water—too often neglected in its planting.

Among the great peoples of old, so far as known to our human story, was one supreme in art, from buildings chiselled as delicately as the petals of the wild rose, to the smallest coins in their pockets, and bits of baked clay in their graves, and this is clear to all men from what remains of their work gathered from the mud and dust of ages. And from that time of deathless beauty in art comes the voice of one who saw this lovely art in its fulness: *The greatest and fairest things are done by Nature and the lesser by Art* (Plato). There is not a garden in Britain, free from convention and carpet gardening, from the cottage gardens nestling beneath the Surrey hills to those fair and varied gardens in Cornwall, which does not tell the same story to all who have eyes to see and hearts to care for the thing itself, and not merely for incoherent talk about it. The only sad thing is that such words must be said again and again; but we live in a time of much printed fog about artistic things—the "New Art" and the "New Æsthetic"; "Evolution," which explains how everything comes from nothing and goes back again to worse than nothing; the sliding bog of "realism and idealism" in which the phrase-monger may dance around and say the same false thing ten times over; and, last and least of all among these imbecilities, the teaching that to form a garden one had better know nothing of the things that should grow in it, from the Cedar of Lebanon to the violets of the mountain rocks.

This teaching is as false as any spoken or written thing can be; there is an absolute difference between the living gardens and conventional designs dealing with dead matter, be it brick or stone, glass, iron, or carpets. There is a difference in kind, and while any pupil in an architect's office will get out a drawing for the kind of garden we may see everywhere, the garden beautiful does not arise in that way. I would much rather trust the first simple person, who knew his ground and loved his work, to get a beautiful result than any of those artificers. We have proof in the gardens of English people abroad that were freed from the too facile plans of the "office"; far more beautiful gardens arise, as in the Isle of Madeira, where every garden differs from its neighbour, and all are beautiful. So it is in a less degree in our own island, where the more we get out of the range of any one conventional idea for the garden the more beauty and happy incident we see.

CHAPTER VII

*Design and Position; Against Styles, Useless
Stonework, and Stereotyped Plans; Time's Effect on
Garden Design; Architecture and Flower Gardens;
Design Not Formal Only; Use in the Garden
of Builders' and Other Degraded Forms of the
Plastic Art*

The first thing is to get a clear idea of the hollowness of much of the
talk about "styles." In books about laying out gardens there are many
dissertations on styles, the authors going even to China and to Mexico
for illustrations. What is the result to anybody who looks from words
to things? That there are two styles: the one strait-laced, mechanical,
with much wall and stone, with fountains and sculpture; the other the
natural, which, once free of the house, accepts the ground lines of the
earth herself as the best, and gets plant beauty from the flowers and
trees arranged in picturesque ways.

There are positions where stonework is necessary; but the beautiful
terrace gardens are those that are built where the nature of the ground
required them. There is nothing more melancholy than the walls,
fountain basins, clipped trees, and long canals of places like the
Crystal Palace, not only because they fail to satisfy the desire for
beauty, but because they tell of wasted effort, and riches worse than
lost. There are, from Versailles to Caserta, a great many ugly gardens
in Europe, but at Sydenham we have the greatest modern example
of the waste of enormous means in making hideous a fine piece of
ground. As Versailles has numerous tall fountains, the best way of
glorifying ourselves was to make some taller ones at Sydenham! Instead
of confining the terrace gardening to the upper terrace, by far the greater

portion of the ground was devoted to a stony extravagance of design, and nearly in the centre were placed the vast and ugly fountain basins. The contrivances to enable the water to go downstairs, the temples, statues and dead walls, were praised by the papers as the marvellous work of a genius.

Many whose lawns were, or might readily have been made, the most beautiful of gardens, have spoiled them for sham terraced gardens, and there is a modern castle in Scotland where the embankments are piled one above another, till the whole looks as if Uncle Toby with an army of Corporal Trims had been carrying out his grandest scheme in fortification. The rude stone wall of the hill husbandman, supporting a narrow slip of soil for olive-trees or vines, became in the garden of the wealthy Roman a well-built one; but it must be remembered that, even where the wall is necessary, the beauty of the true Italian garden depends on the life of trees and flowers more than on the plan of the garden.

Terraced gardens allowing of much building (apart from the house) have been in favour with architects who have designed gardens. The designer, too often led by custom, falls in with the notion that every house, no matter what its position, should be fortified by terraces, and he busies himself in forming them even on level ground, and large sums are spent on fountains, vases, statues, balustrades, useless walls, and stucco work out of place.

Elaborate terraced gardens in the wrong place often prevent the formation of beautiful lawns, though a good lawn is the happiest thing in a garden. For many years past there has been so much cutting up, geometry and stonework, that it is rare to find a good lawn, and many a site so cut up would be vastly improved if changed into a large, nobly fringed lawn.

A style of garden "design" that for a long time has had an injurious effect on many places is the "railway embankment" phase; there we see a series of sharply graded grass slopes like well-smoothed railway embankments—often several sharp banks, one below the other, without a protecting wall at the top, and obtruding their sharp green angles on various points of view, and this perhaps in the face of a beautiful landscape.

A beautiful house in a fair landscape is the most delightful scene of the cultivated earth, all the more so if there be an artistic garden. The union between the house beautiful and the ground near it is worthy of more thought, and the best way of effecting that union artistically should interest men more and more as our cities grow larger and the landscape shrinks back from them.

After we have settled the essential approaches and levels around a house, the natural form or lines of the earth itself are in nearly all cases the best to follow, and it is often well to face any labour to get the ground back into its natural grade where it is disfigured by ugly or needless banks, lines, or angles. In the true Italian garden *on the hills* we have to alter the natural line of the earth, or "terrace it," because we cannot otherwise cultivate the ground or stand at ease upon it, and in such ground the formal is right, as the lawn is in a garden in the Thames valley. But the lawn is the heart of the true English garden, and as essential to it as the terrace to the gardens on the steep hills.

We may get every charm of a garden and every use of a country place without sacrificing the picturesque or the beautiful. There is no reason, either in the working or design of gardens, why there should be a false line in them; every charm of the flower garden may be secured by avoiding the knots and scrolls which subordinate all the plants and flowers of a garden, all its joy and life, to a conventional design. The true way is the opposite. With only the simplest plans to ensure good working, we should see the flowers and feel the beauty of plant forms, and secure every scrap of turf wanted for play or lawn, and for every enjoyment of a garden.

Time's effect on gardens is one of the main considerations. Fortress-town and castle moat are now without further use, where in old days gardens were set within the walls.

To keep all that remains of such gardens should be our first care—never to imitate them now. Many are far more beautiful than the modern gardens, which have been kept bare of plants or flower life. At one time it was rash to make a garden away from protecting walls; but when the danger from civil war was past, then arose the often beautiful Elizabethan house, free from all moat or trace of war.

In those days the extension of the decorative work of the house into the garden had some novelty to carry it off, while the kinds of evergreens were very much fewer than now. Hence if the old gardeners wanted an evergreen hedge or bush of a certain height they clipped a Yew tree to the form and size they wanted. To-day the ever-growing city, pushing its hard face over our once beautiful land, should make us wish more and more to keep such beauty of the earth as may be still possible to us.

CHAPTER VIII

Borders of Hardy Flowers

We now come to the flowers that are worthy of a place in gardens, and to consider ways of arranging them. Their number and variety being almost without limit, the question is, how the garden lover is to enjoy as many of these treasures as his conditions allow of. As during all time a simple border has been the first expression of flower gardening, and as there is no arrangement of flowers more graceful, varied, or capable of giving more delight, and none so easily adapted to almost every kind of garden, some ideas of the various kinds of borders of hardy flowers mainly deserve our first consideration.

The difference in cost of growing hardy flowers or tender should be thought of. The sacrifice of flower gardens to plants that perish every year has often left them poor of all the nobler plants. We must take into account the hothouses, the propagation of plants by thousands at certain seasons, the planting out at the busiest and fairest time of the year—in June—the digging up and storing in autumn, the care in the winter.

There are a number of plants which, given thorough preparation at first, it would be wise to leave alone for some years at a time—as, for example, groups or beds of the various Tritomas, Irises, Lilies, either grouped with others or in families. When all these exhaust the ground or become too crowded, by all means move them and replant, but this is a very different thing from moving all the plants in the flower garden twice a year.

It would be better every way if, so far as the flower garden is concerned, gardeners were to see what could be done unaided by the hothouse; but meanwhile the wise man will reduce the expense of glass, labour, fire, repairs, paint, pipes, and boilers.

The true way to make gardens yield a return of beauty for the labour and skill given them is the permanent one. Choose some beautiful class of plants and select a place that will suit them, even as to their effect in the garden landscape. Let the beds be planted as permanently and as well as possible, so that there will remain little to do for years.

One of the best reforms will be to avoid the conventional pattern plans, and adopt simple beds and borders, in positions suited to the plants they are to grow. These can best be filled permanently because the planter is free to deal with them in a bolder way than if he has to consider their relation to a number of small beds. In this way, also, the delight of flowers is much more keenly felt as one sees them relieved, sees them at different times, and to more advantage than the flowers stereotyped under the window. Roses grouped well together, and not trained as standards, would lend themselves admirably to culture with other things, for example, Tea Roses with Carnations. Then there are many groups made by the aid of the finer perennials themselves, by choosing things that would go well together, such as the Delphiniums and Phloxes. Other plants, such as Yuccas, of which there are now various beautiful kinds, are often best by themselves; and noble groups they form, whether in flower or not. The kinds of Yucca that flower very freely, such as Y. recurva and Y. flaccida, lend themselves to grouping with Flame Flowers (Tritoma) and the bolder autumn plants.

There is no beauty among tender plants to be compared with that of Irises, Lilies, Delphiniums, Evening Primroses, Pæonies, Carnations, Narcissi, and are we to put aside or into the background all this glorious beauty for the sake of a few things that merely give us flat colour? No one who knows even to a slight extent what the plants of the northern and temperate world are, can admit that this sort of gardening should have the first place. There is nothing among tender plants to equal Windflowers in many kinds, flowering in spring, summer, and autumn; Torch Lilies, superb in autumn; Columbines; Hairbells; Delphiniums; Day Lilies; Everlasting Peas; Evening Primroses; Pæonies; Phloxes; Ranunculus, double and single, and the many fine species; all the noble autumn-blooming, Daisy-like flowers; plumy Spiræas; Globe Flowers; Lilies, in noble variety; Polyanthus; Primroses; Auriculas; Wallflowers; Meadow Saffrons; Crocuses, of the spring and autumn; Scillas; Snowflakes; Grape Hyacinths; Narcissi, in lovely variety; Tulips, the old florists' kinds, and many wild species; Carnations and Pinks; Cornflowers; Foxgloves; Stocks; Starworts; great Scarlet and other Poppies; Christmas Roses, Forget-me-nots; Pansies and many of the rock plants of the mountains of Europe—from the Alps to the hills of Greece, cushioned with Aubrietia, and sky-blue Windflowers—all hardy as the Docks by the frozen brooks.

A frequent way in which people attempt to cultivate hardy flowers is in what is called the "mixed border," often made on the edge of a shrubbery, the roots of which leave little food or even light for the flowers. The face of a shrubbery should be broken and varied; the shrubs should not form a hard line, but here and there they should come full to the edge and finish it. The variety of positions and places afforded by the front of a shrubbery so arranged is tempting, but it is generally best to use plants which do not depend for their beauty on high culture—which, in fact, fight their way near shrubs—and there are a great many of them, such as the evergreen Candytufts, the large-leaved Rockfoils, Acanthus, Day Lilies, Solomon's Seal, Starworts, Leopard's Banes, Moon Daisies, and hardy native Ferns.

A scattered, dotty mixed border along the face of a shrubbery gives a poor effect, but a good one may be secured by grouping the plants in the open spaces between the shrubs, making a careful selection of plants, each occupying a bold space. The presence of tree and shrub life is a great advantage to those who know how to use it. Here is a group of shrubs over which we can throw a delicate veil of some pretty creeper that would look stiff and wretched against a wall; there a shady recess beneath a flowering tree: instead of planting it up with shrubs in the common way cover the ground with Woodruff, which will form a pretty carpet and flower very early in the year, and through the Woodruff a few British Ferns; in front of this use only low plants, and we shall thus get a pretty little vista, with shade and a pleasant relief. Next we come to a bare patch on the margin. Cover it with a strong evergreen Candytuft, and let this form the edge. Then allow a group of Japan Quince to come right into the grass edge and break the margin; then a large group of broad-leaved Rockfoil, receding under the near bushes and trees; and so proceed making groups and colonies, considering every aid from shrub or tree, and never using a plant of which we do not know and enjoy the effect.

This plan is capable of much variety, whether we are dealing with an established and grown shrubbery, or a choice plantation of flowering Evergreens. In the last case, owing to the soil and the neat habit of the bushes, we have excellent conditions in which good culture is possible. One can have the finest things among them if the bushes are not jammed together. The ordinary way of planting shrubs is such that they grow together, and then it is not possible to have flowers between them, nor to see the true form of the bushes, which are lost in one solid leafy mass. In growing fine things—Lilies or Cardinal Flowers, or tall Evening Primroses—among open bushes we may form a delightful garden, we secure sufficient space for the bushes to show their forms, and we get light and shade among them. In such plantations one might have in the back parts "secret" colonies of lovely things which it might not be well to show in the front of the border, or which required shade and shelter that the front did not afford.

It is not only in the flower garden where we may have much beauty of flower, but away from it there are many places better fitted for growing the more beautiful things which do not require continual attention. Unhappily, the common way of planting shrubberies has robbed many grass walks of all charm. The great trees which take care of themselves, are often fine, but the common mixed plantation of Evergreens means death to the variety and beauty of flower we may have by grass walks in sun or shade. The shrubs are frequently planted in mixtures, in which the most free-growing are so thickly set as soon to cover the whole ground, Cherry Laurel, Portugal Laurel, Privet, and such common things frequently killing all the choicer shrubs and forming dark heavy walls of leaves. Some of these Evergreens, being very hungry things, overrun the ground, rob the trees, and frequently, as in the case of the Portugal Laurels, give a dark monotonous effect while keeping the walks wet, airless, and lifeless.

Light and shade and the charm of colour are impossible in such cases with these heavy, dank Evergreens, often cut back, but once one is free of their slavery what delightful places there are for growing all hardy flowers in broad masses, from the handsome Oriental Hellebores of the early spring to the delicate lavenders of the Starworts in October. Not only hardy flowers, but graceful climbers like the wild Clematis, and lovely corners of light and shade may be made instead of the walls of sombre Evergreens. If we want the ground green with dwarf plants, we have no end of delightful plants at hand in the Ivies and Evergreens like Cotoneaster.

In many situations near houses, and especially old houses, there are delightful openings for a beautiful kind of flower border. The stone forms fine background, and there are no thieving tree roots. Here we have conditions exactly opposite to those in the shrubbery; here we can have the best soil, and keep it for our favourites; we can have Delphiniums, Lilies, Pæonies, Irises, and all choice plants well grown.

Walls may be adorned with climbers of graceful growth, climbing Rose, Wistaria, Vine, or Clematis, which will help out our beautiful mixed border. Those must to some extent be trained, although they may be allowed a certain degree of abandoned grace even on a wall. In this kind of border we have, as a rule, no background of shrubs, and therefore we must get the choicest variety of plant life into the border itself and we must try to have a constant succession of interest. In winter this kind of border may have a bare look when seen from the windows, but the variety of good hardy plants is so great, that we can make it almost evergreen by using evergreen rock-plants. Where walls are broken with pillars, a still better effect may be obtained by training Vines and Wistaria along the top and over the pillars or the buttresses.

We have here a frequent kind of mixed border often badly made, but which may be excellent. A good plan is to secure from about eight to ten feet of rich soil on each side of the walk, and cut the borders off from the main garden by a trellis of some kind from seven feet to nine feet high. This trellis may be of strong iron wire, or, better still, of simple rough oak branches, on which we may grow Climbing Roses and Clematis and all the choicer climbers. Moreover, we can grow them in their natural grace along the wires or rough branches, or up and across a rough wooden trellis, Rose and Jasmine showing their grace uncontrolled. We fix the main branches to the supports, and leave the rest to the winds, and form a fine type of flower border in this way, as we have the graceful climbing plants in contrast with the flowers in the border.

Mixed borders may be made in various ways; but it may be well to bear in mind the following points: Select only good plants; throw away weedy kinds, there is no scarcity of the best. See good collections. Put, at first, rare kinds in lines across four-feet nursery beds, so that a stock of plants may be at hand. Make the choicest borders where they cannot be robbed by the roots of trees; see that the ground is good, and that it is at least two and a half feet deep, so deep that, in a dry season, the roots can seek their supplies far below the surface. Plant in naturally disposed groups, never repeating the same plant along the border at intervals, as is so often done with favourites. Do not graduate the plants in height from the front to the back, as is generally done, but sometimes let a bold plant come to the edge; and, on the other hand, let a little carpet of a dwarf plant pass in here and there to the back, so as to give a varied instead of a monotonous surface. Have no patience with bare ground, and cover the border with dwarf plants; do not put them along the front of the border only. Let Hepaticas and double and other Primroses, and Rockfoils, and Golden Moneywort and Stonecrops, and Forget-me-nots, and dwarf Phloxes, and many similar plants cover the ground among the tall plants betimes, at the back as well as the front. Let the little ground plants form broad patches and colonies by themselves occasionally, and let them pass into and under other plants.

Thoroughly prepared at first, the border might remain for years without any digging in the usual sense. When a plant is old and rather too thick, never hesitate to replant it on a wet day in the middle of August any more than in the middle of winter. Take it up and put a fresh bold group in fresh ground; the young plants will have plenty of roots by the winter, and in the following spring will flower much stronger than if they had been transplanted in spring or in winter. Do not pay much attention to labelling; if a plant is not worth knowing, it is not worth growing; let each good thing be so bold and so well grown as to make its presence felt.

The plants of the older kind of mixed border were, like the grasses of the meadows of the northern world, stricken to the earth by winter, and the border was not nearly so pretty then as the withered grass of the plain or copse. But since the revival of interest in hardy and Alpine flowers, and the many introductions of recent years, we have a great number of beautiful plants that are evergreen in winter and that enable us to make evergreen borders. The great white blanket that covers the north and many mountain ranges in winter protects also for months many Alpine plants which do not lose their leaves in winter, such as Rockfoils, Stonecrops, Primroses, Gentians, and Christmas Roses. The most delicate of Alpine plants suffer, when exposed to our winter, from excitement of growth, to which they are not subject in their own home, but many others do not mind our winters much, and it is easy by good choice of plants to make excellent borders wholly or in greater part evergreen.

These are not only good as evergreens, but they are delightful in colour, many being beautiful in flower in spring, and having also the charm of assuming their most refreshing green just when other plants are dying in autumn. Along with these rock and herbaceous plants we may group a great many dwarf shrubs that come almost between the true shrub and the Alpine flower—little woody evergreen creeping things like the dwarf Partridge Berry, Canadian Cornel, hardy

Heaths, and Sand Myrtles, often good in colour when grouped. Among these various plants we have plenty for evergreen borders, and this is important, as, while many might object to the bare earth of the ordinary border of herbaceous plants near the house or in other favourite spots, it is different with borders of evergreen plants, which may be charming and natural in effect throughout the year.

Of garden pictures, there are few prettier than Crocus, Snowdrops, or Scilla coming through the green, moss-like carpets in these evergreen borders, far prettier to those who love quiet and natural colour than more showy effects. Often narrow evergreen borders are the best things that can be placed at the foot of important walls, as the way of allowing grass to go right up to the walls is a foolish one, and often leads to injury to the wall trees. A narrow border cut off by a natural stone edging from the grass or walk, is best even a border of this size may have many lovely things, from early Cyclamen to the best Meadow Saffrons in the autumn. Besides the flowers already named, we have Violets, Periwinkles, Carnations, Pinks, Barrenworts, charming in foliage, purple Rock Cresses, Omphalodes, Iris, Acanthus, Indian and other Strawberries, Houseleeks, Thymes, Forget-me-nots, Sandworts, Gentianella, Lavender, Rosemary, hardy Rock Roses, and many native and other hardy evergreen Ferns in all their fine variety; Bamboos, Ruscus and Dwarf Savin, these are an essential aid in the making of evergreen borders.

Many years of trial with the best wooden trellising disclosed to me its defects as to endurance, even the best wooden trellising oak perishing on the ground or being blown over in storms. The same objection applies to Chestnut *or any native wood*. The result of various trials for many years was to compel the use of an iron base for our trellis at the back of mixed borders, and so cut off the oak used from the wet ground. We used the ordinary iron fence in the first instance, adding a foot or so to the height by means of an iron attachment. This was painted oak colour and fitted with upright heart of oak. The battens do not touch the ground and project a little above the top iron rail. The effect is very good. The best plants for it we found to be Clematis, Roses of the nobler climbing type, like Bouquet d'Or, the Japanese and other Vines. The height of the finished trellis is 5 foot oak battens in seasoned oak ½ by ¾ inches. For backgrounds, so essential to the good mixed border, this manner of trellising is the best.

HARDY BORDER FLOWERS
FOR BRITISH GARDENS

From this list all families not quite hardy in Britain are excluded, for whatever we may do with flower-beds, mixed borders should be mainly of hardy plants, and we ought to be able to plant or refresh them at any time through the autumn or winter months. Well-planned mixed borders, covered as they mostly should be with rock plants forming green carpets, should have few gaps in early summer, but where these occur they may be filled up with half-hardy plants as the stock of plants may permit, or with good annuals.

Acanthus	Campanula	Fuchsia	Lythrum	Ranunculus
Achillea	Carnations	Funkia	Malope	Rhodanthe
Acis	Catananche	Gaillardia	Malva	Rockets
Aconitum	Centaurea	Galtonia	Meconopsis	Rudbeckia
Adonis	Cheiranthus	Geranium	Megasea	Salvia
Agapanthus	Chelone	Geum	Mimulus	Saponaria
Agrostemma	Chrysanthemum	Gypsophila	Mirabilis	Saxifraga
Alstrœmeria in var.	Convallaria	Helenium	Monarda	Scabiosa
Alysum	Convolvulus	Helianthemum	Montbretia	Sedum
Amarylli	Coreopsis	Helianthus	Myosotis	Spiræa
Amberboa	Corydalis	Helichrysum	Narcissus	Statice
Anemone	Cyclamen	Helleborus	Œnothera	Stocks
Anthericum	Cypripedium	Hepatica	Omphalodes	Sweet Pea
Antirrhinum	Delphinium	Hesperis	Onosma	Sweet William
Arabis	Dianthus	Hollyhock	Ornithogalum	Symphytum
Arenaria	Dielytra	Iberis	Orobus	Thymus
Argemone	Digitalis	Iris	Pæonia	Tigridia
Armeria	Dodecatheon	Kniphofia	Pancratium	Tradescantia
Arnebia	Doronicum	Lathyrus	Pansy	Trillium
Aster	Echinops	Lavatera	Papaver	Trollius
Aubrietia	Epimedium	Lavendula	Pentstemon	Tropæolum
Bartonia	Eremurus	Leucojum	Phlomis	Tulipa
Bocconia	Erigeron	Lilium	Phlox	Veratrum
Brodiæa in var.	Erodium	Linaria	Plumbago	Verbascum
Calendula	Eryngium	Linum	Polemonium	Veronica
Calliopsis	Erythronium	Lobelia	Potentilla	Viola
Calochortus	Eschscholtzia	Lupinus	Primula	Wallflower
Caltha in var.	Fritillaria	Lychnis	Pyrethrum	Zephyanthes
				Zinnia

CHAPTER IX

The Reserve and Cut-Flower Gardens

Nothing is worse in gardening than the way in which plants of all kinds are huddled together without regard to fitness for association in stature, in time of blooming, or in needs of culture. The common scene of confusion is the shrubbery border, into which Carnations, annuals, Alpine flowers, and rampant herbs are often thrown, to dwindle and perish. There is no shrubbery border that could not be made beautiful by carpeting it with wood and copse plants of the northern world in broad groups, but many of our favourite flowers are not wood plants, and many—for example, Carnations—cannot maintain the struggle against the bushes and trees. Hardy plants should be divided into two broad series at least—those which thrive in and near woody growth, and those which must perish there. Solomon's Seal and the blue Apennine Anemone are types of plants that one may grow in any shady place: Carnation, Pink, Auricula are among the flowers which must have good soil and be kept away from tree roots.

One good plan that all can follow is the growing of certain plants without heed to their place in any design, but not in any kind of "mixed border" or other mixed arrangements. Many hardy flowers are worthy of special culture, and good results cannot often be got without it, whether we grow Carnations, Pinks, Pansies, Phloxes, Lilies, Stocks, double Wallflowers, Cloves, or scarlet Lobelias. Even a choice annual, such as Rhodanthe, or a beautiful grass, it is not easy to succeed with unless it has a fair chance, away from the crowding of the mixed border. This special culture of favourite flowers may be best carried out in a plot of ground set aside for beds of the choicer flowers, in a piece of ground in or near the kitchen garden or any other open position, sheltered, but not shaded. With the aid of such a division of the garden, the cultivation of many fine hardy plants becomes a pleasure. When any plant gets tired of its bed, it is easy to make the Carnation bed of past years the bulb one for the next year, and so on. It would be easy to change one's favourites from bed to bed, so that deep-rooting plants should follow surface-rooting kinds, and thus the freshness of the garden would be kept up. If any edging is used, it should be of natural stone sunk in the earth, but the abolition of all edgings, beyond one or two main lines, would tend to simplify the work. Such a plot is excellent for giving cut flowers in quantity, and is also a great aid as a nursery, while it would also be a help to exchanges with friends or neighbours in the generous way of all true gardeners. The space occupied by it will depend upon the size and wants of the place; but, wherever the room can be spared, an eighth of an acre might be devoted to the culture in simple beds of favourite flowers.

Among the fair flowers which in this way may be cultivated, each separately and well, are the old Clove Carnations—white, crimson, and scarlet, as well as many other kinds; tall Phloxes, so fair in country gardens in the autumn; scarlet Lobelias, splendid in colour; Pinks of many kinds; Persian and Turban Ranunculus; bright old garden Anemones, and the finer species of Anemone; Lilies, and as many as possible of the splendid kinds introduced into our gardens within the past dozen years from California and Japan; Delphiniums; double Rockets; Irises, English, Spanish, Japanese, and German; Pansies in great variety; Tiger Flowers; the Columbine, including the lovely blue Columbine of the Rocky Mountains; Pyrethrums, Chinese Pinks, Scabious, Sweet Williams; Stocks of many kinds; Wallflowers, double and single; the annual Phloxes; China Asters, the Sweet Sultan, in two or three forms; showy Chrysanthemums; Grasses for cutting in winter; Grape Hyacinths; rare Narcissus; Meadow Saffrons; Lilies of the Valley; Crocuses, the autumnal as well as the vernal kinds; Dahlias, cactus and single; Pæonies; Primroses, double and single; Pentstemons; Polyanthus; Oxlips; Tulips, many early and late kinds; sweet Violets; American Cowslips; Gladioli; Christmas Roses; and, lastly, Everlasting Flowers, which may be grown with the pretty Grasses, and, like them, be gathered for the house in winter.

In these special plots for hardy flowers are included the various hardy florists' flowers. The term "florists' flowers" was once applied to flowers supposed to be popular with amateurs and florists, but it had never any clear meaning. A Rose is a florist's flower; but it is more—it is everybody's flower, and we call it a Rose, having no use for any other term. The reserve garden is a good place to grow flowers for cutting for the house. A supply equal to that of a dozen plant houses can be got from an open square in the kitchen garden or any piece of good ground. For eight months there is a procession of open-air flowers, which can easily be grown in sufficient quantity to allow the cutting of plenty for every want. A bed or a few lines of each favourite in a plot of good soil would give a great number of flowers, and these, aided by the Roses and other bush and tree flowers about the garden, would yield all the flowers that a large house would require, and many besides for hospitals and for those who have no gardens. Flowers grown for cutting should be carefully selected as regards odour, form, and colour.

We have had evidence of the good way in which inter-cropping suits plants in nursery beds, and there is reason to believe that the presence in rich ground of two plants wholly different in their nature is a good plan. A collection of Narcissi, with lines between of Delphiniums and hardy Fuchsias, that is to say, two lines of each in a 4-foot bed, will thrive. The same is true of other hardy spring bulbs, which may be alternated with the choicer perennials that bloom in autumn; and this way is a good one for people who live in their gardens chiefly in spring and autumn, as it secures two distinct seasons of bloom in the same ground. This applies to store beds as distinct from the regular flower garden, though some kind of inter-cropping would give an excellent result in the flower garden also; as, for instance, if we have beds of Roses, we might have them carpeted with early bulbs, and be none the worse for it, and so also with Pæonies and many other flowers. It wants some care to find out which go best together; but, given that, all is easy enough.

Apart from the reserve garden, with its flowers in close masses, we may have gardens of a favourite flower and its forms, for the purpose of studying a family or adding to it by collecting or cross-breeding. Such gardens now and then owe their existence to the difficulty of cultivating a flower, as was the case of a charming garden of the lovely forms of our native Primrose formed by a friend of mine, who thus describes it:—

No flower better deserves a garden to itself than the Primrose. It is so old a favourite, and has been cultivated into so many forms, that anyone determined to have a Primrose garden may choose the kind he likes best, and set to work accordingly. There are the single-stalked

Primroses, the earliest of all, flowering from the middle of March onwards, while some may be had in bloom as soon as the end of February. They range in colour from pure white to deep primrose, and from palest pinky-lilac through strong red-purples to a colour nearly approaching blue, and there are also rich reds of many shades. There is not as yet any Primrose of a true pink colour, nor, though the type colour is yellow, are there as yet any strong yellows of the orange class. There are also double Primroses in nearly all the same colourings. The grand Primroses for garden effect are the large bunch-flowered kinds, white, yellow, and orange-coloured, red, crimson, and rich brown; of infinite variety in form, texture, habit, and colouring, easy to raise to any amount by seed, as also by division of the older plants. A Primrose garden (part of which is here illustrated), that for some years has been an ever-increasing source of pleasure and interest to its owners, was formed a few years ago by making an opening about 70 yards long, and varying from 10 to 15 yards wide, through a wild copse of young Birch trees. The natural soil was very poor and sandy, so it was prepared by a thorough trenching and a liberal addition of loam and leaf soil. No formal walks are made, but one main track is trodden down about 2 feet wide near the middle of the space, dividing into two here and there, where a broader clearing makes it desirable to have two paths in the width. The older divided plants are put into groups of a colour together from twenty to fifty of a sort. The groups of seedlings are of necessity more various, though they are more or less true to the parent colour, so that a patch of a hundred seedlings—from yellow, for instance—will give a general effect of yellow throughout the group. The whites and yellows are kept at one end of the garden, and the reds at the other; the deepest yellows next to the reds. Seen from a little distance, the yellow and white part of the Primrose garden looks like a river of silver and gold flowing through the copse. The white stems of the Birches and the tender green of their young leaves help to form a pretty picture, which is at its best when the whole is illuminated by the evening sunlight.

Some of the Plants for Reserve Garden and for Cutting Flowers

Carnations	Double Rockets	Tigridia	Chinese Pinks	Stocks
Phloxes	Iris	Columbines	Scabious	Wallflowers
Scarlet Lobelias	Pansies	Pyrethrum	Blue Cornflower	Grape
Pinks	Alstrœmeria	Schizostylis	Sweet Williams	Hyacinths

Grasses, the more graceful kinds	Lilies	Meadow Saffrons	Pentstemon	American Cowslips
Zinnias	Delphiniums	Roses	Primroses	Gaillardia
Sweet Sultan	Narcissus	Crinum	Polyanthus	Gladiolus
Ranunculus	China Asters	Crocus	Oxlips	Everlastings
Anemone	Campanula	Dahlia	Tulips	Christmas Roses
	Chrysanthemums	Pæonies	Violets	Lenten Roses

CHAPTER X

Hardy Bulbous Flowers

At no distant time lists of these things were mostly looked at for the sake of getting a few bulbs to force, but that day is past, at least for all who now see the great part which hardy bulbous and tuberous plants must take in the outdoor gardens of the future. Since those days the hills of California and of Japan alone have given us a noble Lily garden, and the plants of this order in cultivation now form a lovely host. We are not nearly so likely to want novelties as knowledge of how to make effective use of the nobler plants, such as the Narcissus, the glory of the spring, as the Lily is of the summer garden.

We may indeed be often tempted with Zephyr flowers, and Ixias and other plants, beautiful in warmer countries than ours, but delicate here, and only living with us as the result of care; but there are so many lovely things from the mountains and plains of the northern world, as hardy as the wild Hyacinths of British woods, that our search will be more for the nobler materials and how to make artistic use of them than in quest of novelty.

Who of those who remember the Orange and White Lilies of all English and Irish gardens would have looked for the splendid Lilies that have come to us within less than a generation? For size, and form, and lovely colour they surpass all we had ever dreamt of even among tropical flowers. The variety is great, but the main thing for all who care for them is how to possess their beauty with the least amount of care; and, happily, the question has been solved for many handsome kinds by planting them in the peat beds that were made at first wholly in the interest of the American shrubs, as some of the finest Lilies thrive admirably in these. Nor need we neglect the mixed borders because we have new ways for our Lilies, as several of the European Lilies thrive in ordinary borders. They may be naturalised too, or some of them, in deep moist peat bottoms; for example, the American swamp Lily (L. superbum). Lilies are so varied in their nature and stature that they may adorn almost any aspect in sun or shade. The new and rare among them will have special beds or borders, and we have men who will have Lily Gardens. And as these lovely flowers tumble into our lap from the woods and hills of Western China, Japan, and California, untouched by man until he found them made to his hand a few years ago, it was reasonable to suppose that some of them would take care of themselves, if trusted in likely spots, with us. I put some of the Panther Lily deep in a leafy hollow in a Sussex wood, just to see if it would survive in such conditions. Whether owing to a series of cold wet seasons and the want of the glorious sun of the hills in Nevada County, California, where I found it, I know not, but after the first season it did not come up. I thought no more of it, but a friend going into the same wood some years afterwards found a colony of it in bloom.

Next to the Lily in value as an outdoor flower is the Narcissus, though when we know the Iris better it may find a high place. But the wondrous development of the garden forms of Narcissus during recent years, and their fitness for our climate, give it great value. Mountain plants in origin, for the most part they are as hardy as rushes, and those few southern forms that will only live in dry banks and at the foot of warm walls need not concern us who look for pictures of Narcissus in the open air. We have not to ask where the Narcissus will grow, as there are few places they will not grow in with the usual garden culture, and in some cool, loamy soils they take kindly to the turf. Hence it is easy on many soils to have a garden of these flowers, grouped and massed, set in turf, and giving us many flowers for the house as well as pictures in lawn and meadow. These precious early flowers will also have their place in the garden for cut flowers or the nursery bed, where the many new forms of Narcissus may take their place until plentiful. The true hardiness of the flower allows of its being enjoyed in all parts of these scattered islands. In planting Narcissus in the wild garden the mistake is in planting all over the surface without relief. I have made the mistake myself and have regretted it. When they cover the ground like tiles on a roof, they are not nearly as effective as in simple groups. The practice of the Trade of offering mixed kinds is attractive but quite wrong. Much the best way is to use mixtures rarely and always to have distinct plants.

The Iris is one of the oldest of our garden flowers, in many forms too, but, like the Lily, it has come to us in greater novelty and beauty of recent years, and as districts in Central Asia and Asia Minor are opened to collectors, we must have our Iris gardens too. And what so fair as an Iris garden? They are the Orchids of the north, many of them as hardy as reeds, and with more richness of colour than Orchids. The old Irises of our gardens are usually of the Germanica class; there is much variety among these groups, and they are very hardy and precious, and excellent for the adornment of gardens and even walls and thatched roofs, as we see in France, the Iris of this great group having a valuable power of thriving on such surfaces as well as on good soil.

There is a group of waterside and water-loving Iris, much less seen in our gardens than the above, and some of them not yet come to us, but of great value. They are allied to the common yellow Iris of our watercourses, but are taller and richer in colour, the golden Iris (aurea), Monnieri, and ochroleuca being the best known so far, and very free, hardy, and beautiful plants they are, thriving, too, almost anywhere, but best in rich, moist soil. And we have the distinct gain of the splendid Japanese Iris, in its many strange forms, the Japanese surpassing all waterside Irises in its wide range of colour, though most beautiful perhaps in its simple forms, white and purple. This plant, though its beauty suggests that of the tropics, will grow side by side with our great water dock by any lake-side or even in a clay ditch, where only the coarsest weeds live. The Siberian Iris and the forms near it are very graceful beside streams or ponds, either in open or copsy places, and far more graceful and charming in such positions than in set borders. All these water-loving Irises will do in the wild garden in bold groups when we can spare them.

Then there are the brilliant purple and gold Iris reticulata and its allies, little bulbous Irises, for the spring garden, early and charming things, many beautiful; Irises that flower in winter and early spring, like the Algerian Iris; others happy in Britain on warm soils and warm corners, and some for the rock garden, like the crested Iris; and the many pretty forms of Iris pumila, of some of which edgings were made in old gardens. The foliage of the evergreen Iris is so graceful and usually so nice in colour that artistic use may be made of it in that way. The most novel of all the groups of Iris, however, are the Cushion Irises, which promise much beauty, but are as yet too little known for us to see how far that beauty may be preserved in our gardens. The old Iris

Susiana has been known for many years, and some of its allies, like
I. Lorteti and the Wolf Iris, seem more hardy and not less beautiful.

The old garden Tulip, a favourite for generations, grown in the
so-called florist varieties, and the source once of severe mania, is but
one of a large number of wild Tulipa, many of which have come to
us of late years from Central Asia. The old Tulips are the forms of
an Italian species (T. Gesneriana), and these varieties are worthy of
all the attention they ever had; but the wild form is as good as any
of its varieties for splendid effect, and a selection should be made of
its simpler colours, including a good white and yellow. The bedding
Tulips, which are earlier in blooming, are forms of T. scabriscapa,
and though useful, are not nearly so valuable for their effect as the
late tulips. The new Tulips coming from Central Asia and other lands
promise to be very valuable, too, for their effect, though our climate
may not suit all of them, as it does the fine hardy Gesneriana. The
colour of these Tulips is too fine to be missed, and, as the bloom is
too short-lived to give beds to them, the best way is to plant them
in borders: when scarce, in the nursery, when plentiful, in the wild
garden. The later these wild Tulips come into bloom the better, as
it brings their nobler colour in when the harsh changes of the spring
are nearly over, and in the north they will come in with the early
summer days.

If the Crocus has any fault it is courage in coming so early that it
has to face every trouble of the spring, and green winters induce it to
open too early. Yet what promise it brings us of the many-blossomed
spring in border and in lawn; for, in addition to the old and good way
in garden borders, the Crocus, at least all the forms and series and the
hardy and vigorous European kinds, is easily naturalised in lawns or
meadow turf, and others even under Beech trees, as in Crowsley Park.
As regards this question, it should be remembered that the Crocus is
wild in rich meadow grass in various parts of England, at Nottingham
and in Essex. The autumnal kinds may be naturalised too, but they ask
perhaps for a warmer soil than the vernal kinds. Recent years have
brought us many new Crocuses. Soil has much to do with the effect
of the Crocus, and calcareous and warm soils they love, on cold clays
apt to go back.

The old Snowdrop gives as good an effect as any other, but the
many new varieties give the Snowdrop more value. Whether these new
forms are species or varieties matters little; their value as garden plants
is the only question that concerns flower gardeners. Who would have

thought a few years ago that our Snowdrop was only one of a large number taking care of themselves in the mountains of Asia Minor and near regions? Others are coming, and when these increase in our gardens we shall have fresh aids to make our spring gardens more beautiful. As these new kinds are mostly plants from cool regions, they will probably be easily naturalised in many soils. The Snowflake must not be forgotten—few spring flowers are more free than the vernal Snowflake growing in moist soils, tallest and best in peaty soils.

The lovely early group of plants allied to our Wood Hyacinth—Scilla, Chionodoxa and Hyacinthus—ask for some thought as to their artistic use. The Scillas are well known, but the newer forms of Chionodoxa give an unlooked-for loveliness of blue very early in the spring, and show a pretty variety in their delicate colours; and yet there is no more lovely thing among them than the Taurian Scilla. It is so early and so deep a blue that one may get rich effects with it very early. The more tiny and select of all these plants are Alpine, delightful for rock-gardens, and all the more so if we can use them in visible groups.

Apart from the true Lilies there are certain plants to which the name is also given betimes, such as the Torch Lily (Kniphofia), the Day Lily (Hemerocallis), the Peruvian Lily (Alstrœmeria), the African Lily (Agapanthus), the Belladonna Lily (Amaryllis), the Cape Lily (Crinum), the Plantain Lily (Funkia), the Wood Lily (Trillium), the Mariposa Lily (Calochortus), besides other Lilies that do not come under our present heading, or which do not ask for thought as regards their effective use.

The Torch Lilies are brilliant in colour and have been added to of recent years, but severe winters have thinned them, and they will always be best in dry soils and in sunny positions, protected in winter. They are best kept apart from flowers more refined in colour, such as Tea Rose. The Day Lilies are a really hardy race, and most of them will grow anywhere. With their fine leaves and showy, well-formed flowers, they may be used with good effect in various ways. The Belladonna Lily can be grown in no more effective way than the old one of planting it under south walls. The Cape Lilies have increased of late years from hybrids and otherwise, and are worth attention in deep soil in warm corners near walls that protect them from the north. The African Lily is most important for its unrivalled blue, and there is a hardy kind, Moreanus. It is one of the plants for which the expense of tubs or large pots is worth indulging in, and there are new and handsome kinds, which make the culture more interesting. The Wood Lilies are valuable because they give us effects both distinct and beautiful in peat borders or bog gardens. The best effects are in half-shady spots. The Mariposa Lilies are beautiful, but they come from one of the best climates in the world, and one can hardly hope that they will thrive in our climate without special care. Yet such charming flowers will always have a place in curious gardens, where they will thrive in frames and warm corners.

The Poppy Anemone has been a welcome flower in our gardens for hundreds of years, and it should never be forgotten, save in cold soils where it perishes. Many now grow it well from seed, but the old way of planting the tubers of favourite kinds and colours should be carried out in the flower garden in Rose beds or in any beds to spare. The Scarlet Anemone and its varieties is also precious; the Star Anemone, so charming in Italy and Greece in spring, is rarely seen happy in our gardens, which are too cold for it, no doubt, so it may well be left out in favour of the hardier sorts. Valuable as the brightest Anemones are, the old Turban and Persian Ranunculus and other forms were once a great charm of the flower garden, and should not be forgotten in warm soil, where they thrive, but they perish in severe winters.

The old Dog's-tooth Violet of the mountains of Europe has been joined in our gardens of recent years by a number of its American relations, graceful plants for peat borders, but as yet not so valuable as the European kind in its various forms, which are among the prettiest early spring flowers. They are, moreover, true wild garden plants, which thrive in turf, coming up every year even more faithfully than Crocus or Snowdrop. The Snake's-head too (Fritillaria), is a charming wild garden plant, thriving in wet meadows. The new yellow Fritillaries give a greater interest to this group of plants, some of which are fitted for the wild garden, but we never could see the charms of the Crown Imperials, with their offensive odour. The Stars of Bethlehem (Ornithogalum) thrive in grass, and are pretty in it. The Montbretias are plants of somewhat recent appearance in our gardens, and some have a hardiness we do not look for in Cape plants, and a tenacious way of growing even in cold, poor soil, and are, therefore, valuable where we wish to have close tufts of graceful leaves and gay blossoms below flowering shrubs not set too closely on the ground. Grape Hyancinths (Muscari) are often very pretty, and nearly always hardy. I use them freely in grass, where their blue is very pretty in spring. In close turf they may not thrive in sandy soils more free. One (racemosus) is wild in the Eastern counties. The best is *conicum*, free on many soils. It deserves to be in sandy fields.

Among the new plants we have one of fine distinction in the Giant Asphodel (Eremurus), plants of noble port and vigour, which, best grouped among shrubs, hold their full effect.

So noble a plant as the Gladiolus should not have been left to the end, but the fact that the finest class are only half hardy makes them less important in our country than Lilies and Narcissi, that give so much beauty with little or no care. The years pass so swiftly, and are so full of cares, that things demanding two important attentions yearly—*i.e.*, taking up and planting—must take a minor place, except in the case of growers who make a special care of them. Generally our climate is against the older Gladioli, and disease very often comes with attempt to grow them.

The special or reserve garden includes beds for hardy bulbs—a very good way of growing them, and for supplying flowers for the house. A curious habit of the flowers of bulbs is that, cut from the plants when just opening and put into water, they get larger than they would if left on the plants out of doors, and this should lead us to encourage many lovely flowers among hardy bulbs that are among the best for our rooms. Hitherto the bane of the gardener has been cutting flowers for the house; but if cutting prolongs his bloom, strengthens his plants, and gives all who care for his flowers a fuller enjoyment of them, we may secure his powerful aid. Consider what one may escape in storms, frosts, and other dangers if a flower, cut just on arriving at maturity, lasts longer indoors than out, and actually, as in the case of the Narcissus, gets larger! Narcissi, through their hardiness and drooping heads, endure our climate better than any other flowers, and yet severe storms will beat them about and destroy flowers that might have lived for days in the house. Large showy flowers like Tulips, suffer with every heavy shower. Anything which makes it easier to have flowers in the house is a real gain; their exquisite forms are best seen, and tell their story best when brought near to the eye. A flower of our yellow wood Tulip opening and closing, and showing its changing form in a room, gives ideas of beauty which cannot be gleaned by glancing at a bed of bulbs.

One of the most marked improvements is the planting of handsome bulbs in masses of Rhododendrons and like bushes. These beds, as usually planted, are interesting only when in flower, and not always then, owing to the flat surface into which the shrubs are pressed;

Lilies, therefore, and the finer bulbs may with great advantage be placed among the shrubs. In many cases where this plan has been carried out, it has almost changed the entire aspects of gardens, and given various beautiful types of life instead of only one, and many fine rare bulbs find a home in such beds, which should be sacred from the spade. In placing choice, peat-loving shrubs, give the bushes room to fully attain their natural forms, and plant the interspaces with Lilies, giant Asphodels, the tall Larkspurs and the golden Iris (aurea). Light and shade, relief and grace, are among the merits of this mode of planting. Beds of the smaller shrubs will do admirably for the smaller and more delicate bulbs, the shelter of low shrubs being an advantage to many little bulbs whose leaves are apt to suffer from cold winds. In this way we get relief, variety, and longer bloom, and the shrubs show their forms better when they have free play of light and air about them.

Bold beds of Lilies and the taller bulbs are admirable for the lawn, and for quiet corners of the pleasure-ground. At Moulton Grange some years ago I saw on the turf in a quiet corner a bed of Tiger Lilies which had no other flowers near to mar its beauty. It was a large oval bed, and the colour of the finely grown Lilies was brilliant and effective seen through the trees and glades. In point of colour alone, nothing could be better; the mass of bloom was profuse, and the plants, about 6 feet high, told well in the garden landscape. Among the most lovely beds are those of the nobler Lilies, while Iris, and many beautiful Day Lily, Pæony, Gladiolus, and Cape Hyacinth may be grouped with them or near them. It may be as well to note that what is meant here is not wild gardening with bulbs, but very good cultivation of them, and surfacing and edging the beds with spring flowers.

Some Hardy Bulbous and Tuberous Plants for British Flower Gardens

Acis	Calochortus	Gladiolus	Narcissus	Scilla
Agapanthus	Chionodoxa	Galtonia	Orchis	Sparaxis
Allium	Colchicum	Hyacinthus	Ornithogalum	Sternbergia
Alstrœmeria	Convallaria	Iris	Oxalis	Tigridia
Amaryllis	Crocus	Ixiolirion	Pæonia	Trillium
Anemone	Cyclamen	Leucojum	Pancratium	Triteleia
Anthericum	Erythronium	Lilium	Puschkinia	Tritonia
Arum	Fritillaria	Montbretia	Ranunculus	Tropæolum
Calla	Galanthus	Muscari	Schizostylis	Tulipa

CHAPTER XI

Annual and Biennial Plants

Whatever we may do with perennials, shrubs, or hardy bulbs, the plants in this class must ever be of great value to the flower gardener; and among the most pleasant memories of flower garden things are often those of annual or biennial plants such as tall and splendid Stocks in a farmhouse garden on a chalky soil, seen on a bright day in early spring; Wallflowers in London market gardens and in cottage gardens, when not cut down by cruel winters; Snapdragons on old garden walls, and bright Marigolds everywhere; Hollyhock lines, Sweet Pea hedges, and Mignonette carpets; Evening Primrose, Poppies, Sweet Scabious, and Sweet Williams. However rich a garden may be in hardy flowers or bedding plants, it is wise in our climate to depend much on annual flowers.

Like most other plants, they enjoy fresh ground, and where they are grown in borders by themselves it is easy to enrich the ground, and make it fitted for them, easier than when grown among perennials, Roses, and the like. With this precaution the culture is very simple.

In wet seasons and in wet northern districts annuals surprise us by their vigour and beauty. In warmer counties the defect of the heat may in the case of the hardy kinds be met by autumn sowing in good ground. The autumn sowings are the best. The plants not only flower much sooner, but, where the soil and climate suit them, they are stronger and more beautiful.

Among annual flowers we have the lovely Everlastings of Australia, which have an order of beauty distinct from those we see in gardens into which annuals do not enter. Carefully gathered, they may adorn our houses during the winter. The Pimpernels, which with their pretty blue flowers were once made charming use of in gardens, are much neglected. The Mexican Poppy is a pretty flower and quite distinct. The annual Chrysanthemums of Southern Europe and Northern Africa, and indeed of our own fields, are strong in effect. The annual Bindweeds are pretty, and in southern gardens may be used. The annual Larkspurs are so little used in gardens that it is only in seed farms that we have the pleasure of seeing them now and then in all their beauty. The annual Chinese Pinks are brilliant grown in sunny beds and good soil. Our native Foxglove, seen in many of our woodlands, breaks in the hands of the gardener into varieties well worth growing, if not in the garden, in shrubberies and in copses and woods. It is a good plan, when any ground is broken up for fence-making or rough planting, to scatter a few seeds of the white and other pretty kinds and leave them to take care of themselves. There are many graceful grasses which may be treated as annuals, and their flowers, like the Everlasting flowers, be in bloom through the winter. The annual Hibiscus when well grown are effective plants, and the same may be said of the Hollyhock, for which probably the best way is to raise it from seed, as in that way we can fight better against the killing fungus. The Single Hollyhock is worthy of much care and is often very effective. The Flaxes are very pretty annuals, red and blue, and even the common cultivated Flax is a beautiful plant. In our day quite a series of beautiful form of Mignonette have come to add to the charms of that always welcome plant. The annual and biennial Evening Primroses are often beautiful in evenings and at night.

The Sweet Scabious are pretty and varied in colour and so fragrant. Of Sweet Peas there is a delightful series in our own day, when so many kinds have been raised that one could easily make a garden of them. No words can exaggerate their value, either in mixed or separate colours, and they should be both autumn and spring sown, so as to get a chance of those fine tall hedges of Sweet Peas which come where we sow in autumn and get the plants safely through the winter, and they are doubly valuable owing to the many beautiful new kinds.

Some annual plants, like the Cornflower, Sweet Sultan, Sweet Pea, Scabious, are precious for cutting for the house, and may be grown with the hardy flowers for this purpose where there is room for it; others are good for trellis-work, and others for surfaces we wish to adorn with pretty climbers, such as Canary Creeper, Gourds, and Convolvulus.

The various French and African Marigolds, and the prettier forms of the pot Marigold, are very showy plants, and, for those who love much colour, are almost essential, and the same may be said of the various annual Calliopsis. The China Aster used to be grown much better than it is generally now, and there is no doubt, where people do not get much colour from other plants, such as Roses, the China Aster in its many forms is useful. But more important by far are the various kinds of Stock, which have the added charm of fragrance, and which do so well in many gardens with light and warm soils in the north and in Scotland. Cosmos are pretty plants worthy of a place, and the best of the annual kinds of Datura are picturesque and distinct. Chinese Pinks are very beautiful and charming in variety. The Gilias are very pretty, varied, and hardy, and some forming a carpet for taller plants.

The Godetias, allied to the Evening Primroses, are handsome when well grown, especially the white and simple coloured kinds, and where they live over the winter, from autumn sowing, they are very strong and handsome the following year. The many varieties of the annual Ipomæa are graceful, there being much charming variety among the blooms, and with these may be named the various kinds of Convolvulus minor, which does not climb. Lavatera and Malope are handsome plants in the autumn garden, as are the Lupins, well grown, and the Nemesia from the Cape is charming. We think the various Nigellas very interesting, while every one should have the annual Phloxes, now to be had in such good colours, and the Portulacas, which are so brilliant on warm borders. The Salpiglossis is a beautiful plant, especially where we take the trouble to select the simpler colours, the amber coloured one being very fine. The Sweet Scabious has charming varieties, and is often very fine in colour, though not so good on heavy and cool soils.

The Sweet Sultans are pretty, and useful for cutting for the house, and Love-lies-bleeding (Amaranthus) and its allies are quaintly effective. The Snapdragons, which are often treated as annuals, are frequently excellent when grown in their simple colours, the striped kinds not being nearly so good in effect. The annual Poppies are essential where a good display is hoped for from annuals, also the Mexican and Californian Poppies. Such handsome plants as the varieties of Tropæolum are also many of them beautiful annuals.

It is not everyone who has the means to winter a large number of tender bedding plants, and the keeping of a large stock involves much work, and takes up space that might be better occupied. But a garden may be made very gay in summer with half-hardy plants raised from seed, and without keeping a single plant over the winter in the greenhouse. In seedlings there may be differences in habit and colour, but this should be no objection. Seedling Verbenas make a handsome bed, and usually do much better so grown than from cuttings.

Biennial plants are usually such as make their growth in one year and flower the next, but the line between biennial and annual is not a strict one, because in their native countries annual plants often spring up in one year, and flower the next. In countries with open winters and hot summers, annuals do so naturally, and begin to grow in the first rains through the winter, and flower strongly the next year—these often being kinds sown in spring in gardens. Hollyhocks, Foxgloves, Chimney Campanula, and Sweet Williams come under this head, but in some cases early raising in spring gives us a chance of blooming some of them the same year as they are sown. In any case it is better for simplicity's sake to group all annual and biennial plants together, and with them the half-hardy plants raised from seed for use in the flower garden, as the work of raising all is, to a great extent, the same.

Annuals are a much greater aid in the flower garden than is generally acted upon. Often sown in a hurried way in the spring, they give a good effect, it is true, for those who depend much on annuals; but some of the very finest are best if sown in the early autumn, so that they can get a hold when there is still some warmth in the earth. We usually sow them the first week in September, and among the beautiful things that pass the winter with safety here and flower long in the spring are the Collinsias, *grandiflora* and *bicolor, Nemophila insignis* and *maculata*, the beautiful Phacelia Campanularia. The blue Cornflower is much better and handsomer autumn-sown. And one may say generally of all annuals that naturally shed their seeds in summer and autumn, and in their own country gather strength during the winter, that they are able to throw up a fine bloom in the spring.

Some Annual and Biennial Plants, and Half-Hardy Plants Raised from Seed for the Flower Garden

Acroclinium	Anagallis	Calliopsis	Chrysanthemum	Didiscus
Adlumia	Antirrhinum	Campanula	Clarkia	Digitalis
Agathæa	Arctotis	Cannabis	Clintonia	Erysimum
Ageratum	Argemone	Catananche	Convolvulus	Erythræa
Agrostemma	Bartonia	Celosia	Coreopsis	Eschscholtzia
Alonsoa	Boerkhausia	Celsia	Cosmidium	Eucharidium
Alyssum	Brachycome	Centaurea	Cosmos	Eutoca
Amaranthus	Calandrinia	Centranthus	Datura	Gaillardia
Amberboa	Calceolaria	Cheiranthus	Delphinium	Gilia
Ammobium	Calendula	China Aster	Dianthus	Glaucium

Godetia	Limnanthes	Nemesia	Platystemon	Sphenogyne
Gypsophila	Linaria	Nemophila	Podolepis	Stenactis
Hedysarum	Linum	Nicotiana	Polygonum	Stocks
Helichrysum	Loasa	Nierembergia	Portulaca	Sweet Peas
Heliophila	Lobelia	Nigella	Pyrethrum	Sweet William
Hesperis	Lophospermum	Nolana	Rhodanthe	Tagetes
Hollyhock	Lupin	Nycterinia	Ricinus	Tropæolum
Iberis	Maize	Œnothera	Salpiglossis	Verbascum
Impatiens	Malope	Onopordon	Salvia	Verbena
Ionopsidium	Malva	Oxalis	Saponaria	Viola
Ipomopsis	Martynia	Oxyura	Scabious	Virginia Stock
Ipomæa	Maurandya	Papaver	Schizanthus	Viscaria
Isotoma	Mesembryan-	Pelargonium	Schizopetalon	Waitzia
Kaulfussia	themum	Pentstemon	Senecio	Whitlavia
Lasthenia	Mignonette	Petunia	Silene	Zea
Lavatera	Mimulus	Phacelia	Solanum	Zeranthemum
Leptosiphon	Mirabilis	Pharbitis	Sorghum	Zinnia
Leptosyne	Myosotis	Phlox	Specularia	

CHAPTER XII

Flowering Shrubs and Trees, and their Artistic Use

Spring comes to us wreathed in Honeysuckle, and summer brings the
Wild Rose and the May bloom, and these are but messengers of a host
of lovely shrubs and low trees of the hills and plains of northern and
temperate regions, and also of the high mountains of countries like
India, where there are vast Alpine regions with shrubs as hardy as
our own, as we see in the case of the white Clematis that covers
many an English cottage wall with its fair white bloom. If we think
of the pictures formed in thousands of places in England, Scotland,
and Ireland by the May alone, we may get an idea of the precious
beauty there is in the American, Asiatic, and European kinds, some
of which flower later than our own and make the May bloom season
longer. Nothing is lovelier among flowering trees than a group of the
various Thorns, beautiful also in fruit, and the foliage of some kinds
is finely coloured in autumn. The flowering Thorns are but one branch
of the most important order of flowering trees, embracing the Apples (a
garden in their varied flowers alone); Pears, wild and cultivated; Crabs,
pretty in bloom and bright in fruit; Quinces, Medlars, Snowy Mespilus,
Almonds, Double Cherries, Japan Quinces, Plums (including Sloe and
Bullace).

The Double Peaches are among the most precious of trees of this
order, but for some reason we rarely see them in any but a miserable
state in England. In France they are sometimes lovely, not only in the
flower, but in the mass of colour from healthy growth. It may be that
the failure of the shoots to ripen in our cool climate is owing to some
weakness through grafting on a bad stock. There is such a great and
noble variety among these trees that there is room for distinct effects.
An excellent point in favour of trees like Crabs, Almonds, and Bird

Cherries is that, in their maturity, they, in groups or single specimens, stand free on the turf—free, too, from all care; and it is easy to see how important this is for all who care for English tree-fringed lawns—a long way more beautiful than any other kind of tree garden.

It is not only the flowers on the trees we have to think of, but of their use also in the house—as cut flowers gathered when the buds are ready to open—gathering the branchlets and long twigs before the flowers are quite out and placing them in vases in rooms. In very bad weather this way will prolong the bloom for us, or even save it in the case of very hard frost, and in a cold spring it will advance the bloom a little, the warmth of the house giving a few days' gain in time of opening. As to the kinds of shrubs that may be cut for the house in this way there are many of the same race, from the Sloe to the beautiful kinds of Apple.

What beautiful groups of flowering evergreens we might plant in them! Mountain Laurels (Kalmia), Japan and American Andromeda, Azaleas, choice Evergreen Barberries, alpine Cotoneaster, Evergreen Daphne, Desfontainea, in the south; the taller hardy Heaths, Escallonia, Ledum, Alpine and wild forms of Rhododendron, Sweet Gale, Star bush, and various Laurustinus. Charming gardens might be made of such shrubs, not lumped together, but in open groups, with the more beautiful American hardy flowers between them, such as the Wood Lily and Mocassin flower, many rare Lilies, and bulbous flowers of all seasons. The light and shade and variety in such beds of choice evergreens and flowers mingled are charming, and the plan would be a permanent one as it would tend to abolish the never-ending digging in the flower garden. Beds of flowering shrubs in the flower garden are not always so well suited for small gardens; but in bold ones, now naked in winter, it would make them sightly even at that season, and much easier to deal with in early summer.

Rhododendrons of the hybrid sorts are too much used, and, as they are nearly always grafted, the common stock that bears them in the end kills the plant it should support, and so we too often see the pontic surviving. These shrubs are so easily raised by layering that there is no longer need to face death in the pontic stock as some nurseries have stocks of the plants in their natural roots, the only right way. Yet there are many beautiful things among these hybrids. The good colours are well worth picking out from them, and the aim of the planter should be to show the habit and form of the plant. This does not mean that they may not be grouped or massed just as before, but openings of all sizes should be left among them for light and shade, and for handsome herbaceous plants that die down in the winter, thus allowing the full light for half the year to evergreens.

In the south and west the various Arbutus are charming for lawns and ravines, and for sheltering the flower garden, as is also the sweet Bay Laurel, but the Common Cherry Laurel and the Portugal should not be planted near anything precious.

Azaleas are, considering their great number and variety, perhaps the most precious flowering shrubs we have; they are fine in form of bush, even when they get little freedom, and superb in colour, the foliage in autumn, too, being rich in colour in sunny places. The Hydrangeas are noble plants in warm valleys, and on soils where they are not too often cut down by the winter; not only the common one of the markets, which, in soils where it turns blue, is so effective in the garden, but a variety of good kinds, among which should always be the oak-leaved Hydrangea, as old plants of it are so handsome. As these are plants that cannot be grown everywhere, this is a good reason why they should be made much of where the climate suits them. There are few garden sights more interesting than groups of Hydrangeas well grown and placed, and it is one we rarely see.

The Brooms have many effective plants, and none more so than the common and the Spanish Brooms, which should be massed on banks, or where they will come into the picture, and some of the smaller Brooms are excellent for rock gardens. The Furze in all its obtainable forms is just as precious, as it blooms so early, it will grow almost anywhere, and it brightens up a landscape as no other plant does. We have only to place it in any rough spots to enjoy it without care. Native shrubs should not be neglected; the wild single Guelder Rose is as pretty a shrub as any from across the sea, while all the hardy kinds may give us good and bold effects grouped with or near such bushes as Deutzias, Weigelas, Mock Oranges—all plants of high value and much variety.

From an artistic point of view nothing is better than groups of our hardy Heaths in any open place where room can be found for them, including White Heather and all other strong varieties of heather, as well as all other kinds of hardy Heaths. After planting they give little trouble, and they are good in colour even in winter, being generally happiest out of the garden proper, where any other wild plants may be allowed to grow among them. No doubt, the choicest and smallest of these Heaths deserve careful garden culture, but for effect the forms of our common Heather, the Cornish and Irish Heaths, are the best, and in bold masses not primly kept, but, once well rooted, allowed to mingle with any pretty wild plants. We might even assist this idea by sowing or planting other things, such as Foxgloves, Hairbells, or the small Furze, among the Heaths. When Heaths are grown in this way their bloom is charming from the first peep of spring, when the little rosy Heath of the mountains of central Europe begins to open, till the autumn days, and even the mild winter ones, when the delicately tinted Portuguese Heath (E. codonodes) blooms in the south and west of England.

We take little notice of such minor things as the Fire-bush, so lovely in Cornwall, and pretty also in other seashore districts, as it may not be enjoyed in the country generally, and we also leave out some others, which, though pretty seen near at hand, do not give us those definite effects in the garden landscape which it is well to seek if we wish to get out of the fatal jumble of the common shrubbery. The Escallonias, though very precious in seashore gardens and in the south on warm soils, are apt to go into mourning after hard winters elsewhere. So many of our island gardens are near the sea that we must not undervalue these shrubs, but a constant source of waste is the planting of things not really hardy in districts where they perish in hard winters, such as the Arbutus about London and in the Midlands. And, even where things seem hardy, some of them, like Fuchsias, never give the charming effects we get from them in the west of Ireland, in Wales, and in warm coast gardens, whatever care we take. Such facts should not discourage, because they only emphasise the lesson that the true way in a garden is for each to do what soil and climate allow of, and in that way we arrive at the most important artistic gain of all, *i.e.*, that each garden has its own distinct charms.

A very lovely group is the Lilacs, much enriched of recent years by the introduction of new species and many charming varieties of the common old Lilac—lovely plants, worthy of the finest days of our English spring. Few of the Lilacs raised in France seem to thrive in our gardens, owing to grafting on the Privet, which often, after a year or two's poor bloom, kills the plant and begins to take care of itself. Lilacs, being hardy in all parts of Britain, deserve our best care, and should always be grouped together in the open sun. They should always be bought from nurserymen who raise them from layers or suckers in the good old way, and should be, once grown up, always kept a little open and free by simple pruning, so that we may get handsome trusses.

With these, too, must be grouped such lovely things as the Snowdrop tree, the Stuartias, and Magnolias.

The Magnolias have recently become more numerous, and it will be easy soon to have a Magnolia garden, at least in favoured places. The tree Magnolias should come among the taller flowering trees in the distant parts of our flower grove—Horse Chestnuts, Buckeyes, Tulip Trees, Laburnums, Catalpa, and Yellow Wood. The Alpine Laburnum, so very beautiful in bloom, becomes a tall, slender tree where not overcrowded, and the flowering Ash (Ornus) must not be forgotten among the taller flowering trees.

Some shrubs of modest charm as to their flowers give very pretty effects in well-placed groups, such as the flowering Currant, Tamarix, and Ceanothus on walls. But none are more charming than the wild Roses in summer, the Sweet Brier being taken as representing our native wild Roses; the Glossy Rose (R. lucida), the American wild Roses; the many-flowered Rose (Polyantha), and the Japanese (R. rugosa).

The Judas Tree is neglected in England, and rarely planted in an effective way. In the Parc Monceau in Paris there is a beautiful grove of it in which trees of various ages form one family party, so to say, showing some differences in colour and earliness. Such slight but often valuable differences arise when we raise trees from seed. It is curious that a tree so effective in bloom, and so distinct in habit as the Judas Tree is, should be so little planted with us, and, when planted, so often left to the scant mercy of the shrubbery. All such trees have their own ways and wants, and should not be jumbled up in the crowded way of planting.

Of Indian Azaleas in the open air Mr C. R. Scrase-Dickens writes: "The hardy Azaleas of the American races are very popular, but few know the value of the white Indian Azalea for the open garden in the south of England." Few plants give so little trouble when once established, even though the late frosts may now and again spoil the beauty of the flowers. When planted out and left alone it is not much more than three or four feet in height, dense and spreading. The engraving shows a bush over ten feet across with a shadow thrown over the upper part by a tree of Magnolia which grows at the side. It gets shelter from cold winds and from too fierce a sun on the flowers. Anyone who intends to plant this Azalea should remember that it flowers naturally at a time when there may still be late frosts and cold winds hovering about, and that it would be a mistaken kindness to choose any place, such as under a south wall, which would tend to make the blossoms open earlier in the season. We have some plants under a north wall which do admirably, but they seem to like association with other things. The variety which does best here is the old typical white.

There are no plants so much neglected as flowering shrubs, and even when planted they are rarely well grown, owing to the "traditions" of what is called the shrubbery. The common way is to dig the shrubbery every winter, and this is often carried out as a matter of form while much harm is done by mutilating the roots of the shrubs.

The idea of the murderous common shrubbery is so rooted in the popular mind that it is almost hopeless to expect much change for the better. The true way is to depart wholly from it as a mass of *mixed* shrubs, for beautiful families should be grouped apart. Each family or plant should have a separate place, free from the all-devouring Privet and Laurel, and each part of the shrubbery should have its own character, which may easily be given to it by grouping instead of mixing, which ends in the starvation of the choice kinds. The shrubbery itself need no longer be a dark, dreary mass, but light and shade may play in it, its varied life be well shown, and the habits and forms of each thing may be seen. Shrubs of high quality or rare deserve to be well grown. Any one who thinks how much less trouble is given by hardy plants will not begrudge attention to outdoor things, and some may even consider a garden of beautiful shrubs as a conservatory in the open air, no kind of flower gardening being more delightful or enduring.

Whether they are all distinct species or merely varieties it matters little, the great beauty of the Thorn trees being undoubted, not only in their flowers, but in their fruits, some of which are edible.

Being natives of countries colder than ours, including much of Canada and North-Eastern America, they are as hardy as any of our native trees, and well fitted for planting in any soil or position.

Here, there was a slope above the moat cottage too steep for plough or spade, and many years ago I planted most of the kinds that were obtainable at the time, and while some did very well, half of them failed owing to their being grafted on the wild Quick. The latter being common in every nursery, opportunity is taken to graft exotic kinds upon it, with the result that the native kind will kill the foreigner.

The important thing is that they should be raised from seed, the natural method of increase, and as the shrubs are as free to fruit as to flower, there should be no difficulty in obtaining plenty of seed.

Apart from the beauty of these trees, they interested me for their value in making very good fences. We all know the use of our native Thorn for this purpose, and some of these foreign kinds might give a better fence than any contrivance of barbed wire.

A fault of the native Thorn is the constant labour it requires to keep it in shape, and some of the wild species might give a better fence. This is important, as the beauty of England is in the way of being lost through the use of iron fences. Some estates are quite disfigured for landscape beauty by the iron fence, costly and not so enduring. The only fence for those who wish to preserve the beauty of our country is a "live" one of Thorn.

The Thorn best for this purpose is the Cockspur. It makes a very good fence for woods where frequent trimming is not needed, being well armed with spines, and the leaves turn a fine brown in autumn.

A wood of Cedars of Lebanon which I planted for a friend some years ago was fenced with iron: during a recent visit I saw the fence smashed to pieces by the stock. Such fences are not without danger to animals, whereas a good live fence is wholly free. No doubt such a fence takes time to grow, but by planting seedlings in the full sun rapid growth is made, and stout Quick might even be planted within the iron fence, that being eventually removed. The fairest landscapes are destroyed if one has to look at them through an iron grille.

To enjoy their beauty in a mature state, the best places for these hardy Thorns are the fringes of copses and woods, sandy banks or knolls and rocky places, and they should be grouped, not dotted about. They are vigorous enough to battle with weeds, and can be trusted to take care of themselves.

There is evidence of their picturesque form, endurance and beauty of flower and fruit in some of our parks like Shrubland, and in botanic gardens trees raised from seeds before the art of grafting was used in too many ways.

Some Flowering Trees and Shrubs Hardy in British Gardens

Abelia	Azalea	Ceanothus	Comptonia	Deutzia
Æsculus	Azara	Cerasus	Cornus	Deutzia
Akebia	Berberidopsis	Cercis	Corylopsis	Embothrium
Amelanchier	Berberis	Chimonanthus	Cotoneaster	Erica
Amygdalus	Bignonia	Chionanthus	Cratægus	Escallonia
Andromeda	Buddleia	Cladrastis	Cydonia	Eucryphia
Aralia	Calycanthus	Clematis	Cytisus	Euonymus
Arbutus	Camellia	Clethra	Daphne	Exochorda
Arctostaphylos	Caragana	Colletia	Desfontainea	Fabiana
Asimina	Catalpa	Colutea	Desmodium	Forsythia

Fothergilla	Kerria	Mespilus	Pyrus	Staphylea
Garrya	Kœlreuteria	Olearia	Raphiolepis	Stauntonia
Gaultheria	Laburnum	Ononis	Rhododendron	Stuartia
Genista	Ledum	Ornus	Rhodora	Styrax
Gleditschia	Leiophyllum	Ozothamnus	Rhodotypos	Syringa
Halesia	Lespedeza	Paulownia	Ribes	Tamarix
Hamamelis	Leycesteria	Pavia	Robinia	Ulex
Hibiscus	Liriodendron	Pernettya	Rosa	Veronica
Hydrangea	Lonicera	Philadelphus	Rubus	Viburnum
Hypericum	Lupinus	Phlomis	Sambucus	Virgilia
Illicium	Magnolia	Piptanthus	Sophora	Weigela
Indigofera	Mahonia	Prunus	Spartium	Wistaria
Jasminum	Malus	Pterostyrax	Spiræa	Xanthoceras
Kalmia				

* *Some of the evergreens, though thriving long in the southern and shorelands, may perish in severe winters in cold inland districts.*

CHAPTER XIII

Climbers and their Artistic Use

The splendid squadrons of the Pine, with crests proud in Alpine storm and massed in serried armies along the northern mountains—the Oak kings of a thousand winters in the forest plain are lovely gifts of the earth mother, but more precious still to the gardener are the most fragile of all woody things that garland bush and tree with beautiful forms and blossoms, like Clematis, Jasmine, and Honeysuckle, and the many lace-workers of the woods and brakes. It is delightful to be able to turn our often ugly inheritance from the builder almost into gardens by the aid of these, from great yellow Roses to Ivy in many lovely forms; but it is well to take a wider view of these climbing and rambling bushes and their places in the garden and in the pleasure ground. It is for our own convenience we go through the labour of nailing them to walls, and though it is a charming and necessary way of growing them it is well to remember that many climbers may be grown in beautiful ways without such laborious training. The tendency to over-pruning of the climbers on walls ends often in a kind of crucifixion, and the more freely things are trained the better. Proof of this is in the handsome masses of climbers on the high walls of the Trinity College Gardens at Dublin and in many private places where climbers have been liberally and well planted on walls.

But it should never be forgotten that many of these plants will grow by themselves, like the Honeysuckles, which, while pleasant to see on walls, are not less so on banks, or even on the level ground. Pretty fences and dividing screens may also be easily formed by hardy climbers.

The Ivy of our northern woods has broken into a number of beautiful varieties often distinct in form and even in colour; they deserve far more attention for evergreen bowers, evergreen fences, and dividing lines, apart from their growth on walls and trees. The bush forms of these may make broken hedge-like garlands 2 feet to 3 feet high round little isolated flower gardens. But the Ivy is a destroyer of houses, and ought never to be planted near one. There are ways of enjoying it where it can do no harm—in woods or rocks and as a screen, where an evergreen one is sought. Almost equally beautiful plants in form of leaf are the Green Briers (Smilax), some of which are hardy in England, but seen in few gardens, and rarely treated in an artistic way, though excellent for walls and rocks.

Of the beauty of the Jasmine of all climbers there is least need to speak, yet how rarely one sees the old white Jasmine made good use of in large gardens. It should be in bold wreaths or masses where it thrives, and so also the winter Jasmine, which is a precious thing for our country, should not be put in as a plant or two in bad conditions, but treated as a fine distinct thing in masses round cottages and outhouses. The finest of hardy climbers, the Wistaria, is much more frequently and rightly planted in France than in our gardens, though it thrives in the Thames valley as well as in the Seine valley. It should be, in addition to its use on walls and houses, made into bold, covered ways and bowers and trained up trees.

It is not only that stout climbers are more beautiful and natural, and show their form better growing amongst trees, but it is the best way that many of them can be grown with safety owing to their vigour. The way the common Ivy wreaths the trees in rich woods, and the wild Clematis throws ropes up trees on the chalk hills, shows what the larger hardy climbers do over trees or rough or open copses, or even now and then in hedgerows. Some vigorous climbers would in time ascend the tallest trees, and there is nothing more beautiful than a veil of Clematis montana running over a tall tree. Besides the well-known climbers, there are species of Clematis which have never come into general cultivation, but which are beautiful for such uses, though not all showy. The same may be said of the Honeysuckles, wild Vines, and various other families with which much of the northern tree and shrub world is garlanded. Occasionally one sees a climbing Rose rambling over a tree, and perhaps among our garden pictures nothing is more lovely than such a Rose when in flower. By a selection of the hardiest of climbing Roses very beautiful pictures might be formed in our pleasure grounds and plantations, and we might often see as the result of design what is now mainly an accident, as a number of wild Roses grow "freely" among trees and large shrubs

A home for these is often found on walls, and in our country some variety of wall surface is a great gain to botanic gardens and private gardens like Offington, in which a great variety of shrubs from all countries is grown. In the milder districts of the country and in favoured spots round the coast some of the finest exotics, such as Lapageria, and some greenhouse plants of great beauty, like Clianthus, may be grown on walls in the open air. Some of the fine plants of Chili also may be grown on walls of various aspects. Many who have visited our best gardens will probably have stored away in their memories some of the pictures they have seen given by noble wall plants well grown in this way—as, for example, the New Zealand Edwardsia at Linton, so fine in form and colour, and the handsome Fremontia. Hard winters settle the fate of many beautiful things among these, but, happily, some of the loveliest things are hardy, like the Winter Sweet, Bignonia, and Magnolia.

It may be noted here that among the unfortunate attempts of certain architects who designed gardens to get rid of the gardener and his troublesome plants were instructions that no climbers were to be allowed on walls. There was not a single spray of any climber allowed to grow on the house or extensive terrace walls at Shrubland, some years ago, as if in a garden death were better than life.

Apart from the vigorous climbers that we may trust in shrubberies, woods, and on rough banks, and which, when fairly started, take care of themselves, there are fragile things which deserve to be used in rather a new way as far as most gardens are concerned, namely, for throwing a delicate lacework of flowers over the evergreen and other choice shrubs grown in our gardens—Rhododendron, Kalmia, Azalea, and even taller shrubs. A group of Hollies will not look any the worse for wreaths of fragrant Clematis in autumn. Often stiff, unbroken masses of Rhododendrons and evergreen flowering shrubs will be more varied if delicate flakes of Clematis (white, lavender, or claret-red) or the bright arrows of the Flame Nasturtium come among them here and there in autumn. The great showy hybrid Clematises of our gardens are also good for this use and the more elegant wild Clematises of North America, Europe, and North Africa.

The old Climbers and Garland Roses were almost too vigorous for the garden, and their bloom did not last long enough to justify their getting a place there; but now, with the great climbing Tea Roses we have for the southern parts of these islands, we may count on a bloom for months. We have in these Roses, where they thrive the best, the most precious of all ornaments for walls of houses, trellis work, pergolas. In southern parts of the country we even get fine results from these Roses on the north side of walls, where some Roses flower better than on the south side. Also, we can grow them in the open on trellises or away from walls, but in the northern parts of the country, where these great climbing Tea Roses may not thrive so well, walls come in to help us more and more by their shelter and warmth.

Apart from these great Roses of garden origin, which will long be among the most precious, some Wild Roses are of the highest importance in warm districts and good soils, particularly the Indian R. Brunonis and the many-flowered Roses (R. polyantha) of Japan; but in the presence of the need of so much wall space for the garden Roses these Wild Roses will usually be best in the shrubbery or some place apart, where they may be let alone, and no good can arise from choice garden ground being given to Roses like R. polyantha which are even more vigorous than our own wild Dog Rose.

On walls, in southern parts, never forget the noble Macartney Rose, it thrives on walls and should always be raised from suckers of the natural root.

Going back some thousands of years to the earliest sculptured remains of some of the oldest peoples, we see evidence that the Grape Vine was in common use, and it is, no doubt, much older than the monuments of Assyria. Among the Kabyle villages of North Africa I passed many Vines of great age trailing over very old Olive trees in the little orchard fields. In such countries there was the value of the fruit, but even in ours, where the Grape ripens rarely out of doors, the charm of the plant is so great that we see many cottages in Surrey and Norfolk set deep in Vine leaves. The Grape Vine, however, is but one of a large family, and, though we may not see in our country its garlands from tree to tree purple with fruit, we may see much of its fine forms of leaf. The wild Vines are too vigorous for use on walls, though excellent for banks and trees and for any place outside the flower garden. I have seen them clambering up forest trees, spreading into masses of fine foliage on the ground, and sending out long arms in search of the nearest trees—strong and handsome climbers, hardy, vigorous, and soon covering dry banks, rocks, and trees.

To the Vines (Vitis) have now been joined by the botanists Virginian Creepers (Ampelopsis), and between the two groups it need not be said what noble things they offer for garlanding trees, walls, bowers, rocks, and banks. It cannot be said that we neglect these Virginian and Japanese creepers, but the Vines are so far seldom well used with us, although easy of cultivation.

There are seasons when shaded walks may be enjoyed, and numbers of free-growing, climbing plants give an abundant and lovely choice of living drapery for them, Aristolochia, Wistaria, Virginian Creeper, rambling Roses, Honeysuckles, Jasmines, and the free Clematises doing well over such. In Italy and warm countries one often sees in gardens the pergola—as the creeper-shaded walk is called—serving the twofold purpose of supporting Grape Vines and giving pleasant coolness during the summer heat. As a rule, these pergolas are rude trellis-work structures of wood, sometimes supported by stone posts where these are at hand. In the gardens in the neighbourhood of Rome, Naples, and Florence there are beautiful examples of the pergola—stately structures, the supports of which are massive columns of stone covered and festooned with Banksian Roses, Wistaria, Periploca, Clematises, Honeysuckles, Passion Flowers, scarlet Trumpet Flowers, and other climbers which form cool retreats in the hot days. But such pergolas seldom occurred outside the gardens of the great villas, and near humbler dwellings the pergola was usually a simple structure made for the purpose of supporting the Grape Vine.

These creeper-clad covered ways should usually lead to somewhere and be over a frequented walk, and should not cut off any line of view nor be placed near big trees. A simple structure is the best. The supports, failing the Italian way of making posts of stone—also seen, by the way, in gate-posts in Northern England—should be Oak tree stems, about 9 inches in diameter, let into the ground about 2 feet—the better if on a bed of concrete. The posts must be connected and firmly secured to each other by long pieces along the sides, while the top may be formed of smaller pieces to make a firm structure. On no account let the "rustic" carpenter begin to adorn it with the fantastic branchings he is so fond of. Some experience with wooden supports makes me stick to brick pillars as the best support where stone is not near. Over narrow ways one may use a 9-inch brick pillar—on airy pergolas a 14-inch pillar is best.

Instead of trusting to wire and ugly posts or the many artificial ways for supporting climbers, why should we not do as the Italians and people of South Europe do, use living trees to carry the Vine or climber? Weeping trees of graceful leaf and form might be used in this way with fine effect. Abroad they take for this purpose any kind of tree which happens to be near and keep it within bounds, and those who know our garden flora may select trees which, while beautiful themselves, will not be much trouble to keep in bounds, like the weeping Cherry, weeping Aspen, some Willows even, and any light-leaved weeping tree would be charming for its own sake as well as for what it might carry. Some of them might even be beautiful in flower, and there would be no trouble in getting creepers to run over them.

When a quiet walk leads from one part of the garden to another, and that walk is spanned at intervals with slender light arches clothed with Honeysuckle, Clematis, or Jasmine, it gives an added grace to the walk. This also is a delightful way of framing, so to say, a flower border, the light arches springing up from the line of the trellis, which should be used to cut off the borders from the kitchen garden.

However rich we may be in perennial and shrubby climbers, we must not forget the climbing things among annual and like plants to help us, especially for the smaller class of gardens and those in which we depend more on annual flowers. Hedges of Sweet Peas there are few things to equal; the fragile annual Convolvulus in many colours are pretty for low trellises, the vigorous, herbaceous Bindweeds for rough places outside the flower garden. Most showy of all annual climbers are the many Gourds, which, treated in a bold way, give fine effects when trained over outhouses, sheds, or on strong stakes as columns.

Although in our gardens the shaded walk is not so necessary as it is in Italy and Southern France, in hot seasons shade is welcome in Britain; and, as in many gardens we have four times as many walks as are needed, there is plenty of room for covering some of them with fruit trees which would give us flowers in spring, fruit in autumn, and light shade. The very substance of which walks are made is often good for fruit; and those who know the Apricot district of Oxfordshire and the neighbouring counties may see how well fruit trees do in hard walks. It is not only in kitchen and fruit gardens that their shade might be welcome, but in flower gardens too, if we ever get out of the common notion of a flower garden which insists on everything being seen at one glance.

In some old gardens there was a way of "plashing" trees over walks—trees like the Lime, which grew so vigorously that they had to be cut back with an equal vigour, this leading in the end to ugliness in the excessive mutilation of the trees. One result of the frequent cutting was a vigorous summer growth of shoots, which cast a dense

shade and dripped in wet weather. The purpose of such walks would
be well fulfilled by training fruit trees over them, as they are trees
which much more readily submit to training and give the light and
airy shade which is best in our country. The fruit trellis, whatever it is
formed of, need not be confined to fruit trees only, but here and there
wreaths of Clematis or other elegant climbers might vary the lines.

Those who live in sheltered valleys on warm soils, or among pleasant
hills above the line of hard frosts, may be so rich in evergreens that
they will keep their walls for the fairest of true climbers. But in cold,
exposed, and inland parts people are often glad to have good evergreens
on walls, even bushes not naturally climbers in habit, such as the choicer
evergreen Barberries, and Camellias on the north sides of walls. The
Laurustinus, too, is charming on many cottage walls in winter, and
may escape there when it would suffer in the open; the Myrtle is happy
on walls in southern districts, and even the Poet's Laurel may be glad
of the shelter of a wall in the north. The evergreen Magnolia, which
in warmer Europe is a standard tree, in our country must usually be
grown on walls, even in the south, and there is no finer sight than a
good tree of Magnolia on a house. The beautiful Ceanothus of the
Californian hills often keep company with these evergreens on walls;
but even in the warmer soils of the home counties they are tender, and
their delicate sprays of flowers are much less frequently seen with us
than in France, although we cannot resist trying them on sunny walls,
and on chalky and sandy soils they have better chances.

In clearing up this question, the first thing to do is to state a few facts
about which there can be no dispute among any who are interested.
The first is the extraordinary beauty of the Clematis. No conservatory
in Europe shelters any plant so graceful in habit or so fine in colour of
flowers. Added to this is the precious quality of hardiness and power
to resist the rainstorms of our isles. I have grown every obtainable
kind in various positions, and never lost a plant from cold. When day
after day in July my Roses became bags of ugly mould, and even native
plants were sickened by the rain day and night, the large Clematises,
on their natural roots, suffered not the slightest injury.

The next fact, of which there can be no doubt, is that the gardens of
Britain and of France have been robbed of the most beautiful race of
climbers of the northern world. Large gardens, with every advantage
of site, soil, and air, are quite bare of them. It is not only in our country
this loss has arisen through mistaken ways of increasing the plants. It
is so everywhere in France, where we may see in the great nurseries at

Orleans and Angers masses of the finest Clematises huddled together in pots, but never a plant on its natural roots. If one asks any question as to the diseases of the plants, only guesses are given. The loss to the trade is great. To suppose that clever propagators could not increase these hardy climbers in the natural way is absurd. The final test of the practice is not in the nursery, but in the grounds of the buyers of the plants. Any practice of increase which drives plants out of general cultivation is a loss to the trade as well as to the planter. From experiments carried on for many years here I have proved that the cause of the loss is the practice of grafting these plants.

The nature of the Clematis in the wild state is to run over bushes and copses, as one may see on the shores of Northern Africa. So if we plant beneath a bush a little shade is afforded and though the growth is not so free as when the plants are set apart, the life of the plant is longer and the effect is more beautiful. Lastly, more dangerous than eelworms and fungi are slugs, which bark the fragile stems as far up as they can get, and that means the death of the shoot in summer, but not the death of the plant if on its own roots. Lawn-mower, hoe, or rake may smash the delicate stems if the plants are set out singly, especially if grafted, as the union of the choice variety and the wild stock used is often fragile, whereas the plant on its natural roots never is. On hot, sunny days partial loss occurs by shoots dying off, but when on its own roots we do not lose the plant.

The rest is the story of my planting and success here by following a completely different way from the common one. It at first struck me that the grafting of plants of different species was not always justified in results. In the nursery practice the rule is to graft the Clematis of Japan on the toughest climber of our chalk hills—a wholly different plant and from a different country—and, therefore, there might be a cause of death through the sap arising at different times in the two plants in the spring of the year. The next thing was to test the matter by planting—not an easy matter, as in every nursery there were only the grafted plants, and, like so many others, I lost many. At the same time, there was evidence in many places that the Indian Mountain Clematis and other wild kinds, which are grown on their natural roots, are vigorous climbers. The stool ground in which the old nurserymen layered their plants was done away with in favour of the new way of buying stocks by the thousand with no thought as to the result to the planter.

In only one nursery in France—that of the late Ferdinand Jamin, of Bourg-la-Reine, Seine, a much-trusted French nurseryman—did I find the stools of Clematis, the little plants simply layered into pots set around the old plants in the open air. I had many of these, and never failed with them.

I have planted the very finest kinds in every sort of position, some in the hedgerow, round an orchard, in open ground, and in close shade of trees and shrubs, and have had success in all. With the plants from cuttings, layers, or seedlings there is no risk. Is there any sound reason for grafting a plant so easy to raise from layers as the Clematis? There is none, either as to tenderness or difficulty of increase.

It was thought that calcareous soil was a need, no doubt arising from the fact that our native species abounds on the chalk hills, but for the Japanese Clematis chalk is not needed. The plants may grow in calcareous soil, but so they do in sandy loam. If anything is helpful in planting a Clematis it is plenty of sharp sand. We never give either mulch or special fertiliser—none is needed.

Having proved beyond a doubt the vigour and beauty of naturally-grown plants, my next step was to bring them into the flower garden—their right place, though from gardens they are generally excluded. So they were planted on tripods, pergola, wall, and Oak fence as a background to the mixed border, and on almost every surface at hand. And all these places they adorn from early summer to mid-autumn.

Miss Willmott tells me she raises Clematis easily from cuttings. From seed of the nobler kinds it is well to raise varieties of merit, though the seed is slow to germinate. The wild species come freely from seed. I sowed the Virgin's Bower (C. Viticella) out of hand when forming a new live fence around an orchard, and there it has been ever since, throwing a lace-work of delicate form and flowers over the fence.

There is no more need to graft a Clematis than to graft a Raspberry. It is a short-sighted practice which has driven the loveliest of all hardy climbers from the gardens of Europe. On the contrary, both as to root and branch, they are among the most vigorous of hardy climbers. In the loss of Rhododendrons by thousands on the ponticum type on which they were grafted, the planter has the satisfaction of seeing the bloom of his favourite for a few years before it gives up the ghost. In the Clematis even this poor satisfaction is denied him, and in large gardens, with every advantage of soil and climate, they are often unseen. The idea that grafting is a cheaper way of increase is not true. Layers in March give strong plants for full planting in October—a more rapid way to increase.

There is scarcely any limit to the different uses that plants of a climbing or rambling habit may be put to, for many of them are extremely beautiful when employed for the draping of arbours, pergolas, or even living trees, while for hiding unsightly fences or clothing sloping banks, the more vigorous kinds are well adapted. For draping buildings or furnishing walls there is a great variety of plants, either quite hardy or sufficiently tender to need the protection of a wall in order to pass through an ordinary winter without much injury. The majority of those enumerated below are hardy enough to succeed as wall plants in any part of England, while a few are adapted only for particularly mild districts.

Those plants marked with an asterisk are either half-hardy or require some slight protection in cold districts or special care in some cases.

Abelia	Celastrus	Exochorda	Lycium	Ribes
Abutilon	Chimonanthus	Exogonum	Magnolia	Roses
Actinidia	Choisya	Forsythia	*Mandevilla	Rubus
Adlumia	Clematis	Fremontia	Maurandya	Schizandra
Akebia	Clianthus	Fuchsia	Menispermum	Schizophragma
*Aloysia	Cocculus	Garrya	*Mitraria	Smilax
Apios	Convolvulus	Grevillea	Muhlenbeckia	Solanum
Aristolochia	Cotoneaster	Hedera	Myrtus	*Sollya
Azara	Crataegus	Illicium	Paliurus	Stauntonia
*Berberidopsis	Cydonia	Indigofera	*Passiflora	Stuartia
Berberis	Desfontainea	Jasminum	Periploca	*Thunbergia
Bignonia	Eccremocarpus	Kerria	Physianthus	Tropæolum
Buddleia	Edwardsia	*Lapageria	Piptanthus	Vitis (now including
Calystegia	*Embothrium	*Lardizabala	*Pittosporum	Ampelopsis)
Camellia	Escallonia	Leptospermum	Pueraria	Wistaria
*Carpenteria	Eucryphia	Lonicera	*Punica	Xanthoceras
Ceanothus	Euonymus	Lophospermum	Rhus	

CHAPTER XIV

Alpine Flower, Rock, and Wall Gardens

Alpine plants grow naturally on high mountains, whether they spring from sub-tropical plains or green northern pastures. Above the cultivated land these flowers begin to occur on moorland and in the fringes of the hill woods; they are seen in multitudes in the broad pastures with which many mountains are robed, enamelling their green, and where neither grass nor tall herbs exist; where mountains are crumbled into slopes of shattered rock by the contending forces of heat and cold; even there, amidst the glaciers, they spring from the ruined ground, as if the earth-mother had sent up her loveliest children to plead with the spirits of destruction.

Alpine plants fringe the fields of snow and ice of the mountains, and at such elevations often have scarcely time to flower before they are again buried deep in snow. Enormous areas of the earth, inhabited by Alpine plants, are every year covered by a deep bed of snow, and where tree or shrub cannot live from the intense cold a deep mass of down-like snow falls upon Alpine plants, like a great cloud-borne quilt, under which they rest safe from alternations of frost and biting winds with moist and spring-like days as in our green winters.

But these conditions are not always essential for their growth in a cool, northern country like ours. The reason that Alpine plants abound in high regions is because no taller vegetation can exist there; were these places inhabited by trees and shrubs, we should find fewer Alpine plants among them; on the other hand, were no stronger vegetation found at a lower elevation, these plants would often appear there. Also, as there are few hard and fast lines in Nature, many plants found on the high Alps are also met with in rocky or barish ground at much lower elevations. Gentiana verna, for example, often flowers very late in summer when the snow thaws on a very high mountain; yet it is also found on much lower mountains, and occurs in England and Ireland. In the close struggle upon the plains and low, tree-clad hills, the smaller species are often overrun by trees, trailers, bushes, and vigorous herbs, but, where in far northern and high mountain regions these fail from the earth, the lovely Alpine flowers prevail.

In the culture of these plants, the first thing to be remembered is that much difference exists among them as regards size and vigour. We have, on the one hand, a number of plants that merely require to be sown or planted in the roughest way to flourish—Arabis and Aubrietia, for example; and, on the other, there are some kinds, like Gentians and the Primulas of the high Alps, which are rarely seen in good health in gardens, and it is as to these that advice is chiefly required. Nearly all the misfortunes which these little plants have met with in our gardens are due to a false conception of what a rock garden ought to be, and of what the Alpine plant requires. It is too often thought that they will do best if merely raised on tiny heaps of stones and brick rubbish, such as we frequently see dignified with the name of "rockwork." Mountains are often "bare," and cliffs devoid of soil; but we must not suppose that the choice jewellery of plant-life scattered over the ribs of the mountain lives upon little more than the air and the melting snow. Where else can we find such a depth of stony soil as on the ridges of shattered stone and grit flanking some great glacier, stained with tufts of crimson Rockfoil? Can we gauge the depth of that chink from which peep tufts of the beautiful little Androsace helvetica, which for ages has gathered the crumbling grit, into which the roots enter so far that we cannot dig them out? And if we find plants growing from mere cracks without soil, even then the roots simply search farther into the heart of the flaky rock, so that they are safer from drought than on the level ground.

We meet on the Alps plants not more than an inch high firmly rooted in crevices of slaty rock, and by knocking away the sides from bits of projecting rock, and laying the roots quite bare, we may find them radiating in all directions against a flat rock, some of the largest perhaps more than a yard long. Even smaller plants descend quite as deep, though it is rare to find the texture and position of the rock such as will admit of tracing them. On level or sloping spots of ground in the Alps the earth is of great depth, and, if it is not all earth in the common sense of the word, it is more suitable to the plants than what we commonly understand by that term. Stones of all sizes broken up with the soil, sand, and grit prevent evaporation; the roots lap round them, follow them down, and in such positions they never suffer from want of moisture. It must be remembered that the continual degradation of the rocks effected by frost, snow, and heavy rains in summer serves to "earth up," so to speak, many alpine plants.

The part of the gardens around the rock garden should be picturesque, and, in any case, be a quiet, airy spot with as few jarring points as may be. No tree should be in the rock garden; hence a site should not be selected where it would be necessary to remove favourite trees. The roots of trees would find their way into the masses of good soil for the alpine flowers, and soon exhaust them. Besides, as these flowers are usually found on treeless wastes, it is best not to place them in shaded places.

As regards the stone to be used, sandstone or millstone grit would perhaps be the best; but it is seldom that a choice can be made, and almost any kind of stone will do, from Kentish rag to limestone. Soft and slaty kinds and others liable to crumble away should be avoided, as also should magnesian limestone. The stone of the neighbourhood should be adopted, for economy's sake, if for no other reason. Wherever the natural rock crops out, it is sheer waste to create artificial rockwork instead of embellishing that which naturally occurs. In many cases nothing would be necessary but to clear the ground, and add here and there a few loads of good soil with broken stones to prevent evaporation, the natural crevices and crests being planted where possible. Cliffs or banks of chalk, as well as all kinds of rock, should be taken advantage of in this way; many plants, like the dwarf Hairbells and Rock Roses, thrive in such places

No walk with regularly trimmed edges should come near the rock garden. This need not prevent the presence of good walks through or near it, as by allowing the edges of the walk to be broken and stony, and by encouraging Stonecrops, Rockfoils, and other little plants to crawl into the walk at will, a pretty margin will result. There is no surface of this kind that may not be thus adorned. Violets, Ferns, Forget-me-nots, will do in the shadier parts, and the Stonecrops and many others will thrive in the full sun. The whole of the surface of the alpine garden should be covered with plants as far as possible, except a few projecting points. In moist districts Erinus and the Balearic Sandwort will grow on the face of the rocks; and even upright faces of rock will grow a variety of plants. Regular steps should never be in or near the rock garden. Steps may be made quite picturesque, and even beautiful, with Violets and other small plants jutting from every crevice; and no cement should be used.

In cases where the simplest type of rock garden only is attempted, and where there are no steps or rude walks in the rock garden, the very fringes of the gravel walks may be graced by such plants as the dwarfer Stonecrops. The alpine Toadflax is never more beautiful than when self-sown in a gravel walk. A rock garden so made that its miniature cliffs overhang is useless for alpine vegetation, and all but such wall-loving plants as Corydalis lutea soon die on it.

The great majority of alpine plants thrive best in deep soil. In it they can root deeply, and when once rooted they will not suffer from drought, from which they would quickly perish if planted in the usual way. Three feet deep is not too much for most kinds, and in nearly all cases it is a good plan to have plenty of broken sandstone or grit mixed with the soil. Any free loam, with plenty of sand or broken grit, will suit most alpine plants. But peat is required by some, as, for example, various small and brilliant rockplants like the Menziesia, Trillium, Cypripedium, Spigelia, and a number of other mountain and bog-plants. Though the body of the soil may be of loam, it is well to have a few masses of peat here and there. This is better than forming all the ground of good loam, and then digging holes for the reception of small masses of peat. The soil of some portions might also be chalky or calcareous, for the sake of plants that are known to thrive best on such formations, like the Milkworts, the Bee Orchis, and Rhododendron Chamæcistus. Any other varieties of soil required by particular kinds can be given as they are planted.

It is not well to associate a small lakelet or pond with the rock garden, as is frequently done. If a picturesque piece of water can be seen from the rock garden, well and good; but water should not, as a rule, be closely associated with it. In places of limited extent water should not be thought of.

In the planting of every kind of rock garden, it should be remembered that *all* the surface should be planted. Not alone on slopes, or favourable ledges, or chinks, should we see this exquisite plant-life, as many rare mountain species will thrive on the less trodden parts of footways; others, like the two-flowered Violet, seem to thrive best in the fissures between steps; many dwarf succulents delight in gravel and the hardest soil.

In cultivating the very rarest and smallest alpine plants, the stony, or partially stony, surface is to be preferred. Full exposure is necessary for very minute plants, and stones are useful in preventing evaporation and protecting them in other ways.

Few have much idea of the number of alpine plants that may be grown on fully exposed ordinary ground. But some kinds require care, and there are usually new kinds coming in, which, even if vigorous, should be kept apart for a time. Therefore, where the culture of alpine plants is entered into with zest, there ought to be a sort of nursery spot on which to grow the most delicate and rare kinds. It should be fully exposed, and sufficiently elevated to secure perfect drainage.

Artificial rock is formed now and then in the districts where the natural rock is beautiful, as in the country round Tunbridge Wells. Why anybody should bring the artficial rockmaker into a garden or park where there is already fine natural beautiful rock it is not easy to see. Also, in certain districts, it is a mistake to place this artificial rock under conditions where rock of any kind does not occur in nature. It would be much better, as far as alpine and rock plants are concerned, to dispense with much of this ugly artificial rockwork, and take advantage of the fact that many of these plants grow perfectly well on raised borders and on fully exposed low banks.

Many vigorous alpine flowers will do perfectly well on level ground in our cool climate, if they are not overrun by coarser plants. Where there are natural rocks or good artificial ones it is best to plant them properly; but people who are particular would often be better without artificial "rockwork" if they wished to grow these plants in simpler ways. There is not the slightest occasion to have what is called "rockwork" for these flowers. I do not speak only of things like the beautiful Gentianella, which for many years has been grown in our gardens, but of the Rock-foils, the Stonecrops, and the true alpine plants in great numbers.

The next point is the great superiority of natural grouping over the botanical or labelled style of little single specimens of a great number of plants. In a few yards of border, in the ordinary way there would be fifty or more kinds, but nothing pretty for those who have ever seen the beautiful mountain gardens. Many rightly contend that, in a sense, Nature includes all, and that therefore the term "natural" may be misapplied, but it is a perfectly just one when used in the sense of Nature's way of arranging flowers as opposed to the lines, circles, and other set patterns so commonly followed by man. Through bold and natural grouping we may get fine colour without a trace of formality.

Those who have observed alpine plants must have noticed in what arid places many flourish, and what fine plants may spring from a chink in a boulder. They are often stunted and small in such crevices, but longer-lived than when growing upon the ground. Now, numbers of alpine plants perish if planted in the ordinary soil of our gardens from over-moisture and want of rest in winter. But if placed where their roots are dry in winter, they may be kept in health. Many plants from countries a little farther south than our own, and from alpine regions, will find on walls, rocks, and ruins that dwarf, sturdy growth which makes them at home in our climate.

In garden formation, especially in sloping or diversified ground, what is called a dry wall is often useful, and may answer the purpose of supporting a bank or dividing off a garden quite as well as masonry. Where the stones can be got easily, men used to the work will often make gently "battered" walls which, while banks, will make homes for many plants which would not live one winter on a level surface in the same place. In my own garden I built one such wall with large blocks of sandstone laid on their natural "bed," the front of the stones almost as rough as they come out, and chopped nearly level between, so that they lie firm and well. No mortar was used, and as each stone was laid slender rooted alpine and rock plants were placed along in lines between with a sprinkling of sand or fine earth enough to slightly cover the roots and aid them in getting through the stones to the back, where, as the wall was raised, the space behind it was packed with gritty earth. This the plants soon found out and rooted firmly in. Even on old walls made with mortar rock plants and small native ferns very often establish themselves, but the "dry" walls are more congenial to rock plants, and one may have any number of beautiful alpine plants in perfect health on them.

One charm of this kind of wall garden is that little attention is required afterwards. Even on the best rock gardens things get overrun by others, and weeds come in; but in a well-planted wall we may leave plants for years untouched beyond pulling out any interloping plant or weed that may happen to get in. So little soil, however, is put with the plants that there is little chance of weeds. If the stones were stuffed with much earth weeds would get in, and it is best to have the merest dusting of soil with the roots, so as not to separate the stones, but let each one rest firmly on the one beneath it.

Almost the whole of the beautiful rock and alpine flowers may be trusted to do well in this way, such things as Arabis, Aubrietia, and

Iberis being among the easiest to grow: but as these can be grown without walls it is hardly worth while to put them there, pretty as some of the newer forms of the Aubrietia are. Between these stones is the very place for mountain Pinks, which thrive better there than on level ground; the dwarf alpine Hairbells, while the alpine Wallflowers and creeping rock plants, like the Toad Flax (Linaria), and the Spanish Erinus, are quite at home there. The Gentianella does very well on the cool sides of such walls, and we get a different result according to the aspect. All our little pretty wall ferns, now becoming so rare where hawkers abound, do perfectly on such rough walls, and the alpine Phloxes may be used, though they are not so much in need of the comfort of a wall as the European alpine plants, the Rocky Mountain dwarf Phloxes being very hardy and enduring in our gardens on level ground. The advantage of the wall is that we can grow things that would perish on level ground owing to excitement of growth in winter, or other causes. The Rockfoils are charming on a wall, particularly the silvery kinds, and the little stone covering Sandwort (A. balearica) will run everywhere over such a wall. Stonecrops and Houseleeks would do too, but are easily grown in any open spot of ground.

There is in fact no limit to the beauty of rock and alpine flowers we may enjoy on the rough wall so often and most easily made about gardens in rocky and hill districts, dressed or expensive stone not being needed.

ALPINE AND ROCK PLANTS FOR BRITISH GARDENS

Where the name of a large and varied family is given as in Phlox, Iris, Rhododendrum, Pentstemon, Salix Antirrhinum, it is the alpine or dwarf mountain kinds that are meant.

Acæna	Arenaria	Chimaphila	Dryas	Globularia
Acantholimon	Armeria	Colchicum	Epigæa	Helianthemum
Achillea	Asperula	Cornus	Erigeron	Helleborus
Acis	Astralagus	Coronilla	Erinus	Houstonia
Æthionema	Aubrietia	Crocus	Erodium	Hutchinsia
Alyssum	Bellis	Cyclamen	Erpetion	Hyacinthus
Andromeda	Bryanthus	Cypripedium	Erysimum	Iberis
Androsace	Bulbocodium	Daphne	Erythronium	Iris
Anemone	Calandrinia	Dianthus	Galanthus	Isopyrum
Antennaria	Campanula	Diapensia	Gaultheria	Jasione
Anthyllis	Cardamine	Dodecatheon	Genista	Leiophyllum
Aquilegia	Cerastium	Draba	Gentiana	Leontopodium
Arabis	Cheiranthus	Dracocephalum	Geranium	Leucojum

Linaria	Narcissus	Phlox	Saponaria	Thlaspi
Linnæa	Nertera	Polemonium	Saxifraga	Thymus
Linum	Œnothera	Polygala	Scilla	Trientalis
Lithospermum	Omphalodes	Potentilla	Sedum	Trillium
Loiseleuria	Ononis	Primula	Sempervivum	Triteleia
Lychnis	Onosma	Puschkinia	Senecio	Tulipa
Lycopodium	Ophrys	Pyrola	Silene	Tunica
Mazus	Orchis	Pyxidanthera	Smilacina	Vaccinium
Meconopsis	Orobus	Ranunculus	Soldanella	Veronica
Menziesia	Oxalis	Rhexia	Spigelia	Vesicaria
Mertensia	Papaver	Rhododendron	Statice	Viola
Muscari	Parnassia	Sanguinaria	Thalictrum	Waldsteinia
Myosotis	Petrocallis			

CHAPTER XV

The Wild Garden

O universal Mother, who dost keep
From everlasting thy foundations deep,
Eldest of things, Great Earth, I sing of thee.

In a rational system of flower gardening one of the first things to do
is to get a clear idea of the aim of the "Wild Garden." When I began
to plead the cause of the innumerable hardy flowers against the few
tender ones put out in a formal way, the answer sometimes was, "We
cannot go back to the mixed border"—that is to say, to the old way of
arranging flowers in borders. Thinking, then, much of the vast world of
plant beauty shut out of our gardens by the "system" then in vogue, I
was led to consider the ways in which it might be brought into them,
and of the "Wild Garden" as a home for numbers of beautiful hardy
plants from other countries which might be naturalised, with very
little trouble, in our gardens, fields, and woods—a world of delightful
plant beauty that we might make happy around us, in places bare or
useless.

The term "Wild Garden" is applied to the placing of perfectly hardy
exotic plants in places where they will take care of themselves. It has
nothing to do with the "wilderness," though it may be carried out in
it. It does not necessarily mean the picturesque garden, for a garden
may be picturesque and yet in every part the result of ceaseless care.
What it does mean is best explained by the winter Aconite flowering
under a grove of naked trees in February; by the Snowflake abundant
in meadows by the Thames; and by the Apennine Anemone staining
an English grove blue. Some have thought of it as a garden allowed
to run wild, or with annuals sown promiscuously, whereas it does not
meddle with the flower garden proper at all.

I wish the idea to be kept distinct from the various important phases of hardy plant growth in groups, beds, and borders, in which good culture may produce many happy effects; from the rock garden or borders reserved for choice hardy flowers; from growing hardy plants of fine form; from the ordinary type of spring garden. In the smaller class of gardens there may be little room for the wild garden, but in the larger gardens, where there is often ample room on the outer fringes of the lawn, in grove, park, copse, or by woodland walks or drives, new and beautiful effects may be got by its means.

Among reasons for advocating this system are the following:—
1. Because many hardy flowers will thrive better in rough places than ever they did in the old border. Even small ones like the Ivy-leaved Cyclamen, are naturalised and spread all over the mossy surface of woods. 2. Because, in consequence of plant, fern and flower and climber, grass, and trailing shrub, relieving each other, they will look infinitely better than in stiff gardens. 3. Because no ugly effects will result from decay and the swift passage of the seasons. In a semi-wild state the beauty of a species will show in flowering time; and when out of bloom they will be succeeded by other kinds, or lost among the numerous objects around. 4. Because it will enable us to grow many plants that have never yet obtained a place in our "trim gardens"—multitudes that are not showy enough to be considered worthy of a place in a garden. Among the plants often thought unfit for garden cultivation are a number like the coarser American Asters and Golden Rods, which overrun the choicer border-flowers when planted among them. Such plants would be quite at home in neglected places, where their blossoms might be seen in due season. To these might be added plants like the winter Heliotrope, and many others, which, while interesting in the garden, are apt to spread so rapidly as to become a nuisance. 5. Because in this way we may settle the question of spring flowers, and the spring garden, as well as that of hardy flowers generally; and many parts of the grounds may be made alive with spring flowers, without in the least interfering with the flower garden itself. The blue stars of the Apennine Anemone will be seen to greater advantage when in half-shady places, under trees, or in the meadow grass, than in any flower garden, and this is but one of many of sweet spring flowers that will succeed in like ways.

Perhaps an example or two of what has already been done with Daffodils and Snowdrops may serve to show the way, and explain the gains of the wild garden, and there is no more charming flower to begin with than the Narcissus, which, while fair in form as any Orchid or Lily of the tropics, is as much at home in our climate as the Kingcups in the marsh and the Primroses in the wood. And when the wild Narcissus comes with these, in the woods and orchards of Northern France and Southern England it has also for companions the Violet and the Cowslip, hardiest children of the north, blooming in and near the still leafless woods. And this fact should lead us to see that it is not only a garden flower we have here, but one which may give glorious beauty to our woods and fields and meadows as well as to the pleasure grounds.

In our country in a great many places there is plenty of room to grow them in other ways than in the garden proper, and this not merely in country seats, but in orchards and cool meadows. To chance growth in such places we owe it already that many Narcissi or Daffodils which were lost to gardens, in the period when hardy plants were wholly set aside for bedding plants, have been preserved to us, at first probably in many cases thrown out with the garden refuse. In many places in Ireland and the west of England Narcissi lost to gardens have been found in old orchards and meadows.

Three months after our native kind has flowered in the weald of Sussex and in the woods or orchards of Normandy, many of its allies are beneath the snow in the mountain valleys of Europe, waiting till the summer sun melts the deep snow. On a high plateau in Auvergne I saw many acres in full bloom on July 16, 1894, and these high plateaux are much colder than our own country generally. Soils that are cool and stiff and not favourable to a great variety of plants suit Narcissi perfectly. On the cool mountain marshes and pastures, where the snow lies deep, the plant has abundance of moisture—one reason why it succeeds better in our cool soils. In any case it does so, and it is mostly on dry light soils that Narcissi fail to succeed. Light, sandy or chalky soils in the south of England are useless, and Narcissus culture on a large scale should not be attempted on such soils. We must not court failure, and however freely in some soils Narcissi grow in turf, there is no law clearer than that all plants will not grow in any one soil, and it is a mercy, too, for if all soils were alike, we should find gardens far more monotonous than they are now.

The fine distant effect of Narcissi in groups in the grass should not be forgotten. It is distinct from their effect in gardens, and it is most charming to see them reflect, as it were, the glory of the spring sun. It is not only their effect near at hand that charms us, but as we walk about we may see them in the distance in varying lights, sometimes through and beyond the leafless woods or copses. And there is nothing we have to fear in this charming world save the common sin—overdoing. To scatter Narcissi equally over the grass everywhere is to destroy all chance of repose, of relief, and of seeing them in the ways in which they often arrange themselves. It is almost as easy to plant in pretty ways as in ugly ways if we take the trouble to think of it. There are hints to be gathered from the way wild plants arrange themselves, and even from the sky. Often a small cloud passing in the sky will give a very good form for a group, and be instructive even in being closer and more solid towards its centre, as groups of Narcissi in the grass should often be. The regular garden way of setting things out is very necessary in the garden, but it will not do at all if we are to get the pictures we can get from Narcissi in the turf, and it is always well to keep open turf here and there among the groups, and in a lawn or a meadow we should leave a large breadth quite free of flowers.

A picture of snowdrops in the glass at Straffan, Kildare gives one a glimpse of the pretty and natural way in which the Snowdrops have grouped themselves on the greensward beneath the red-twigged Limes and on the soft and mossy lawns. Originally, no doubt, these flowers were planted, but they have seeded themselves so long that they are now thoroughly naturalised, and one of the sights to see at Straffan Gardens is the Snowdrops at their best under the leafless trees. The common single and double forms are still the best for grouping in quantity and for naturalisation everywhere. There are finer varieties, but none grow and increase so well in our gardens as do these northern kinds. The best of the eastern Snowdrops are very bold and beautiful; they are unsurpassed for vigour of leafage and size of bloom if carefully cultivated, but they may not grow and increase on the grass as do G. nivalis and all its forms.

For solid green leafage and size of flower, G. Ikariæ when well grown is the finest of all Snowdrops, but it is from Asia Minor, and seems to really love our climate, and is likely to naturalise itself with us as G. nivalis has done. The best of all the really hardy and truly northern Snowdrops is a fine form of G. nivalis, leaning to the broad-leaved or G. caucasicus group, which was found in the Crimea in 1856 and introduced from the Tchernaya valley to Straffan. It is called G. nivalis grandis, or the Straffan Snowdrop, or G. caucasicus var. grandis, and to see it at its best is a great pleasure. It is really a tall, vigorous-habited, and free-flowering form of the wild Snowdrop (G. nivalis) as found in the Crimea. The flowers are very large and pure in colour, and being borne on stalks a foot or more in length they bunch better than do those of the common type. G. plicatus is also from the Crimea, but is, as I have said, quite different, having much broader plicate leaves and smaller flowers.

Snowdrops generally like deep, moist soils and half shade, as their flowers wither and brown quickly on dry, light soils in full sunshine. In damp wood, copses, and hedgerows they seem most at home, and like Narcissi and many other early flowering bulbs, they rather enjoy flooding or occasional irrigation after root and top growth have begun. At Straffan the lawn lies low down near the river Liffey, and it is sometimes submerged for a day or two after the snow melts in early spring or after heavy rains. From May until September, however, the bulbs are dry among the tree roots with the dense canopy of Lime leafage overhead, as are also the roots of the sky-blue Apennine Anemone that bear them company. We are beginning to perceive that, as a broad rule, some bulbous plants enjoy growing amongst the roots of other plants, or of trees and shrubs, or in the grass of lawn or meadow. The wild Daffodil and Bluebells do this as well as the Snowdrop, and those who have tried to dig up bulbs of any kind abroad with a knife or even with a botanical trowel, will remember how tightly wedged they frequently are in roots of various kinds, or jammed tightly in both roots and stones.

All planting in the grass should be in natural groups or prettily fringed colonies, growing to and fro as they like after planting. Lessons in this grouping are to be had in the woods, copses, heaths, and meadows, by those who look about them as they go. At first many will find it difficult to get out of formal masses, but they may be got over by studying natural groupings of wild flowers. Once established, the plants soon begin to group themselves in pretty ways.

In the cultivation of hardy plants and especially in wild gardening the important thing is to find out what things really do in the soil, without which much good way cannot be made. Many people make errors in planting things that are tender in our country and very often fail in consequence; but apart from such risky planting perfectly hardy plants may disappear owing to some dislike of the soil. They flower feebly at first and afterwards gradually wane in spite of all our efforts. The Narcissus, which is so free and enduring in cool damp soil, does little good on warm, light or chalky soil. Some things are so omnivorous in their appetites that they will grow anywhere, but some, the more beautiful races of bulbous and other early flowers, will only thrive and stay with us where they like the soil. It should be clearly seen therefore that what may be done with any good result in the wild garden cannot be determined beforehand, but must depend on the nature of the soil and other circumstances which can be known only to those who study the ground.

Where the branches of trees, both evergreen and summer-leafing, sweep the turf in pleasure grounds many pretty spring-flowering bulbs may be naturalised beneath the branches, and will thrive without attention. It is chiefly in the case of deciduous trees that this can be done; but even in the case of Conifers and Evergreens some graceful objects may be dotted beneath the outermost points of their lower branches. We know that a great number of our spring flowers and hardy bulbs mature their foliage and go to rest early in the year. In spring they require light and sun, which they obtain abundantly under the summer-leafing tree; they have time to flower and grow under it before the foliage of the tree appears; then, as the summer heats approach, they are overshadowed, and go to rest; but the leaves of the tree once fallen, they soon begin to reappear and cover the ground with beauty.

SOME PLANTS FOR THE WILD GARDEN

The following are the chief families of plants that may be used in the wild garden. Where families are named which are British as well as natives of the Continent of Europe, as in the case of, say, Scilla, the foreign kinds are meant. In considering what may be done in naturalising plants in a given position, it may be well to cast the eye over the families available.

Acanthus	Comfrey	Ferns, Hardy	Holly, Sea	Mallow
Aconite, Winter	Compass Plant	Forget-me-not	Honesty	Meadow Rue
Asphodel	Cornflower	Foxglove	Honeysuckle	Meadow Saffron
Aubrietia	Coronilla	French Willow	Houseleeks	Meadow Sweet
Barrenwort	Cotton Thistle	Giant Fennel	Iris	Mimulus
Bee Balm	Cow Parsnip	Giant Scabious	Knotwort	Monk's Hood
Bellflower	Crane's-bill	Globe Flower	Lavender	Mountain Avens
Bindweed	Crocus	Globe Thistle	Leopard's-bane	Mullein
Blood Root	Cyclamen	Golden Rod	Lily	Narcissus
Borage	Daffodil	Grape Hyacinth	Lily-of-the-valley	Omphalodes
Broom	Dane's Blood	Heath	Loosestrife	Ox-eye Daisy
Clematis	Day Lily	Heliotrope, Winter	Lungwort	Pæony
Columbine	Dog's-tooth Violet	Hepatica	Lupine	Pea, everlasting

Periwinkle	Rocket	Snake's Head	Stonecrop	Virginian Creeper
Phlox	Rose, wild kinds	Snapdragon	Sun Rose	Virginian Poke
Plaintain Lily	St Bruno's Lily	Snowdrop	Sunflower	Wallflower
Pond-flower	St John's Wort	Snowflake	(Perennial)	Water-Lily
Poppy	Sandwort	Solomon's Seal	Thyme	Windflower
Primrose, Evening	Scabious	Star of Bethlehem	Tulip	Wistaria
Rest Harrow	Scilla	Starwort	Viola	Wood Lily

CHAPTER XVI

Spring Gardens

"I have seen foreign flowers in hothouses of the most beautiful nature, but I do not care a straw for them. The simple flowers of our spring are what I want to see again."—JOHN KEATS (Letter to James Rice).

In our islands, swept by the winds of iceless seas, spring wakes early in the year, when the plains of the north and the mountains of the south and centre are cold in snow. In our green springs the flowers of northern and alpine countries open long before they do in their native homes; hence the artistic error of any system of flower gardening which leaves out the myriad flowers of spring. It is no longer a question of gardens being bare of the right plants; nurseries and gardens where there are many good plants are not rare, but to make effective use of these much thought is seldom given. Gardens are often rich in plants but poor in beauty, many being stuffed with things, but ugly in effect.

A common kind of "spring gardening" consists of "bedding out" Forget-me-nots, Pansies, Daisies, Catchflies, and Hyacinths; but this way is only one of many, and the meanest, most costly, and inartistic. It began when we had few good spring flowers, now we have many; and hence this chapter must deal with other and better ways.

There are so many hardy plants among rock plants that flower in spring (many alpine plants blooming as soon as the snow goes), that there is not room to name them all. We must omit any detailed notice of plants like Adonis, Cyclamen, Draba, Erodium, and the smaller Rockfoils and Stonecrops, Dicentra, Fumaria, Orobus, Ramondia, Silene, and many other flowers of the rocks and hills, which though beautiful individually do not tell so well in the picture as many here named.

Among rock plants the first place belongs to certain mountain plants of the northern world, which, in our country, come into bloom before the early shrubs and trees, and among the first bold plants to cheer us in spring are those of the Wallflower order—the yellow Alyssum, effective and easy to grow, the white Arabis, even more grown in Northern France than in England (it well deserves to be spread about in sheets and effective groups), and the beautiful purple Rock Cresses (Aubrietia), lovely plants of the mountains of Greece and the countries near, which have developed a number of varieties even more beautiful in colour than the wild kinds. Nothing for gardens can be more precious than these plants, the long spring bloom being effective in almost every kind of flower gardening—banks, walls, edgings, borders of evergreen rock plants, or carpets beneath sparsely set shrubs. The white evergreen Candytufts are also effective plants in clear sheets for borders, edgings to beds, tops of walls, and the rougher flanks of the rock garden. These are among the plants that have been set out in hard lines in flower gardens, but it is easy to have better effects from them in groups, and even in broken lines and masses, or as carpets beneath bushes, thus giving softer and more beautiful, if less definite, effects. Happy always on castle wall and rocks, the Wallflower is most welcome in the garden, where, on warm soils and in genial climates, it does well, but hard winters injure it often in cold and inland districts, and it is almost like a tender plant in such conditions. Yet it must ever be one of the flowers best worth growing in sheltered and warm gardens; and even in cold places one may have a few under the eaves of cottages and on dry south borders.

The Windflowers are a noble group among the most beautiful of the northern and eastern flowers, some being easily naturalised (like the blue Italian and Greek Anemones), while the showy Poppy Anemones are easily grown where the soils are light and warm, and in genial warm districts; but they require some care on certain soils, and are among the plants we must cultivate and even protect on cold soils in hard winters. The same is true of the brilliant Asiatic Ranunculus and all its varied forms, Persian, Turkish, and French, as they may be called, all forms of one wild North African buttercup, unhappily too tender to endure our winters in the open air, but they should be abundantly grown on the warm limestone and other soils which suit them, as about our coasts and in Ireland. There is no more effective way of growing these than in simple 4-foot beds in the kitchen or reserve garden. The Wood Anemone is so often seen in the woods that there is rarely need to grow it; but some of its varieties are essential, most beautiful being A. Robinsoniana, a flower of lovely blue colour, and a distinct gain in the spring garden grown in almost any way. The Hepatica is a lovely little Anemone where the soil is free, though slow in some soils, and where it grows well all its varieties should be encouraged, in borders and margins of beds of American bushes as well as in the rock garden. The Snowdrop Windflower (A. sylvestris) is most, graceful in bud and bloom, but a little capricious, and not blooming well on all soils, unlike in this way our Wood Windflowers, which are as constant as the Kingcups. The Pasque-flower is lovely on the chalk downs and fields of Normandy and parts of England in spring, but never quite so pretty in a garden. It would be worth naturalising in chalky fields and woods or banks.

Columbines are very beautiful in the early part of the year, and if we had nothing but the common kind (Aquilegia vulgaris) and its forms, they would be precious; but there are many others which thrive in free soils, some of which are very graceful in form and charming in colour. The Kingcup or Marsh Marigold, so fine in wet meadows and by the riverside, should be brought into gardens wherever there is water as it is a most effective plant when well grown, and there are several forms, double and single. The Clematis, the larger kinds, are mostly for the summer, but some (C. montana, C. alpina, C. cirrhosa) are at their best in the spring; they should be made abundant use of on house walls and over banks, trees and shrubs. The Winter Aconite (carliest of spring flowers) naturalises itself in some soils, but on others dwindles and dies out, and it should not be grown in the garden, but in shrubberies, copses, or woods where the soil suits it. Some kinds of hardy Ranunculus, the herbaceous double kinds, are good in colour, and in bold groups pretty; but taller and bolder and finer in effect are the Globe-flowers, easily naturalised in moist, grassy places or by water, and also free and telling among stout herbaceous plants. The most distinct addition to the spring garden of recent years is the Oriental Hellebore in its many beautiful varieties. They are most effective, sturdy, impressive plants for opening the flower year with, often blooming abundantly at the dawn of spring, and have the essential merit of not requiring annual culture, tufts remaining in vigour in the same spot for many years.

The European Dog's-tooth Violet is pretty in the budding grass, where it is free in growth and bloom, but it is more enduring in the shade of shrubs. The Fritillary is one of the most welcome flowers for grass, and is best in moist meadows; the rarer kinds do well in good garden soil, those with pale yellow bells being beautiful. Every plant such as these, which we can so easily grow at home in grassy places, makes our cares about the spring garden so much the less, and allows of keeping all the precious beds of the flower garden itself for the plants that require some care and rich soil always.

The Snowdrop is of even greater value of late years owing to new forms of it, some of which have been brought from Asia Minor. In some soils it is quite free and becomes easily naturalised, in others it dwindles away, and the same is true of the vernal Snowflake (Leucojum vernum), a beautiful plant. The larger Snowflakes are more free in ordinary soils, and easily naturalised in river bank soil. The Crocus, the most brilliant of spring flowers, does not always lend itself to growing naturally in every soil, but on some it is quite at home, especially those of a chalky nature, and will naturalise itself under trees.

To the Scilla we owe much, from the wild plants of our woods to the vivid Siberian kind; some kinds are essential in the garden, and some, like the Spanish Scilla (S. Campanulata), may be naturalised in free soils. Allies of these lovely early flowers have come of recent years to our gardens—the beautiful Chionodoxa from Asia Minor, of about the same stature and effect as the prettiest of the Scillas, and some of them even more precious for colour.

About the same time come the precious Spanish Iris in many colours, lovely as Orchids, and very easily grown, and the English Iris. The Grape Hyacinths are pretty and early plants of Southern Europe, beautiful in colour. They increase rapidly, and some kinds do very well in the grass in free and peaty soils, but the rarer ones are best on warm borders and groups in the rock garden. In our country, where there are so many cool and rich soils allowing of the Narcissus being naturalised and grown in many ways, it is, perhaps, on the whole, the most precious of all our spring flowers. But the Tulip is the most showy in colour of all the flowers of spring, and for its effectiveness is better worthy of special culture than most; indeed, the florists' kinds and the various rare garden Tulips must be well grown to show their full size and beauty.

Pæonies are nobly effective in many ways. Where single or other kinds are plentiful they may be well used as broad groups in new plantations, among shrubs and low trees, and as to the choice double kinds, no plants better deserve a little garden or border to themselves while the tree kinds make superb groups on the lawn and are safer from frost on high ground. The great scarlet Poppies are showy in spring, and best grown among trees and in the wild garden, and with them may be named the Welsh Poppy, a very effective plant in spring as well as summer, and often sowing itself in all sorts of places. The various garden forms of the opium Poppy and of the field Poppy, both double and single, are very showy where any space is given to annual flowers.

The common perennial Lupin is a very showy, pretty plant grown in a free way in groups and masses, and may sometimes be naturalised, and, associated with Poppies and free-growing Columbines in the wild garden, it is very effective.

Primroses are a lovely host for the garden, especially the garden varieties of the common Primrose, Cowslip, and Oxlip. Few things deserve a better place, or are more worthy of good culture in visible groups and colonies or rich garden borders. Apart from the lovely races of garden forms raised from the Primrose, the Cowslip, and the Oxlip, and also the Alpine Auriculas, double Primroses should not be forgotten, as in all moist districts and in peaty and free soil they give such tender and beautiful colour in groups, borders, or slightly shaded among dwarf shrubs. Primroses and Polyanthus of native origin are well backed up by the beautiful Indian Primrose (Primula rosea), which thrives apace in cool soils in the north of England and in Scotland, and which, when grown in bold groups, is very good in effect, as are the purplish Indian Primroses under like conditions.

The large-leaved Indian Rockfoils (Saxifraga) are in many soils very easily grown, and they are showy spring flowers in bold groups, especially some of the improved varieties. Although it is only in places where there is rocky ground or large rock gardens that one can get the beauty of the smaller Mountain Rockfoils (Saxifraga) we cannot omit to notice their beauty—both the white, yellow, and crimson-flowered kind—when seen in masses. The same may be said of Gentians; beautiful as they are in the mountains, few gardens have positions where we can get their fine effect, always excepting the old Gentianella (G. acaulis), which in old Scotch and English gardens used to make such handsome broad edgings, and which is easily grown in a cool soil, and gives, perhaps, the noblest effect of blue flowers that one can enjoy in our latitudes in spring. The tall Phloxes are plants of the summer, but there is a group of American dwarf alpine Phloxes of the mountains which are among the hardiest and most cheery flowers of spring, thriving on any dry banks and in the drier parts of rock gardens, forming mossy edgings in the flower garden, and breaking into a foam of flowers early in spring.

The Viola family is most precious, not only in the many forms of the sweet Violet, which will always deserve garden cultivation, but in the numerous varieties of the Pansy, which flower so effectively in the spring. The best of all, perhaps, for artistic use are the Tufted Pansies, which are delightfully simple in colour—white, pale blue, or lavender, and various other delicate shades. Almost perennial in character, they can be increased and kept true, and they give us distinct and delicate colour in masses as wide as we wish, instead of the old "variegated" effect of Pansies.

Forget-me-nots are among the most welcome flowers of spring. Before the common and most beautiful of all—the marsh Forget-me-not—comes, there are the wood Forget-me-not (M. Sylvatic) and M. dissitiflora and M. alpestris, all precious early flowers. Allied to the ever-welcome Forget-me-not is the common Omphalodes, or creeping Forget-me-not, valuable for its freedom in growth in half shady or rough places in almost any soil—one of the most precious of the early flowers which take care of themselves if we take a little trouble to put them in likely places.

Among annuals that bloom in spring where the soil is favourable, excellent results are often obtained by sowing Sweet Peas in autumn. When this is done, and they escape the winter, they give welcome hedges of flowers in the early year. So, too, the Cornflower, a lovely spring flower, and perhaps the finest blue we have among annual plants; but to have it good and early it should be always sown in autumn, and for effect it should be in broad masses, sometimes among shrubs or in recently broken ground which we desire to cover. Some of the Californian annuals are handsome and vigorous when sown in autumn, always provided they escape the winter. The White Godetia is very fine in this way. In all chalky, sandy, and warm soils the Stocks for spring bloom are handsome and fragrant.

Some of the finest effects come from the early trees and shrubs. Among the most stately are the Buckeyes (Æsculis), particularly the red kinds, fine in all stages, but especially when old. The snowy Mespilus is a hardy, low-sized tree, blooming regularly, and well deserves a place in the pleasure garden or the fringes of shrubberies. The Almonds, more than any shrubs, perhaps, in our country and in

France, light up the earliest days of spring, and, like most southern trees, are best in warm valley soils. They should be in groups to tell in the home landscape. The double Peaches are lovely in France, but as yet rarely so with us, owing, perhaps, to some defect of the stock used. Perhaps of all the hardy shrubs ever brought to our country the Azaleas are the most precious for effect, often wild on the mountains of America, and many forms have been raised in gardens which are of the highest value. Many places do not as yet show the great beauty of the different groups of hardy Azalea, particularly the late kinds raised of recent years. A neglected tree with us is the Judas-tree, which is very handsome in groups, as it ought always to be grown, and not as a starved single tree. The various double Cherries are noble flowering trees, being showy as well as delicate in bloom, and the Japanese kinds do quite as well as the old French and English double Cherries, though the trees are apt to perish from grafting. The American Fringe-tree (Chionanthus) is pretty, but some American flowering trees do not ripen their wood well enough in England generally to give us the handsome effects seen in their own country. Hawthorns, those of our own country, make natural spring gardens of hills and rocky places, and should lead us to give a place to the many other species to be found in the mountains of Europe and America, which vary the bloom and prolong the season of early-flowering trees. There are many varieties of our native Hawthorn—red, pink, double, and weeping. The Alpine Laburnum has for years been a joy with its golden rain, and of late we are doubly well off with improved forms, with long chains of golden flowers.

Among the early charms in the spring garden are the slender wands of the Forsythia, hardy Chinese bushes, pale yellow, delightful in effect when grown in picturesque ways; effective also on walls or grouped in the open air on banks. Another plant of refined beauty, but too little planted, is the Snowdrop-tree (Halesia). Unlike other American trees, it ripens its wood in our country, and often flowers well. The Mountain Laurel of America (Kalmia) is one of the most beautiful things ever brought to our country, and as a late spring flower is precious, thriving both in the open and in half shady places.

There is no more showy plant or one more beautiful in effect in masses than the common Broom and all its allies that are hardy enough, even the little Spanish Furze giving fine colour. The common Broom should be encouraged on bluffs and sandy or gravelly places, so as to save us the trouble of growing it in gardens, for in effect there is nothing better. The same may be said of the Furze, which is such a beautiful plant in England and the coast regions of France, and the Double Furze deserves to be massed in the garden in picturesque groups. In country seats, especially those commanding views, its value in the foreground is very great, and it is so easily raised from seed that fine effects are very easily secured, though it may be cut down now and then in hard winters.

The glory of spring in our pleasure grounds are the Rhododendrons, but they are so overmastering in their effect on people's minds that very often they lead to neglect of other things. It would be difficult to overrate their charms; but even amongst them we require to discriminate and avoid the too early and tender kinds. Many of the kinds raised from R. ponticum and the Indian Rhododendron, while they thrive in mild districts in the south of England and west of France, near the sea, are not hardy in the country generally. Some of these tender hybrids certainly flower early, but we get little good from that. The essential thing, when we give space to a hardy shrub, is that we should get its bloom in perfection, and therefore we should choose the broad-leaved hardy kinds, which are mostly raised from the very hardy North American R. catawbiense, and be a little particular in grouping the prettiest colours, never using a grafted plant. For many years the Yulan Magnolia, when well grown, has been one of the finest trees in English southern gardens, and nothing is more effective than the Lily-tree in gardens like Syon and others in the Thames valley; while of late years we have seen precious additions to this, the noblest family of flowering trees. Some of these, like M. stellata, have proved to be valuable; all are worth a trial, and, as to the kinds we are sure of, the great thing is to group them.

Amongst the most beautiful of the smaller alpine bushes ever brought to our country is the alpine forest Heath, which is cheery and bright for weeks in spring. It is one of the plants that never fails us, and only requires to be grown in bold ways, fully exposed to the sun. Other Heaths, like the Mediterranean Heath, are also beautiful in some favoured parts of the country, but not so hardy generally as the little alpine forest Heath which has the greatest endurance and perfect hardiness.

Pyrus japonica, a handsome old shrub often planted on cottage garden walls, may in many soils be used with good effect in groups and hedges. The evergreen Barberries in various forms are beautiful early shrubs, with soft yellow flowers, and excellent when grouped in some quantity. Two very important families are the Deutzias and Syringas, which are varied and beautiful, mostly in white masses. The flowering Currant (Ribes) of the mountains of N.W. America is in all its forms a very cheery and early bush, which tells well in the home landscape if rightly placed; but perhaps the most welcome and important of all early trees and shrubs is the Lilac, which in Britain is often grown in a few kinds only, when there are many in France. Beautiful in almost any position, Lilacs are most effective when planted together, so as to enjoy the full sun to ripen their wood; and they should be planted on their own roots always.

Apart from the many orchard trees grown for their fruit, we have in our own day to welcome some of their allies—lovely in flower, if often poor in fruit. Our country has never been without some of this kind of beauty, as the Crab itself is as handsome a flowering tree as are many of the Apples which are descended from it in all the countries in Europe, from Russia to Spain, and in our gardens there were for many years the old Chinese double Pyrus, a handsome tree which became popular, and the American Crab, which never became so. But of late years we have been enriched by the Japan Crab, a lovely tree for some weeks in spring and other handsome kinds, including Parkman's Crab, which comes to us under more than one name, and a red form of the Japanese flowering Crab before mentioned. All these trees are as hardy as our native Crab, and differ much in colour and sometimes also in form. It is difficult to describe how much beauty they give where well grown and well placed; they are not the kind of things we lose owing to change of fashion, and in planting them it is well to put them in groups where they will tell. Apart from these more or less wild species there are numbers of hybrid Crabs raised between the Siberian and some common Apples in America and in our country that are beautiful also in flower, and remarkable too for beauty of fruit, so that a beautiful grove of flowering trees might be formed of Crabs alone. With these many fine things, and the various Honeysuckles, we are carried bravely down to the time of Rose and Lily, summer flowers, though Roses often come on warm walls in spring.

It is worth while thinking of the difference in the blooming of spring flowers in various aspects, as differences in that way will often give us a longer season of bloom of some of our most precious things. Daffodils do better in half shade than in full sunshine, and Scillas and other bulbs are like the Daffodils in liking half shady spots; so also Crown Imperials, which, like the Scillas, bleach badly if fully exposed to the sun. We may see the Wood Hyacinth pass out of bloom on the southern slopes of a hill, and in fresh and fair bloom on its northern slopes. Flowering shrubs, creepers on walls, and all early plants are influenced in the same way. Such facts may be taken advantage of in many ways especially with the nobler flowers that we make much use of. If different aspects are worth securing for hardy flowers generally, they are doubly so for those of the spring, when we often have storms of snow and sleet that may destroy an early bloom. If fortunate enough to have the same plant on the north side of the hill or wall, we have still a chance of a second bloom, and a difference of two or three weeks in the blooming of a plant.

Early Summer Flowers Hardy in English Gardens

Adonis	Convallaria	Fritillaria	Muscari	Sanguinaria
Alyssum	Crocus	Fumaria	Myosotis	Saponaria
Androsace	Cyclamen	Galanthus	Narcissus	Saxifraga
Anemone	Dentaria	Geum	Omphalodes	Scilla
Aquilegia	Dianthus	Gypsophila	Ornithogalum	Sedum
Arabis	Dicentra	Helleborus	Orobus	Silene
Arenaria	Dodecatheon	Hepatica	Pæonia	Trillium
Armeria	Doronicum	Hesperis	Papaver	Triteleia
Asperula	Draba	Hyacinthus	Phlox	Trollius
Asphodelus	Epimedium	Iberis	Polemonium	Tulipa
Aubrietia	Eranthis	Iris	Potentilla	Uvularia
Bellis	Erinus	Leucojum	Primula	Veronica
Caltha	Erodium	Linum	Pulmonaria	Vinca
Centaurea	Erythronium	Lychnis	Ramondia	Viola
Cematis	Ficaria	Meconopsis	Ranunculus	

Spring-Flowering Trees and Shrubs

Æsculus	Cratægus	Genista	Mespilus	Styrax
Amelanchier	Cydonia	Halesia	Philadelphus	Syringa
Amygdalus	Cytisus	Kerria	Prunus	Tamarix
Andromeda	Daphne	Laburnum	Pyrus	Ulex
Azalea	Deutzia	Lonicera	Rhododendron	Viburnum
Berberis	Erica	Magnolia	Ribes	Weigela
Cerasus	Exochorda	Mahonia	Spartium	Wistaria
Cercis	Forsythia	Malus	Spiræa	

THE SUMMER GARDEN
CHAPTER XVII

The New Rose Garden

There is great loss to the flower garden from the usual way of growing the Rose as a thing apart, and its absence at present from many flower gardens. It is surprising to see how poor and hard many places are to which the beauty of the Rose might add delight, and the only compensation for all this blank is what is called the rosery, which in large places is often an ugly thing with plants that usually only blossom for a few weeks in summer. This idea of the Rose garden arose when we had a much smaller number of Roses, and a greater number of these were kinds that flowered in summer mainly.

The nomenclature, too, in use among Rose-growers by which Roses that flower the shortest time were given the name of Hybrid Perpetuals has had something to do with the absence of the Rose from the flower garden. Shows, too, have had a bad effect on the Rose in the garden, where it is many times more important than as a show flower. The whole aim of the man who showed Roses was to get a certain number of large blooms grown on the Dog Rose, Manetti, or any stock which enabled him to get this at the least cost.

It is instructive to study the influence of Rose books upon the Rose as well as that of the Rose exhibitions, as they brought about an idea that the Rose was not a "decorative" plant in the language of recent days. In these books it was laid down that the Rose did not associate properly with other flowers, and it was therefore better to put it in a place by itself, and, though this false idea had less influence in the cottage garden, it did harm in all large

gardens. In a recent book on the Rose by Mr Foster-Melliar
we read:

> I do not consider the Rose pre-eminent as a decorative plant; several
> simpler flowers, much less beautiful in themselves, have, to my mind,
> greater value for general effect in the garden, and even the blooms are,
> I imagine, more difficult to arrange in water for artistic decoration
> than lighter, simpler, and less noble flowers.

He, the author, is only describing the practice and views of the Rose
exhibitors which most unfortunately ruled the practice of gardeners,
and it is very natural many should take the prize-taker as a guide.

There was some reason in the older practice, because until recent
years the Roses most grown were summer flowering, that is to say,
like our wild Roses, they had a fixed and short time of bloom, usually
not more than a few weeks; but in our days, and within the last fifty
years, there have been raised a number of Roses, which flower for
much longer periods. There are, for example, the Monthly Roses
and the lovely Tea Roses, which also come in some way from the
Indian Rose, and which, when well grown, will flower throughout
the summer. So that, while our forefathers might have been excused
for taking the view that Roses are only fit to plant in a place apart,
there is no need for the modern grower to do so, who is not tied to
the show bench as his one ideal and aim.

The Rose is not only "decorative" but is the queen of all decorative
plants, not in one sort of garden, but in many—not in one race or
sort, but in many, from Anna Olivier, Edith Gifford and Tea Roses of
that noble type in the heart of the choicest flower garden, to the wild
Rose that tosses its long arms from the hedgerows in the rich soils of
midland England, and the climbing Roses in their many forms. And
fine as the old climbing Roses were, we have now a far nobler race of
climbing Teas which, in addition to the highest beauty, have the great
quality of flowering, like Bouquet d'Or, throughout the fine summer
and late into the autumn.

The outcome of it all is that the Rose must go back to the flower
garden—its true place, not only for its own sake, but to save the
garden from ugliness, and give it fragrance and beauty of leaf and
flower. The idea that we cannot have prolonged bloom from Roses is
not true, because the finer Monthly and Tea Roses flower longer than
any half-hardy plants, even without the advantage of fresh soil every

year which such plants enjoy. I have Roses growing in the same places for many years, which bloom into autumn. And they must come back not only in beds, but in the old ways—over bower and trellis, and as bushes where they are hardy enough to stand our winters, so as to break up flat surfaces and give us light and shade where all is usually so level and hard. But the Rose must not come back in ugly ways, in Roses stuck and mostly starving on the tops of sticks standards, or set in raw beds of manure and pruned hard and set thin so as to develop large blooms; but, as the bloom is beautiful in all stages and sizes Roses should be seen closely massed, feathering to the ground, the queen of the flower garden in all ways.

A taking novelty at first, few things have had a worse influence on the flower garden than the Standard Rose. Grown throughout Europe and Britain by millions, it is seen usually in a wretched state, and yet there is something about it which prevents us seeing its bad effect in the garden, and its evil influence on the cultivation of the Rose, for we now and then see a fine and even a picturesque Standard, when the Rose suits the stock it is grafted on, and the soil suits each; but this does not happen often. The term grafting is used here to describe any modes of growing a Rose on any stock or kind, as the English use of the term budding as distinct from grafting is needless, budding being only one of the many forms of grafting.

Of the evil effect of the Standard Rose anyone may judge in the suburbs of every town, but its other defects are not so clear to all, such as the exposure high in the air to winter's cold of varieties more or less delicate. On the tops of their ugly stick supports they perish by thousands even in nurseries in the south of England. If these same varieties were on their own roots, even if the severest winter killed the shoots, the root would be quite safe, and the shoots come up again as fresh as ever; so that the frost would only prune our Rose bushes instead of killing them. Even if "worked" low on the "collar" of the stock, grafted Roses have a chance of rooting and keeping out of the way of frost, which they never have when grafted high in the air.

Another element of uncertainty is the kind of stock used. Even if the propagator knows the right stock for the sort he may not for some reason use it, as many have found to their cost who have bought Tea Roses grafted on the Manetti, a stock that in any case has no merit beyond giving a few large blooms for a show the first year; and in many cases it paralyses all growth in the kind grafted on it.

The first care should be to get plants on own roots about as strong as those worked, and it is not difficult to do this with a little patience, as some gardeners and even cottagers strike Roses from cuttings. But no trial would be of any use which did not go over the first year or two, because of the dread phase of the practice alluded to, that the things are grown to sell, and although they look well when they come to us, after a year or two perish.

If we go into the Rose garden of the Luxembourg at Paris or any of the regular roseries in England, we may find half the Roses in a sickly, flowerless state. So sickly are the bushes, or what remains of them, that it is common to see a rosery without any Roses worth picking after the first flush of bloom is past. Think of the number of beautiful things which this has to do with to their harm:—the flowers fairest of all in form, colour, and odour, from the more beautiful tea-scented Roses raised in our own days to the oldest Roses.

Often I have reason to wish that Signor Manetti of Naples had never been born to give his name to the wretched Rose stock that bears it, as among my blighted hopes is a plant of Maréchal Niel Rose, the plants on which have remained as they were at first for the last five years; but this year beside one of them is in bloom the poor Manetti Rose, on which the Maréchal was grafted, and as the Tea Rose will not grow, the Manetti begins to take its place. In some soils and conditions, the Manetti may give some apparent advantages for the first year in making the plant grow rapidly, and perhaps giving one or two flowers to be cut off for a show, but afterwards it is all the other way; the Rose fails on it and Tea Roses do not grow on it at all. It is quite distinct in nature from them, and nurserymen who use the Manetti for Tea Roses do no good to their own craft.

In most gardens where people pay any attention to Roses the ground in which they grow is in winter densely coated with manure, often raw and ugly to see in a flower garden—perhaps under the windows of the best rooms of the house. This is the regulation way of catalogues and books, but it is needless and impossible in a beautiful Rose garden. Most of our garden Roses are grafted on the Dog Rose of our hedgerows, which does best in the heavy, cool loams of the midlands, so that if we want the ordinary grafted garden Rose to do well we must give it not less than 30 inches in depth of like soil. This is often of a rich nature, and it is very easy to add in putting the soil in all the manure which the Rose may want for some years, so that the surface of the bed might be planted with light-rooting rock and like plants, one of the prettiest ways being to surface it with Pansies and Violets. I have beds of Tea Roses over which rock plants have been growing for years without the Roses suffering.

If we free our minds from the incubus of these wrong teachings and practices, many beautiful things may be done with Roses for garden adornment. What is wanted mainly is that the very finest Roses, and above all long-blooming ones like Monthly Roses and such Tea Roses as G. Nabonnand, Marie Van Houtte, and Anna Olivier, should be brought into the flower garden in bold masses and groups to give variety and prolonged bloom, using the choicest Tea Roses in the flower beds, with wreath of yellow climbing Roses swinging in the air, and on walls, especially the climbing Tea Roses.

Perhaps it may be worth while to tell the story of a trial that succeeded as it may be of more use to the beginner. My idea was to get the best of the Roses into the flower garden instead of bedding plants or coarse perennials, and show at the same time the error of the common ways of growing Roses. Another point was to help to get the flower garden more permanently planted instead of the eternal ups and downs of the beds in spring and autumn and the ugly bareness of the earth at those seasons, and to see if one could not make a step towards the beautiful permanent planting of beds near the house and always in view. Tea Roses only were used for the sake of their great freedom of bloom, and these were all planted in large groups, so that one might judge of their effect and character much better than by the usual ineffective mixed planting. The success of the plan was remarkable both for length of bloom and beauty of flower and foliage, variety of kind and charming range of colour, and also curious and unlooked for variety in each kind. Each Tea Rose varied as the weather varied, and the days passed on: the buds of Anna Olivier in June were not the same as the buds of the same Rose in September, and all kinds showed ceaseless changes in the beauty of bud or bloom from week to week.

It was easy to abolish the standard as hopelessly diseased and ugly in effect, but not so easy to get out of the way of grafting on something else, which is the routine in nurseries, and here I had to follow the usual way of getting all the Tea Roses grafted on the common Dog Rose, but always getting the plants "worked" low either on the base of the stock or on the root, so that it is easy in planting to cover the union of the stock with the more precious thing which is grafted on to it, and so protect the Rose from intense cold. There is also a chance in this way of letting the plant so grafted free itself by rooting above the union. Certainly it is so in my garden in a cool and upland district. Some kinds flower, do well for a year or two, and then rapidly diminish in size and beauty; some are very vigorous the first year but die off wholly in the second. The Wild Rose stock has the power to push the Rose into great growth the first year, and then, owing to the stock and graft being of a wholly different origin and nature, there is a conflict in the flows of the sap, and death often ensues. Some Roses that grew freely did not open their buds in our country, and others broke away into small heads and buds which made them useless. However, out of the thousands planted some kinds did admirably, and quite enough of them to make a true garden of Roses, lasting in beauty throughout the summer and autumn.

Knowing that we had to face the fact of all the Roses being grafted on the Dog Rose it was important to give them a deep, cool loam, and the beds in most cases were dug out to a depth of 30 inches below the surface. Although a rocky bottom no drainage was used, no liquid manure was ever given, and no water even in the hot summers.

Instead of mulching the beds in the usual way, and always vexing the surface with attentions I thought needless, we covered them with Pansies, Violets, Stonecrops, Rockfoils, Thymes, and any little rock plants to spare. Carpeting these Rose beds with life and beauty was half the battle. We do not mulch except with these living plants, many of which are so fragile in their roots that they cannot have much effect in a bed of 3 feet of moist, good soil. So that instead of the bare earth in hot days, the flower shadows are thrown on to soft carpets of fragile rock or mountain plants that we think worth growing for their own sake also.

There are a great number of Roses that lend themselves to this, the old climbing Roses being now aided by a splendid series of long-blooming climbing Tea Roses which are more valuable still. They should be trained abundantly over well-formed pergolas, covered ways, trellises, and fences. In countries a little warmer than ours we see what can be done with Roses as noble climbers; in Algeria, and in Madeira, the climbing Tea Roses running up trees in the loveliest bloom.

I have grown Roses here for over a quarter of a century with success and without the usual excess of manure below and on the surface, this last called mulching. It seems to me that to cover beds near the house with excreta from the farm and other yards is anything but a sanitary or even a necessary thing to do. So our Rosebeds are done without it either above or below. We never mulch the beds, but cover them with beautiful plants instead. We set the Roses rather thinly and add many plants beneath them, mostly low in stature. The beds were dug deep, a base of poor shale thrown out for 3 feet. The turf on the surface was buried, and that we found to be a mistake, as it was full of grubs of daddy-long-legs and other pests, which destroyed the Carnations for two years afterwards. We ought to have *burned* the turf. The soil was cool loam rather heavier than I should make it now, being then misled by the catalogues, which told us that Roses must have heavy soil and heaps of manure. Now we only cover the surface with beautiful life, and practise rotation on that. For example, one year's Mignonette is followed by the Missouri Evening Primrose.

In past years an enormous amount of manure was used in gardens in excess of what the plants really needed. Deep soil and a good free texture soil is quite as important. Let us not forget that some so-called artificial manures are really natural, such as bone and other fertilisers, which may be used when helpful; but in my garden, where we have certainly the finest Roses, for many years we use no stable manure.

Tea and China Roses were grown for many years, and as they were invariably bought grafted on the Dog Brier of the hedgerow, much trouble arose from suckers. But in this case the plants were kept in view in bold groups for ten or more years. In that way the effect of soil, climate, and growth could be seen better than in growing single plants. The main result was that more than half the kinds of Tea Roses perished on the Dog Brier, some after flowering badly for years and some dying altogether; others did well and remained in health. Some like Comtesse du Cayla flowered bravely for some years, and then came the briers in strong force and, being anchored on the great roots of the Dog Brier, were very hard to get up. The right way with all the Chinese Roses is to raise plants from cuttings.

Some Roses of very great value go back in the most provoking way, like a beautiful Rose, Mrs D. M'Kee. With them we had great success from cuttings put not in the heavy loam of the Rose beds but in the lighter soil of the fruit garden.

The main difficulty is transplanting, the roots being more fragile than those of the Brier. The best way of all is to put the cuttings where the plants are wanted to grow, and so ensuring to them a long life. The best time to make cuttings of the half-ripened wood is in September, or, in warm valleys, a little later. Our cuttings are usually about 10 inches long and often with a heel, and are inserted for the greater part of their length in the freest sandy loam in the place. We began with heavy soil, which in catalogues is said to be the best—that is because the Brier being universally used the soil must suit it; but for the Teas and Chinas the best soil is a free sandy loam in which the roots can find all they need.

THE SUMMER GARDEN
CHAPTER XVIII

Carnation, Lily, Iris, and the Nobler Summer Flowers

The flowers of our own latitudes, when they are beautiful, are entitled to the first place in our gardens, and among these flowers after the Rose, should come the Carnation, in all its brilliancy of colour, where the soil and climate are fitted for it, as is the case over a large area of our sea-girt land.

It is not enough that the laced, flaked, and other varieties of Carnation should be grown in frames or otherwise; we should show the flower in all its force of colour in our flower gardens. Many who have not the skill, or the time, for the growth of the "florists'" flower, would yet find the brilliant "self" Carnations delightful in their gardens in summer and autumn, and even in winter, for the Carnation, where it does well, has a fine colour-value of foliage in winter, which makes it most useful to all who care for colour in their gardens, adorning the garden throughout the winter and spring, and full of promise for the summer and autumn.

Behind the florists' plates of this century we have the pictures of the Dutch flower painters containing fine Carnations, well grown and admirably drawn after nature. These artists were not confused by any false ideal, and so we have a true record of what the Carnation was three hundred years ago. In these pictures we generally see the finer striped and flaked kinds given the first place, which is natural, as such varieties are apt to strike people the most; and in those days little consideration had yet been given to the question of *effect* in open gardens. In our own day this question has been forced upon us in very unpleasant ways by masses of crudely arranged, and not always pretty flowers.

Over a very large area of the United Kingdom Carnation culture may be carried out well, and perhaps most successfully near the sea. The gentler warmth of the shore in some way influences this, and in any case the best results I have seen from out-door culture have been in places like Scarborough, Edinburgh, Anglesey, the shores of Dublin Bay, and in sea-shore gardens generally where the soil is warm and good. It is wonderful what one may do in such places as compared with what is possible, say, in the Weald of Kent. At Scarborough we may see Carnations almost forming a bush; near Edinburgh tufts of the Clove Carnation 5 feet in diameter, whereas in the Weald we have to plant annually.

The Lily had to go too from the flower garden of our own day; it was too tall, and no doubt had other faults, but like the Rose it must come back, and one of the gains of a free way of flower gardening is that we are able to put Lilies or any other flowers in it at any season that suits their planting, and that their bloom is welcome whenever it comes, and leaves us content with brown stems when it goes. If in the large flower garden we get some diversity of surface through groups of the rarer flowering evergreen shrubs, we have for these the very soil that our Lilies thrive in, and we break up in pretty ways these groups by planting Lilies among them, gaining thereby two seasons of bloom, light and shade in the masses, and diversity of form.

The Iris, too, with its Orchid-like beauty and flower, and with a higher value of leaf than either Lily or Orchid, is in summer-flowering kinds fit to grace the flower garden with some permanent beds. Some will tell us that we may not do these things in the set flower garden under the windows, but from an artistic point of view this is not true and very harmful. There is no flower garden, however arid or formal in its plan, which may not be planted in picturesque ways and without robbing it of fine colour either. But to do that in the face of ugly plans we must be free to choose among all beautiful things of the open air, not forgetting the best of the half-hardy plants that enjoy our summer; annual summer flowers, too, from Sweet Pea to Stocks, Mignonette, and Pansy.

There is no reason for excluding the best of the summer flowers, from Hollyhocks to Sea Hollies, choosing always the best and those that give the most pleasure, and never coarse or weedy plants. For these the true place is the shrubbery and wild garden. It was the use of these coarse and weedy plants that did much harm in old mixed borders when they were allowed to eat up everything. In those days they had not the choice of fine plants we now have, many of the finest we have coming in our day, like the Lilies of Japan and of Western America, and also the new Water-Lilies. These last are above all flowers of the summer, and whenever there is any garden water, they add a distinct and enduring charm to the summer garden. We should not only represent them, but also the other water plants of the summer; and as shown in the chapter on the water garden, many handsome plants can be grown in rich soil that often occurs near water, massed in picturesque groups, like Loosestrife, Meadow Sweets, and Japanese Iris.

THE SUMMER GARDEN
CHAPTER XIX

Plants in Vases and Tubs in the Open Air

In old days and for ages it was not easy nor always possible to many to have a garden in the open air. The need of mutual aid against the enemy threw people into closely packed cities, and even small towns in what might seem to us now the open country. In our own country, free for many years from external enemies, we have spread our gardens over the land more than others; but in France farmers still go home to a town at night from the open and often homeless and barnless plain where they work. And so it came to pass that the land of Europe was strewn with towns and cities, often fortified, and many of those most able to enjoy gardens had to do the best they could with little terraces, walls, tubs by the door, and even windows. Often in Italy and other countries of the south of Europe and north Africa we see beautiful plants in tubs, on balconies, on flat roofs, and every imaginable spot where plants can be grown in a house in a street.

In many gardens plants in tubs are often used without good reason as when hardy evergreen trees are grown in tubs; in front of the Royal Exchange in London there are hardy Poplars in tubs! Some may pursue this sort of gardening with advantage—first, those who have no gardens, and secondly, those who have and who may desire to put half-hardy bushes in the open air, for example, Myrtle or Oleander or Orange, which cannot be grown out of doors throughout the year, and which yet may have fragrance or other charms for us. Many plants can be grown in the open air in summer which will not endure our winters, but which, placed in a cellar, dry room, or cool greenhouse, would be quite safe, and might then be put out of doors in summer. This way is commonly the case abroad with large Datura, Pomegranate, and Myrtles, and a great variety of plants such as we see put out in tubs in certain old palace gardens, like those of Versailles. What was called the orangery, and has almost disappeared from English gardens, was for keeping such plants alive and well through the winter, and in old times, if not now, had a very good reason to be.

There are many charming plants too tender for the open altogether that are happy in tubs, and may be sheltered in an outhouse or greenhouse through the winter—such as the Pomegranate and the Myrtle. The blue African Lily is often happy in tubs, its blue flowers when seen on a terrace walk having a distinct charm, but in England, generally, it must be kept indoors in winter.

Excellent use may be made of the great handsome oil-jars, which are used to bring olive oil from Italy to London, and the best things to put in them are half-hardy plants, which can be taken intact into the cool greenhouse or conservatory at the approach of frost.

One of the most curious examples of routine and waste I saw in the Tuileries gardens on the last day of September 1896, when the Paris people were preparing for the Czar, and among their labours was the refurbishing of the old Orange trees in these gardens. There was a regiment of them set all along the gardens at regular intervals in immense and costly tubs, involving herculean labour to move in and out of the orangery. One might suppose this labour to be given for some beautiful end in perfecting the flower or fruit of the plant, but nothing of the kind; the trees are trained into mop heads, and when the plants make any attempt to take a natural growth they are cut sharply back, and often have an uglier shape than any mop. The ground was strewn with shoots of the orange trees which had been cut back hard. When the tree was in poor health, as it was often, the dark stems were the most visible things seen against the blue sky. This costly and ugly work is a survival of the time when the "golden apples" were a novelty, and it was not so easy to go and see them growing in the open air as it now is, and so what was worth doing as a curiosity hundreds of years ago is carried out still. Since the idea of growing these trees in such an ugly fashion arose we have had a noble garden flora brought to us from all parts of the earth, and it would be easy to take our choice of different ways of adorning this garden in more artistic ways with things in the open ground, and of far greater beauty. If this thing at its best and done with great cost has such a result, what are we to think of the English imitations of it, such as those at Panshanger, in which hardy shrubs, like Portugal Laurels, are used, and sham tubs placed around them?

I saw the vast orangery terrace at Sans Souci in July 1897, and was deeply struck by its "ornaments" in tubs; the branches of the poor distorted trees like black skeletons against the summer sky showing that even with all the aids of artifice, no good result with tubbed oranges is got in northern Germany any more than in northern France. In the warmer south a little better result may be had from trees in tubs, but a few days' journey brings us to orange trees growing as freely and gracefully as willows in Tunis and Algeria and the countries round the Mediterranean.

The Laurel is a winter garden plant over a large area of northern and central Europe, where the true Laurel (our gardeners and nurserymen erroneously give the name to the vigorous evergreen Cherry, of which we have too much in England) is a tender evergreen, requiring the protection of a house in winter. It is grown to a vast extent in tubs to place in the open garden, on terrace, or in courtyard during the summer. The cultivation of the Laurel for this purpose is carried on to such an extent that miles of handsome trees in various forms may be seen in one nursery. There is no plant more worthy of it than the true Laurel, which we usually call the Sweet Bay, and those who cannot enjoy the plant out of doors, as we may in many of the warmer districts of the British Isles, would do well to grow it in tubs, in which state they may enjoy it both in winter and summer. It would be worth while growing it in the same way in cold and northern districts, where it is killed or much hurt in winter, and this sometimes occurs in parts of southern England. Near the sea it may flourish, and 20 miles inland be cut down to the ground, or so badly hurt that it gives no pleasure to see. In gardens where one may have fine groups of the tree on sunny slopes, we should never think of it in any other way, and no evergreen tree gives us more beauty when old and untrained and unclipped. Once the plants are stored for the winter, sometimes in sheds with little light, it is best to give no water. In the same way we may also enjoy the Laurustinus in districts where it is killed by frost out of doors, which in hard winters happens even in the southern countries. This is all the more unfortunate as this shrub and its varieties flower so prettily. If grown well in tubs we may flower them in the cool house and place them out of doors in summer.

CHAPTER XX

Beauty of Form in the Flower Garden

The use in gardens of plants of fine form has taught us the value of grace and verdure amid masses of flowers, and how far we have diverged from artistic ways. In a wild state brilliant blossoms are often usually relieved by a setting of abundant green, and where mountain or meadow plants of one kind produce a sea of colour at one season, there is intermingled a spray of pointed grass and leaves which tone down the colour masses.

We may be pleased by the wide spread of colour on a heath or mountain, but when we go near we find that it is best where the long moss cushions itself beside the ling and the fronds of the Polypody come up around masses of heather. If this be so on the hills, a like state of things is more evident still in the marsh or wood. We cannot attempt to reproduce such conditions, but the more we keep them before our eyes the nearer shall we be to success, and we may have in our gardens all the light and shade, the relief, the grace, and the beauty of natural colour and form too.

A recent demand for £2000, for the building of a glass house for Palms for the sub-tropical garden of Battersea Park, throws light on the costly system of flower gardening in this and other public gardens. This was only a small part of the cost of keeping the tender and half-hardy plants in a glass nursery and was not a demand for money for a Palm-house which the public might enjoy; but was to be part of the expenditure on some glass-sheds which they would never see, and were merely to grow the plants to be put out for a few months in summer.

In our flower gardens Palms can only be seen in a small state; nor can they in pots and tubs give one any idea of the true beauty of the Palm on the banks of the Nile or the Ganges. But, worse than this, the system leads to the neglect of the many shrubs and trees of the northern world, which are quite as beautiful as any Palm. The number of public gardens that are being opened in all directions makes it all the more important that the false ideal they so often set out should be made clear. The concentration of so much attention and of the greater part of the cost on such feeble examples of tropical plants as can be grown in this country out of doors for a few months in the summer has a very bad effect. The things which may be grown to perfection in the open air in any country are always the most beautiful, and should always have the first place in our thoughts.

Many plants that are quite hardy give fine effects, such as the Aralias, herbaceous and shrubby; Aristolochia among climbers; Arundo, hardy and very pretty beside water; the hardy Bamboos of Japan and India; these last increasing in number, and are very distinct and charming, and often rapid growers in genial parts of the country, especially near the sea. A considerable number will probably be found hardy everywhere. The large-leaved evergreen Barberries are beautiful in shade, and grouped in picturesque ways effective for their noble leaves as well as flowers.

The Plume Poppy (Bocconia) is handsome for its foliage and flowers, even in ordinary soil. A great number of the larger hardy Compositæ (Helianthus, Silphium, Senecio, Telekia, Rudbeckia) are fine in leaf, as are some of the Cotton Thistles and plants of that family. The common Artichoke of our gardens and its allies are fine in form of leaf and flower, but apt to be cut off in hard winters in some soils. The Giant Fennels are most graceful early leafing things, thriving admirably in sandy and free soils. Plantain Lilies (Funkia) are important, and in groups their foliage is excellent. The Pampas Grass is precious where it grows well, but in many districts is gradually killed by hard winters. Where it has the least chance, it should be planted in bold masses. The great leaved Gunneras are superb near water and in rich soil. The giant Cow Parsnips are effective, but apt to take possession of the country side, and are not easily exterminated, and, therefore, should be put in with a sparing hand in islands and rough places only. The large Indian evergreen Rockfoils are fine in form, and in their glossy foliage are easily grown and grouped in picturesque ways, and they are very hardy.

In sandy and free soils a handsome group of beautiful leaved things may be formed of Acanthus. The new Water-Lilies will help us much to fine foliage, especially in association with the many graceful plants, including certain hardy Ferns which may be grown near water, like the Royal Fern, which in rich soil and shade makes leaves as fine as any tropical Fern.

As to arrangement, the best beds or sets of beds are those of the simplest design. Shelter is a great aid, and recesses in shrubberies or in banks clothed with foliage, form the most fitting background for beds or groups to nestle in. Avoid Musas or Caladiums, the leaves of which tear to shreds if winds cannot be shut out, and also plants that look unhappy after a cold night or two. Make the most of plants that grow under nearly all conditions, and use any dell overhung by trees for half-hardy fine-leaved plants.

As an example of fine form from hardy plants, we cannot do better than give the New Zealand Reed (Arundo conspicua) a place. This handsome Grass produces its blossom-spikes earlier than the Pampas and is more elegant in habit, the silky white tufts bending like ostrich plumes at the end of slender stalks.

The first and the last word to say about form is, that we should try and see beauty of form everywhere among plants that suit our climate. The willows of Britain are as beautiful as the olives of Italy, or the gum trees of Algeria and the South of France; so that, although the sub-tropical as a system of flower gardening has failed throughout our country generally, and can only be carried out well in the south of England and the warmer countries of Europe, we need not deprive ourselves of the enjoyment of the finest forms near and in our gardens. The new Water-Lilies take us to the waterside, and there are many good forms even among our native flowers and weeds. The new hardy Bamboos are also very graceful and most distinct, of which several of the highest value promise to be hardy in our country. The common hardy Japan Bamboo has thriven even in London, and it is not only waterside or herbaceous plants of all kinds we have to think of, but the foliage of trees, which in many cases is quite as beautiful as that of the dwarfer plants. The hardy trees of North America are many of them beautiful in foliage, from the Silver Maple to the Scarlet Oak, and Acacias from the same country have broken into a number of beautiful forms; some are as graceful as Ferns. These trees, if obtained on their own roots, will afford us fine aid as backgrounds. The Aralias of Japan and China are quite hardy and almost tropical in foliage, while the beauty that may be got from Ferns is very remarkable indeed, our native Royal Fern being of noble proportions when well grown in half-shady and sheltered places in deep soils, as at Newick Park, and the same is true of all the bold American Ferns, plants too often hidden away in obscure corners, whereas the boldest of them should be brought out in our cool British climate to form groups on the lawn and turf. This applies also to our larger native Ferns, which, massed and grouped away from the old-fashioned fernery, often tell better.

During recent years the most graceful things and of permanent value in our gardens are Bamboos.

The Bamboo garden formed a few years ago at Kew has proved so well adapted for the plants, that a few notes as to its position and soil may be of value to the numerous readers who intend to grow the Bamboos. A position was selected in the middle of a wood near the Rhododendron dell, and taking advantage of a hollow already existing there, the ground was lowered some 5 feet or 6 feet below the surrounding level. A belt of shrubs on the north and east sides, between the trees and the Bamboos, together with the low level, affords them a shelter almost as perfect as can be furnished out of doors. Even the bitterest north-easter loses a good deal of its sting before it reaches these Bamboos. What the cultivator of Bamboos has most to fear is not a low temperature merely—most of the Bamboos will stand 20° or 25° of frost in a still atmosphere—but the dry winds of spring.

Bamboos like best a free, open, sandy loam, and the greater part of the soil at Kew is poor and sandy, but there is, in one part, a belt of good stiff loam extending for a few hundred yards, and it is on the border of this that the Bamboo garden is situated. At the commencement the ground was trenched to a depth of 3 feet, and enriched with leaf-soil, and where necessary lightened with sandier soil. These plants can scarcely be overfed, and in well-drained soil can scarcely be overwatered, and an annual mulching with rich manure is of the greatest advantage.

In regard to transplanting, the best time to plant is in spring, when growth begins. The renewal of growth is indicated by the unrolling of the young leaves, which may be in April or May, according to the winter. Bamboos are very difficult to kill outright, but treated improperly they are apt to get into a stunted condition, which it takes them a long time to recover from. I would advise those who wish to try these plants to obtain them from the nurserymen in autumn or winter, if they have been grown in pots, and to give them greenhouse treatment till the end of May, when they can be planted out in a growing state; but, on the other hand, if they have been planted out in the nursery ground, not to have them sent off till the end of April or later, when they can be set out at once.

CHAPTER XX(B)

Colour in the Flower Garden

One of the first things which all who care for gardens should learn, is the difference between true and delicate and ugly colour—between the showy dyes and much glaring colour seen in gardens and the beauties and harmonies of natural colour. There are, apart from beautiful flowers, many lessons and no fees:—Oak woods in winter, even the roads and paths and rocks and hedgerows; leaves in many hues of life and death, the stems of trees: many birds are lovely studies in harmony and delicate gradation of colour; the clouds (eternal mine of divinest colour) in many aspects of light, and the varied and infinite beauty of colour of the air itself as it comes between us and the distant view.

Nature is a good colourist, and if we trust to her guidance we never find wrong colour in wood, meadow, or on mountain. "Laws" have been laid down by chemists and decorators about colours which artists laugh at, and to consider them is a waste of time. If we have to make coloured cottons, or to "garden" in coloured gravels, then it is well to think what ugly things will shock us least; but dealing with living plants in their infinitely varied hues, and with their beautiful flowers, is a different thing! If we grow well plants of good colour, all will be right in the end, but often raisers of flowers work against us by the raising of flowers of bad colour. The complicated pattern beds so often seen in flower gardens should be given up in favour of simpler beds, of the shapes best suiting the ground, and among various reasons for this is to get true colour. When we have little pincushion-beds where the whole "pattern" is seen at once through the use of dwarf plants, the desire comes to bring in colour in patterns and in ugly ways. For this purpose the wretched Alternanthera and other pinched plant rubbish are grown—plants not worth growing at all.

When dwarf flowers are associated with bushes like Roses, and with plants like Carnations and tall Irises, having pointed and graceful foliage, the colours are relieved against the delicate foliage of the plants and by having the beds large enough we relieve the dwarfer flowers with taller plants behind. In a shrubbery, too, groups of flowers are nearly always right, and we can follow our desire in flowers without much thought of arranging for colour. But as the roots of the shrubs rob the flowers; the best way is to put near and around shrubberies free-running plants that do not want much cultivation, like Solomon's Seal and Woodruff, and other plants that grow naturally in woods and copses, while with flowers like Pansies, Carnations, Roses, that depend for their beauty on good soil, the best way is to keep them in the open garden, away from hungry tree-roots.

By having large simple beds we relieve the flowers, and enjoy their beauty of colour and the forms of the plants without "pattern" of any kind. Instead of "dotting" the plants, it is better to group them naturally, letting the groups run into each other, and varying them here and there with taller plants. A flower garden of any size could be planted in this way, without the geometry of the ordinary flower garden, and the poor effect of the "botanical" "dotty" mixed border. As, however, all may not be ready to follow this plan, the following notes on colour, by a flower gardener who has given much thought to the subject, will be useful:—

"One of the most important points in the arrangement of a garden is the placing of the flowers with regard to their colour-effect. Too often a garden is an assemblage of plants placed together haphazard, or if any intention be perceptible, as is commonly the case in the bedding system, it is to obtain as great a number as possible of the most violent contrasts; and the result is a hard, garish vulgarity. Then, in mixed borders, one usually sees lines or evenly distributed spots of colour, wearying and annoying to the eye, and proving how poor an effect can be got by the misuse of the best materials. Should it not be remembered that in setting a garden we are painting a picture,—a picture of hundreds of feet or yards instead of so many inches, painted with living flowers and seen by open daylight—so that to paint it rightly is a debt we owe to the beauty of the flowers and to the light of the sun; that the colours should be placed with careful forethought and deliberation, as a painter employs them on his picture, and not dropped down in lifeless dabs.

"HARMONY RATHER THAN CONTRAST.—Splendid harmonies of rich

.and brilliant colour, and proper sequences of such harmonies, should be the rule; there should be large effects, each well studied and well placed, varying in different portions of the garden scheme. One very common fault is a want of simplicity of intention; another, an absence of any definite plan of colouring. Many people have not given any attention to colour-harmony, or have not by nature the gift of perceiving it. Let them learn it by observing some natural examples of happily related colouring, taking separate families of plants whose members are variously coloured. Some of the best to study would be American Azaleas, Wallflowers, German and Spanish Iris, Alpine Auriculas, Polyanthus, and Alstrœmerias.

"BREADTH OF MASS AND INTERGROUPING.—It is important to notice that the mass of each colour should be large enough to have a certain dignity, but never so large as to be wearisome; a certain breadth in the masses is also wanted to counteract the effect of foreshortening when the border is seen from end to end. When a definite plan of colouring is decided on, it will save trouble if the plants whose flowers are approximately the same in colour are grouped together to follow each other in season of blooming. Thus, in a part of the border assigned to red, Oriental Poppies might be planted among or next to Tritomas, with scarlet Gladioli between both, so that there should be a succession of scarlet flowers, the places occupied by the Gladioli being filled previously with red Wallflowers.

"WARM COLOURS are not difficult to place: scarlet, crimson, pink, orange, yellow, and warm white are easily arranged so as to pass agreeably from one to the other.

"PURPLE and LILAC group well together, but are best kept well away from red and pink; they do well with the colder whites, and are seen at their best when surrounded and carpeted with gray-white foliage, like that of Cerastium tomentosum or Cineraria maritima; but if it be desired to pass from a group of warm colour to purple and lilac, a good breadth of pale yellow or warm white may be interposed.

"WHITE FLOWERS.—Care must be taken in placing very cold white flowers such as Iberis correæfolia, which are best used as quite a high light, led up to by whites of a softer character. Frequent repetitions of white patches catch the eye unpleasantly; it will generally be found that one mass or group of white will be enough in any piece of border or garden arrangement that can be seen from any one point of view.

"BLUE requires rather special treatment, and is best approached by delicate contrasts of warm whites and pale yellows, such as the colours of double Meadow Sweet, and Œnothera Lamarckiana, but rather avoiding the direct opposition of strong blue and full yellow. Blue flowers are also very beautiful when completely isolated and seen alone among rich dark foliage.

"A PROGRESSION OF COLOUR in a mixed border might begin with strong blues, light and dark, grouped with white and pale yellow, passing on to pink; then to rose colour, crimson, and the strongest scarlet, leading to orange and bright yellow. A paler yellow followed by white would distantly connect the warm colours with the lilacs and purples, and a colder white would combine them pleasantly with low-growing plants with cool-coloured leaves.

"SILVERY-LEAVED PLANTS are valuable as edgings and carpets to purple flowers, and bear the same kind of relation to them as the warm-coloured foliage of some plants does to their strong red flowers, as in the case of the Cardinal Flower and double crimson Sweet William. The bright clear blue of Forget-me-not goes best with fresh pale green, and pink flowers are beautiful with pale foliage striped with creamy white, such as the variegated forms of Jacob's-ladder or Iris pseudacorus. A useful carpeting plant, Acæna pulchella, assumes in spring a rich bronze between brown and green which is valuable with Wallflowers of the brown and orange colours. These few examples, out of many that will come under the notice of any careful observer, are enough to indicate what should be looked for in the way of accompanying foliage—such foliage, if well chosen and well placed, may have the same value to the flowering plant that a worthy and appropriate setting has to a jewel.

"IN SUNDAY PLACES warm colours should preponderate; the yellow colour of sunlight brings them together and adds to their glowing effect.

"A SHADY BORDER, on the other hand, seems best suited for the cooler and more delicate colours. A beautiful scheme of cool colouring might be arranged for a retired spot, out of sight of other brightly coloured flowers, such as a border near the shady side of any shrubbery or wood that would afford a good background of dark foliage. Here would be the best opportunity for using blue, cool white, palest yellow, and fresh green. A few typical plants are the great Larkspurs, Monkshoods, and Columbines, Anemones (such as japonica, sylvestris, apennina, Hepatica, and the single and double forms of nemorosa), white Lilies, Trilliums, Pyrolas, Habenarias, Primroses, white and yellow, double and single, Daffodils, white Cyclamen, Ferns and mossy Saxifrages,

Lily-of-the-Valley, and Woodruff. The most appropriate background
to such flowers would be shrubs and trees, giving an effect of rich
sombre masses of dusky shadow rather than a positive green colour,
such as Bay Phillyrea, Box, Yew, and Evergreen Oak. Such a harmony
of cool colouring, in a quiet shady place, would present a delightful
piece of gardening.

"BEDDED-OUT PLANTS, in such parts of a garden as may require
them, may be arranged on the same general principle of related,
rather than of violently opposed, masses of colour. As an example,
a fine effect was obtained with half-hardy annuals, mostly kinds of
Marigold, Chrysanthemum, and Nasturtium, of all shades of yellow,
orange, and brown. This was in a finely designed formal garden before
the principal front of one of the stateliest of the great houses of England.
It was a fine lesson in temperature, this employment of a simple scheme
of restricted colouring, yet it left nothing to be desired in the way
of richness and brilliancy, and well served its purpose as a dignified
ornament, and worthy accompaniment to the fine old house.

"CONTRASTS—HOW TO BE USED.—The greater effects being secured,
some carefully arranged contrasts may be used to strike the eye when
passing; for opposite colours in close companionship are not telling
at a distance, and are still less so if interspersed, their tendency then
being to neutralize each other. Here and there a charming effect may
be produced by a bold contrast, such as a mass of orange Lilies against
Delphiniums or Gentians against alpine Wallflowers; but these violent
contrasts should be used sparingly and as brilliant accessories rather
than trustworthy principals.

"CLIMBERS ON WALLS.—There is often a question about the suitabil-
ity of variously coloured creepers on house or garden walls. The same
principle of harmonious colouring is the best guide. A warm-coloured
wall, one of Bath stone or buff bricks, for instance, is easily dealt with.
On this all the red-flowered, leaved, or berried plants look well—Japan
Quince, red and pink Roses, Virginian Creeper, Cratægus Pyracantha,
and the more delicate harmonies of Honeysuckle, Banksian Roses,
and Clematis montana, and Flammula, while C. Jackmanni and other
purple and lilac kinds are suitable as occasional contrasts. The large
purple and white Clematises harmonise perfectly with the cool gray of
Portland stone; and so do dark-leaved climbers, such as White Jasmine,
Passion Flower, and green Ivy. Red brickwork, especially when new, is
not a happy ground colour; perhaps it is best treated with large-leaved
climbers—Magnolias, Vines, Aristolochia—to counteract the fidgety

look of the bricks and white joints. When brickwork is old and overgrown with gray Lichens, there can be no more beautiful ground for all colours of flowers from the brightest to the tenderest—none seems to come amiss.

"COLOUR IN BEDDING-OUT.—We must here put out of mind nearly all the higher sense of the enjoyment of flowers; the delight in their beauty individually or in natural masses; the pleasure derived from a personal knowledge of their varied characters, appearances, and ways, which gives them so much of human interest and lovableness; and must regard them merely as so much colouring matter, to fill such and such spaces for a few months. We are restricted to a kind of gardening not far removed from that in which the spaces of the design are filled in with pounded brick, slate, or shells. The best rule in the arrangement of a bedded garden is to keep the scheme of colouring as simple as possible. The truth of this is easily perceived by an ordinary observer when shown a good example, and is obvious without any showing to one who has studied colour effects; and yet the very opposite intention is most commonly seen, to wit, a garish display of the greatest number of crudely contrasting colours. How often do we see combinations of scarlet Geranium, Calceolaria, and blue Lobelia—three subjects that have excellent qualities as bedding plants if used in separate colour schemes, but which in combination can hardly fail to look bad? In this kind of gardening, as in any other, let us by all means have our colours in a brilliant blaze, but never in a discordant glare. One or two colours, used temperately and with careful judgement, will produce nobler and richer results than many colours purposely contrasted, or wantonly jumbled. The formal garden that is an architectural adjunct to an imposing building demands a dignified unity of colouring instead of the petty and frivolous effects so commonly obtained by the misuse of many colours. As practical examples of simple harmonies, let us take a scheme of red for summer bedding. It may range from palest pink to nearly black, the flowers being Pelargoniums in many shades of pink, rose, salmon, and scarlet; Verbenas, red and pink; and judicious mixtures of Iresine, Alternanthera, Amaranthus, the dark Ajuga, and red-foliaged Oxalis. Still finer is a colour scheme of yellow and orange, worked out with some eight varieties of Marigold, Zinnias, Calceolarias, and Nasturtiums—a long range of bright rich colour, from the palest buff and primrose to the deepest mahogany. Such examples of strong warm colouring are admirably suited for large spaces of bedded garden. Where a small space has to be dealt with it is better to have arrangements of blue, with white and the palest yellow, or of purple and lilac, with gray foliage. A satisfactory example of the latter could be worked out with beds of purple and lilac Clematis, trained over a carpet of Cineraria maritima, or one of the white-foliaged Centaureas, and Heliotropes and purple Verbenas, with silvery foliage of Cerastium, Antennaria, or Stachys lanata. These are some simple examples easily carried out. The principle once seen and understood (and the operator having a perception of colour), modifications will suggest themselves, and a correct working with two or more colours will be practicable; but the simpler ways are the best, and will always give the noblest results. There is a peculiar form of harmony to be got even in varied colours by putting together those of nearly the same strength or depth. As an example in spring bedding, Myosotis dissitiflora, Silene pendula (not the deepest shade), and double yellow Primrose or yellow Polyanthus, though distinctly red, blue, and yellow, yet are of such tender and equal depth of colouring, that they work together charmingly, especially if they are further connected with the gray-white foliage of Cerastium.—G. J."

CHAPTER XXI

The Flower Garden in Autumn

Now who hath entered my loved woods,
    And touched their green with sudden change?
Who blanched my Thistle's rosy face,
    And gave the winds her silver hair?
Set Golden-rod within her place,
    And scattered Asters everywhere?
Lo! the change reaches high and wide,
    Hath toned the sky to softer blue;
Hath crept along the river side,
    And trod the valleys through and through!

Recent additions to our garden flora have made such a difference to the flower garden in the autumn that it may be even more beautiful than the spring, rich as that is in flowering trees and shrubs.

It would be easy to give the names of many things that are to be found in flower in gardens in autumn, but that is not nearly so important as getting an idea of many of the nobler class of plants which may be effectively used at that time, no matter almost what the season may be. Certain plants may depend for success on soil and situation, or even climate, even when they are hardy, as the Fuchsia, which is so much better in the coast and west country gardens; but, when everything is left out that wants any extra culture or advantages of climate and soil, there remain for every garden many beautiful things for the garden in the fall.

Of those that can generally be trusted for our country, I should say that, of all the gains of the past generation, the brilliant groups of plants of the Sunflower order were the finest, handsomest, and most generally useful for their disregard of any weather likely to occur. The masses of fine form and colour one may have with these when grouped in picturesque ways are remarkable. With the Sunflowers are included not only the Helianthus strictly, of which there are so many good kinds now, but also other showy Prairie flowers of the same natural order, which approach them in character, such as Rudbeckia, Silphium, Helenium, and other vigorous families of this numerous tribe of plants. Many of these thrive in any soil, and make their way in rough places and among shrubs, or in parts of gardens less precious than those we keep for our best flowers.

But the most precious, perhaps, of all flowers of autumn for all parts of the country, grouped in an artistic way, are the hardy Asters of the American woods, which lived for ages in our gardens in mean bundles tied up in mixed borders like besoms. The best of these massed and grouped among shrubs or young plantations of trees, covering the ground, give an effect new and delightful, the colour refined and charming, and the mass of bloom impressive in autumn. Some kinds come in flower in summer, but nearly all the loveliest Asters in colour flower in September and October, and no such good colours of the same shades have ever been seen in the flower garden.

It is not only the Asters of America we have to consider, but the still more precious Asters of Europe, which by their extraordinary beauty make up for their rarity. Professor Green, of California, who knows the American Aster well, on seeing here a plant of Aster acris, said, "We have none so beautiful as that." This is the Aster with the beautiful blue purple flower which is so effective when massed. Under different names this plant is grown in nearly allied forms, some having specific names, enabling us to enjoy plants of different stature but the same high beauty, flowering at slightly different times, but always at their best in autumn. With these should be grouped the handsome large Italian Aster, which also has its half-dozen forms, not differing much, but precious for their variety, and among the prettiest plants ever seen in our gardens.

We give the first place to the Stewarts because they are almost independent of soil or cool climates. Hardy as the Chrysanthemum is, the same cannot be said for it, because, as an outdoor flower, it must have a sandy soil and warm positions, and cool soils, even in southern England, are against it. In warm and free soils, like that at Hazlemere, one may see delightful results from the cottage Chrsyanthemums, which are very pretty where they can be grown against low walls or pailings. Other plants which are of the highest value in endurance and freedom of bloom are the Heaths of our own islands. Their effect is good, summer and winter; but in autumn some of them flower in a pretty way, particularly the Cornish and the little Dorset Heath, and the Irish Heath in its purple and white forms.

Among the half-hardy plants of the garden perhaps the first place belongs to the Dahlia, which was always a showy autumn flower, but of late has become more precious through the beauty of what are called Cactus Dahlias, which are so much better in form and colour than the roundheaded Dahlias.

The hardy Fuchsia is in the warmer and milder districts often very pretty in autumn, especially where it is free enough to make hedges and form large bushes; but in cold and midland places the growth is often hindered by hard winters. Gladiolus is a splendid flower of the south, but coming more into a class of flowers requiring care, and if they do not get it soon disappearing, liable also to disease, and, on the whole, not so precious as showy.

The addition of Lilies to our garden flora within the past generation has had a good effect on the autumn garden. Where the finer kinds are well grown, the varieties of the Japanese Lilies, with their delicate and varied colours, are splendid autumn flowers for the open air. The Anemones, usually flowers of the spring, come in some forms for the autumn garden, particularly the white and pink kinds. The handsome Bignonia, or trumpet creeper, is precious on all warm soils, but generally it has not done so well with us as in France. Several kinds of Clematis come in well in autumn, particularly the yellow and the fragrant kinds. The Pentstemons are handsome and very valuable in warm soils and districts where they may live out of doors in winter, but in London districts they are not so good. A splendid autumn flower is the Cardinal Flower, and happy should be those who can grow it well. It fails in many gardens in loamy soil, and where there is insufficiency of water, being a native of the bogs, and thriving best in moist and peaty soil.

Torch Lilies are extremely effective in autumn, and in warm soils they are often among the handsomest things, but, not being northern plants, are unable to face a northern winter. Happily this is not so with the beautiful new Water-Lilies raised by M. Latour Marliac, which are hardy in the open air, even with such weather as that of the early part of 1895. Though perhaps the best bloom comes in summer, they flower through the autumn, varying, like the Tea

Rose, according to the weather, but interesting always up to the end
of September. We should also name the Hollyhock, which is, however,
so liable to accident from disease, and those who care for it will do
well to use seedling plants. Seedsmen are now saving seed of different
colours which come fairly true.

A handsome group of vigorous perennials for the autumn are the
Polygonums. Some of the large kinds, such as the Japanese and Indian,
are not showy, but massed picturesquely on margins of a wide lawn,
and on pieces of stiff soil which are useless in any garden sense, are
effective for many weeks in autumn, as the flower is pretty, and the
foliage of one kind is often fine in colour.

Thus we have a noble array before coming to some old flowers of
autumn, the Meadow Saffrons or "autumn Crocuses," many of the
common kind of which fleck the meadows in autumn. There are other
kinds, too, which of recent years have been added in greater numbers
to our gardens, some of them pretty, and the double kinds prettier than
most double flowers. As they grow naturally in meadows, in turf is a
delightful way to have them in gardens, though new and rare kinds
should be grown in nursery beds until they are plentiful. They are not
difficult to grow, and should often be placed in moist grassy places.

The true autumn Crocuses are very little seen in gardens, but are
most delicate and lovely in colour. Coming for the most part from sunny
lands, they do best in light soils; but some, like C. speciosus, grow in
any soil, and all are worth growing. Among the best is C. nudiflorus,
naturalised in Britain, in colour one of the most lovely flowers. To get
little pictures from such plants we must have them happy in grass or
among dwarf plants, and on sunny banks and grassy corners of the
lawn or pleasure ground.

No doubt severe frosts may destroy any kind of flower soon, but
for those who live in the country in the autumn it is something to
have bright colours and beautiful plants about them late, and these are
afforded as well by the Starworts and other hardy plants in October, as
the fairest flowers that come in June. When we have a severe September
about London, many gardens of tender plants are shorn of their beauty,
whereas, the hardy flowers go on quite untouched for a month or six
weeks later, and not merely bloom, as do Heliotrope and Geranium,
in a fine autumn, but as the meadow flowers in summer, with vigour
and perfect health. Therefore, it is clear that, whatever the charms of
tender plants may be for the summer, those who live in the country in
autumn are unwise to trust to anything but the finer hardy plants.

Thus, without touching on rarities or things difficult to grow, we have a handsome array of beauty for the autumn garden, even leaving out of the question the many shrubs and trees which are beautiful in foliage or fruit in autumn, and there are many of these in any well-stored garden.

Some Hardy and Half-Hardy Plants Blooming in British Gardens September—October

Abutilon	Crocus	Hyacinthus	Œnothera	Snapdragon
Aconitum	Cuphea	Hypericum	Pampas Grass	Solanum
Agapanthus	Cyclamen	Iberis	Pansy	Solidago
Ageratum	Dahlia	Impatiens	Papaver	Statice
Amaryllis	Delphinium	Lantana	Pentstemon	Strawberry
Anagallis	Desmodium	Laurustinus	Petunia	Sweet Peas
Anemone	Dianthus	Lavender	Phlox	Sweet William
Arnebia	Diplacus	Liatris	Phygelius	Telekia
Aster	Diplopappus	Lilium	Physalis	Trachelium
Berberidopsis	Eccremocarpus	Linaria	Physostegia	Tradescantia
Bignonia	Erica	Linum	Plumbago	Tritoma
Brugmansia	Escallonia	Lobelia	Polygonum	Tritonia
Calceolaria	Fuschia	Lonicera	Prince's-feather	Tropæolum
Campanula	Gaillardia	Lupin	Pyrethrum	Tuberose
Canna	Geum	Lychnis	Rose	Valerian
Cassia	Gladioli	Lythrum	Rudbeckia	Venidium
Ceanothus	Godetia	Magnolia	Salpiglossis	Verbascum
Celsia	Gypsophila	Marigold	Salvia	Verbena
Centaurea	Helenium	Matthiola	Scabious	Veronica
Chrysanthemum	Helianthus	Mignonette	Sedum	Viola
Clematis	Heliotrope	Mimulus	Senecio	Yucca
Colchicum	Hieracium	Montbretia	Silene	Zephyranthes
Convolvulus	Hollyhock	Nicotiana	Silphium	Zinnia
Coreopsis	Honeysuckle	Nigella		

CHAPTER XXII

The Flower Garden in Winter

The idea that winter is a doleful time for gardens must not be taken seriously even by those who only grow hardy things out of doors; because between the colour of the stems and leaves of trees, or shrubs, there is much beauty left, even in winter, and in mild winters good things venture to flower. Mr Moore, of Dublin, wrote to me in midwinter:

> After a very open winter we have had a sharp snap of cold, and to-day (Jan. 20) it is blowing a bitterly cold storm from the east. To-day has opened Winter Sweet and Winter Honeysuckle; Iris Stylosa, blue and white, Christmas Roses and Winter Heliotrope are beautiful; in fact, I never saw them so good.

But even where, owing to hard winters, we cannot enjoy our flowers in this way, there is much beauty to be had from trees and shrubs, evergreen and summer-leafing. Hitherto we have been all so busy in planting evergreens in heavy masses, that the beauty one may realise by using a far greater number of summer-leafing shrubs and fine herbaceous plants among the evergreens is not often seen.

Gardens are too often bare of interest in winter, and some of the evil arises from the common error that plants are not worth seeing in winter. The old poet's wail about the dismal winter is a false one to those who have eyes for beauty. Woods are no less beautiful in winter than in summer—to some they are more beautiful for the refined colour, tree form and the fine contrast of evergreen and summer-leafing trees. In any real garden in winter there is much beauty of form and colour, and there are many shrubs and trees which are beautiful in the depth of winter, like the Red and Yellow Willow and Dogwoods, and even the stems of hardy flowers (Polygonum). The foliage of many alpine plants (Epimedium) are not only good in colour, but some of these plants have their freshest hues in winter, as the mossy Rockfoils of many kinds. In the country garden, where there are healthy evergreens as well as flowering shrubs and hardy plants, how much beauty we see in winter, from the foliage of the Christmas Roses (Helleborus) to the evergreen Barberries! The flower gardener should be the first to take notice of this beauty and show that his domain as well as the wild wood might be interesting at this season.

The stems of all herbaceous plants, reeds, and tall grasses in winter, are very good in colour, and should always be allowed to stand through the winter and not be cut down in the fidgety-tidy way that is so common, sweeping away the stems in autumn and leaving the surface as bare and ugly as that round a besieged city. The same applies to the stems of all waterside and herbaceous plants, stems of plants in groups often giving beautiful brown colours in many fine shades. Those who know the plants can in this way identify them in winter as well as in summer—a great gain in changing one's plantings and in increasing or giving away plants. Moreover, the change to all these lovely browns and greys is a distinct gain as a lesson in colour to all who care for refined colour, and also in enabling us to get light and shade, contrasts and harmonies in colour. If these plants are grouped in a bold and at the same time picturesque way, the good of letting the stems remain will be far more evident than in the weak "dotty" way generally practised, the seed pods and dead flowers of many plants helping the picture. There is no need to remove any stem of an herbaceous plant until the spring comes and the growing shoots are ready to take the place of the brown and dead ones.

Apart from our evergreen shrubs, so happy as these are in many parts of the British Isles, there are the oft-neglected evergreen rock and herbaceous plants, such as Christmas Roses, Barrenworts, Heuchera, Alexandrian Laurel, the bolder evergreen Ferns, and the large Indian Rockfoils, Saxifraga, or Megasea. In early winter these fine evergreen plants become a deeper green some forms getting red. They have been in our gardens for years, but are seldom made a right use of. Thrown into borders without thought as to their habits, and soon forgotten or overshadowed by other things, we never get any expression of their beauty or effect in masses or groups. If grouped in effective ways, they would go on for years, giving us fine evergreen foliage in winter.

The Alexandrian Laurel (Ruscus racemosus) is a most graceful plant, somewhat shrubby in character, with glossy dark green leaves and

Willow-like shoots. It is most free and happy on peaty and friable soils, growing 3 feet or 4 feet high; in winter the effect is very good, and it is valuable for the house, to give a graceful and distinct foliage to accompany various flowers at this season. In clay soils it may want a little encouragement, and it thrives well in partial shade.

The Christmas Rose is a noble winter flower where well grown, and lovely in its wild state in the foot-hills of the Alps, in Italy, and countries near; happily, it flowers in our gardens very well also, varying a little in its ways. The stout kind (H. maximus) flowers in the early winter in front of walls and in sheltered spots, and is hardy in ordinary soil but best in chalky soils. The true Christmas Rose (H. niger) is a little more particular; it thrives much better on chalky and warm soils, and grows best on a northern aspect or shaded place; and even in its own country the finest plants are found in places where it escapes the sun. These are true winter flowers; but hardly less so are the Lenten Roses, or forms of the Oriental Hellebores. In the southern counties, five seasons out of six, no weather stops them from being fine in flower before the winter is past; they often bloom in January and make a handsome show in February, and they are the finest of all flowers to end the winter.

The Algerian Iris flowers in warm sandy borders in the country around London, and in mild winters is a great treasure, not merely for its beauty in warm sheltered corners, but also its precious qualities for the house, in which the flowers, if cut in the bud state, open gracefully if placed in basins in moss. In warm and sheltered gardens on warm soils, others of the winter blooming Iris of the East may be grown, while in such gardens, in the south at least, the good culture of the sweet Violet will often be rewarded with many flowers in winter.

A beautiful Italian Crocus (Imperati) often flowers in winter in the southern counties at least, as, where people take the trouble to get them, do C. Sieberi, Dalmaticus, Etruscus, Suaveolens and others. This habit of some of the winter flowers of the south of Italy and Mediterranean region to open in our green and open winters should be taken advantage of. The fate of these Crocuses is interfered with by the common field vole, and the common rat is also a great destroyer of the Crocus. Where these enemies do not prevail, and the soil favours these charming winter and early flowers, we can grow them, not only in the garden, but on the turf of sunny meadows and lawns in which these beautiful Crocuses will come up year after year in winter and early dawn of spring.

The Winter Sweet (Chimonanthus fragrans) is in bloom often before

Christmas in the country around London, and every shoot full of fragrant buds opening on the trees against south and west walls. The many bright berries which adorn our country, both in the wild land and in well-stored gardens, are rather things of the autumn. By mid-winter the birds are apt to clear them off Wild Roses, Briers, Barberry, and Thorns, American as well as British. The Pyracantha, however, stays with us late; and Hollies, Aucuba, Cotoneaster, Snowberry, and the pretty little hardy Pernettya, from the Straits of Magellan, which has broken into such variety of colour in our country, are among those that stay late. The bright berries may fail us in hard winters, but the colour of the trees and bushes that bear them never does; and the red and yellow Willow, Dogwood, Thorns, Alders, Birch, and many Aspens and Maples, give fine colour when massed or grouped in any visible way. Still more constant are the flowering shrubs of winter, where in sheltered gardens and warm valleys any attention is given to them—Winter Jasmine, Winter Sweet, Winter Honeysuckles, Wych Hazel, Japan Quince in many forms, Laurustinus, several Heaths, Arbutus, at least one variety of Daphne Mezereon, the pale Southern Clematis (Calycina) happy in our warmer gardens, Eleagnus, the Nepal Barberry, a Chinese Plum (P. Davidiana), and the catkin bearing Garrya and Hazel. The Winter Honeysuckles are a bit slow in some districts, and a better result is got from them on free soils, and from walls in sheltered corners, an immense difference resulting if we can have them near the sea, with its always genial influence in favour of things from climates a little warmer than our own. In heavy soils in the inland country and around London the Laurustinus often comes to grief or fails to flower well, but has great beauty in seashore districts, and often on sandy and gravel soils is charming, even in inland places.

The hardy and beautiful Winter Jasmine, which is so free on cottage walls and wherever it gets a chance, is most precious, owing to the way it opens in the house, especially if gathered in the bud state. If we have it in various aspects, the sun scorching the shoots after a frost and killing the flowers may be avoided. The plant is so free that, if the shoots are allowed to hang down, they root in the ground like twitch, and therefore it can be increased very easily, and should be seen in visible groups and lines, and not only on the house or on walls, as in the milder districts it forms pretty garlands and bushes in the open.

When the Dogwood has lost all its leaves and is a deep red by the lake, and the Cardinal Willow has nearly taken its winter colour, the dwarf autumn blooming Furze flowers far into winter, and is in perfect bloom on the drier ground, telling us of its high value where dwarf vegetation is desired. It is seen in abundance on many hills and moors, but is hardly ever planted by design. A good plant for all who care for low foreground vegetation, it may be planted like Common Furze, but by far the best way is to sow it in spring in any bare or recently broken ground. The Common Furze, too, of which the season of bloom is spring and mild winters, often flowers at Christmas; odd plants here and there in the colonies of the plant bearing quite fresh flowers; and if from the nature of these native shrubs they do not find a place in the flower garden, there are few country places where they may not be worth growing not far from the house, in covert, or by drives or rough walks, as no plants do more to adorn the late autumn and winter.

Hardy heaths excellent for the winter garden in their brown and grey tuftiness. The forms of the common Heather and the Cornish Heath are best for rough places outside the flower garden, but some kinds of Heath are among the best plants for the choicest winter garden of the open air, particularly the Portuguese Heath (E. Codonodes), which in mild winters is of great beauty; also a hybrid between the Alpine forest Heath (E. carnea) and the Mediterranean Heath, with the port and dense flowering habit of the Alpine Heath and the earlier bloom of the Mediterranean Heath. The Alpine forest Heath, the most precious of all hardy Heaths, often flowers in mild winters, and in all winters is full of its buds ready to open.

So far we are speaking of districts where there are few advantages of climate; if we include others there might be more flowers in the winter garden, and many varied flowers are seen in gardens in the Isle of Wight, and many other favoured gardens not always confined to the Southern part of England and Ireland: the Cornish, Devon, South Wales or Cork Coasts being far more favourable.

If the snow shrouds the land, all's well, as the leaves of evergreen plants, like Carnations, are at rest in it, and some plants are all the better for the peace of the snow for a time. Even if our eyes are not open to the beauty of the winter let us make the flower garden a real one for spring, summer, and fall, as if it were true that in winter

> The year
> On the earth her deathbed, in a shroud of leaves dead,
> Is lying.

But it is not true: there is in winter no death, every root works and every bud is active with life; the wooded land is tender with the colour of Alders by the busy wintry stream and Birch on the airy hill, Reeds fine in colour round the lake or marsh. If even our wild marsh or rough woodland be beautiful in winter, our gardens with the flora of three continents to gather from, should not then be poor in beauty. No! Winter is not a time of death, but of happy strife for plants and men.

Until her
Azure sister of the spring shall blow
Her clarion o'er the dreaming earth, and fill
(Driving sweet birds like flocks to feed in air)
With living hues and odours plain and hill.

CHAPTER XXIII

Water Gardens

It is not only from the mountain's breast dyed with Violet and Gentian, the Sunflower-strewn prairie of the north, or the sunny fields where Proserpine gathered flowers, that our garden flora comes. River and stream are often fringed with handsome plants, and little fleets of Water-Lily—silvery fleets they look as one sees them from the bank—sail on the lakelets far away in North America and Asia. One need not go so far to see beautiful plants, as our own country rivers and back-waters of rivers possess many. Our gardens are often made about towns where there are few chances of seeing our native water plants, but by the back-waters of rivers and by streams in many situations, and by lakes like the Norfolk Broads one may often see as handsome plants in these places, and also in the open marsh land, as in any garden, and some that we do not often see happy in gardens, such as the Frogbit, the Bladderwort, and Water Soldier.

Where, as often is the case in artificially made ponds, the margin of the water is not the rich deep soil that we have by the Broads and by the sides of rivers, which themselves carry down deep beds of rich soil, a good way is to plant the mud which we take out of the pond around its sides a little above and below the water-line. This will encourage a rich growth of such Reeds as are found beside natural waters. Water with a hard, naked, beaten edge and little or no vegetation is not good to look at, and a margin of rich living plants is better for fish and game as well as for effect. The waterside plants one may establish in that way are worth having and give good cover for duck.

The most beautiful of all water gardens are the river and stream gardens, as their form is so much better than anything we can make and the vegetation is often good even without care. With a little thought we can make it much more so, and in our river-seamed land there are so many charming opportunities for water-garden pictures.

The water margin offers to lovers of hardy flowers a site easily made into a fair garden. Hitherto we have used in such places aquatic plants only, and of these usually a very meagre selection; while the improvement of the waterside may be most readily effected by planting the banks near with vigorous hardy flowers, as many of the finest plants, from Irises to Globe Flowers, thrive in moist soil. Waterside plants have this advantage over water plants that we can fix their position, whereas water plants spread so much that some kinds over-run others. The repeating of a favourite plant at intervals would mar all; groups of free hardy things would be best: Day Lilies, Meadow Sweets, tall Irises, which love wet places; Gunnera, American swamp Lilies in peaty soil, the rosy Loosestrife, Golden Rods, Starworts, the Compass plants, Monkshoods, giant Knotworts, Moon Daisies, the Cardinal Flower, the common Lupine—these are some of many types of hardy flowers which would grow freely near the waterside. With these hardy plants, too, a variety of the nobler hardy Ferns, such as the Royal Ferns and Feather Ferns, would associate well.

Water plants of northern and temperate regions associated with our native water plants, add much beauty to a garden. If the soil be rich, we usually see the same monotonous vegetation all round the margin of the water, and where the bottom is of gravel there is often little vegetation, only an unbroken, ugly line of washed earth. A group of Water-Lily is beautiful, but Water-Lilies lose their charm when they spread over the whole of a piece of water, and even waterfowl cannot make their way through them. The American white Water-Lilies (Nymphæa odorata and N. tuberosa) are hardy, and of recent years much beauty has been given our water plants in the hybrid hardy Water-Lilies raised by M. Latour Marliac, who has added the noble forms and the lovely colour of the Eastern Water-Lilies to the garden waters of northern countries.

Even where natural ponds exist it frequently happens that the banks of the pond, as well as the water itself, are either bare, or are covered only by the rankest weeds. The ponds chiefly considered here are those mostly formed without cement, by natural flooding from a brook, streamlet or river. If the water supply is abundant and continuous, it matters little whether a portion of the water is wasted by percolating through the sides of the pond, but when only a small supply can be had the bottom and sides of the pond must be either concreted or puddled with clay. It often happens that when the excavations for a pond are completed the bottom is found to consist of impervious clay, but the sides consist of ordinary soil, which would allow a large portion of the water to waste. In such cases the best way out of the difficulty is the cutting of a narrow trench, say 18 inches wide, to a depth a little beyond the surface of the natural clay subsoil. This trench, which should skirt the whole pond at some little distance from the actual edge of the water, is then filled with clay "puddle" till just above the water-line and forms an effective remedy against waste, while the water-soaked soil between the trench and the actual outline of the pond forms an excellent home for all kinds of marsh plants of the bolder type. The outline of a pond is of the utmost importance. Regular curves of circles or ovals are utterly out of place and look ridiculous in a landscape with naturally undulating ground.

The water-soaked margins of our ponds and brooks would furnish a home for many graceful fine-foliaged and flowering plants. Rheum Emodi from the Himalayas, Rheum palmatum from Northern Asia, and the Siberian Rheum undulatum are effective plants for the waterside. Of an entirely different type is the noble Arundo donax. The Pampas Grass (Gynerium argenteum) and its early flowering companion, Arundo conspicua, from New Zealand, may also be mentioned as graceful plants for the waterside. Much dwarfer, but also effective, is the Elymus, with broad glaucous foliage contrasting well with the fine deep green foliage cyperus longus, a graceful native.

The plants just mentioned as suitable for the waterside are valued mostly on account of their foliage. But among flowering plants also handsome varieties may be found that might with great advantage be used for decoration at the waterside much oftener than is at present the case. Few things are brighter than the brilliant flowers of purple loosestrife. Groups of Iris Kæmpferi and the bolder Iris, also look exceedingly well on the margin of a pond, and the "Royal" Fern (Osmunda regalis) delights in that position. Senecio japonica grows really well only when its roots can find abundance of moisture; its large deeply cut leaves are as handsome as its deep yellow flowers, 4 inches across, and borne on a stem 3 feet to 4 feet high. Spiræa gigantea, which bears its flowers on stems 5 feet to 6 feet above the ground. Spiræa Aruncus, though not so tall, is, nevertheless suitable, as are also its smaller, but still companions, Spiræa palmata, and others.

For many years I have planted these Lilies with pleasure and happy results, and, in view of their importance, their story is worth telling. Their discovery by a modest amateur in a small town near Bordeaux was the best ever done for hardy flowers. It seemed doubtful at first if these Water-Lilies, showing as they do such lovely colours, could be hardy; as it happens, they are as hardy as the great Water Dock by the lake side. In all these years many groups have been in position without change or attention. No preparation whatever was made for planting beyond sinking in the ordinary mud which is washed into the lake by the woodland streamlets. They were planted tied to pieces of stone dropped into the water, or sometimes in a small wicker basket weighted with stones. From some of the groups many scores of flowers might be gathered at one time: perfect blooms fine in colour. The earlier kind sent out, some of them, were not decided as to colour, but of late years they are fine in that way. The lake is rather deep, 12 feet or more in places, so there was little chance of attending to the "toilet" of the plants, as may be done in shallow lakelets or fountain basins in thinning out the plants, which is certainly a gain. Here we had no means of doing this, except by emptying the lake, which was not done except on rare occasions. The plants are such vigorous growers that an occasional thinning out is to be desired.

The only thing that has really mattered has been that great enemy of Water-Lilies, the water-rat. He never goes far from the waterside, but is as destructive there, enjoying himself very much carrying the flowers to the bank and cutting the centres out at his leisure. For many years we set traps for him, with some success, but since the war we have had to discontinue this, with the result that many of the blooms disappear. Shooting and trapping is essential in this case. Another enemy is the water-hen, which comes in shoals out of the woods. Though not nearly so bad as the water-rat, she also must be kept down.

A mistake is any kind of artificial rearing of ducks in ponds where Water-Lilies are grown. The heron occasionally visits us, and also the swan, the kingfisher, and a few small birds; but none of them do harm to the Water-Lilies. The case is different when ducks are artificially reared and bred, for then farewell to all the beauty of the flowers. In one or two instances I have given way to this in the interests of shooting friends, but never again!

Many water plants will grow almost anywhere and bid defiance to game or rats, but the newer and rarer Water-Lilies will not show half their beauty if they are subjected to the attacks of certain animals. They may, indeed, when young be easily exterminated by them, and even when old and established the common water-rat destroys the flowers, and, taking them to the bank, eats them at its leisure. When the plants are small; the attacks of the common moorhen and other water-fowl may mean all the difference between life and death to a Water-Lily. Perhaps, therefore, the first thing to be done in establishing these plants is to put them in some small pond apart from the rougher waterside plants, and especially where they will be safe from the attacks of the water-rat and other creatures which cannot be kept out of ponds fed by streamlets. By these and river banks or back-waters water-rats are hard to destroy, and guns, traps, ferrets, or any other means must be used. The common brown rat is not so fond of these flowers as the true water-rat, but it is so destructive to everything else that it is essential to destroy it at the same time, as it often abounds near water. The water or moorhen is continuously destructive to all the Water-Lilies, pecking at the flowers until mere shreds are left, and no one can fairly judge of the rare beauty of these plants where these birds are not kept down.

Our island homes, with a vast storm-vexed shore-line, abounding rivers and beautiful inland waters, offer interesting work to the planter. And not without difficulties; but these difficulties are pleasant to remember when we get over them, as we may. Wild shores, often bare and free to the wild, sharp kisses of the sea; innumerable lovely sites now desolate will in time invite men to plant: hence the importance of good work on such ground. And we may bear in mind its great advantages in some ways, as we get these good things talked of in books, but seldom seen in home landscape work, breath, air, repose, graceful contours of earth, fair backgrounds of Willow and many trees. Few need be told of the beauty of our inland waters, loved for many reasons. Yet it is when we think of lands without the gift of water, such as some parts of our own Eastern and Southern country, and the land around Lyons in France and about Berlin, that we feel more than ever the precious gain of abounding rivers, lakes like those of England and Western Ireland and noble estuaries and bays of many parts of our islands. Even those who care for good planting in ordinary ground are apt to neglect the waterside, and we see much land near it without any of the lovely effects which well-chosen river or lake-side trees give. The best waterside trees are often those of our own country and Europe, easily procured, fine in colour and good in form. There are certainly gains in waterside position which we do not find elsewhere; we get air and light, shade and breadth, from the water itself, which prevents the dotting of plants over the whole area. Again, there are often good lands beside rivers liable to flood, which we cannot well plant with ordinary trees, and cannot wisely build upon, and these give us those rich levels that are such a gain to lowland landscape when fringed by noble planting. Flooding is not against the right trees upon islands, lake margins and riversides. Some of the best trees, like the Eastern Plane that we often associate with hot dry soils, seem happy in ground sometimes flooded, as we may see in the good soils in Southern valleys.

Of all the sites for planting there are none in which we may have clearer guidance as to what is best than we have in islands and the margins of water, be it lake or river. The vegetation should be mostly of a spiry-leaved sort—Willows in many forms, often beautiful in colour, both in summer and winter, with Poplars. Even the Willows of Britain and Europe are ample to give fine effects, and some, like the White Willow, form tall timber trees. There is also a lovely group of weeping trees among these Willows, some of them more precious than the Babylonian Willow. The best trees for waterside-planting are those of our own country or of Europe and the Northern world generally. There are many Willows, but for good effect the best are the Tree Willows, those which may be had on their natural roots and of some timber value. The best of these for our country is the White Willow, lovely at all times, but especially on days of storm, when other things are often at their worst. The hybrids of the White Willow (Bedford Willow) are good also, and next best for colour is the Yellow Willow (Salix vitellina), classed by the botanists as a variety of the White Willow, but distinct in stature, form and colour. It is often seen beside Northern rivers, and when massed in a marsh or bog or beside a wide river it is fine in effect, and best of all on wintry days. The Red Willow (Cardinal Willow) is a form of it, of even brighter colour. The Crack Willow (S. fragilis) is not so showy in colour, but is very picturesque in form upon the river banks, and quite worthy of a place among the Tree Willows.

After Willows the Poplars come in best in all Northern countries. The White Poplar is beautiful in colour as a riverside tree, and superb in form when well grown. The Poplars by the French rivers are also beautiful, though none is prettier than the Aspen. The Lombardy Poplar is sometimes very fine in valleys near water. The Grey Poplar comes next to the White in beauty, and the Black Poplar is often good beside water.

Some of the American marsh trees are very pretty near water in particular one called the Tupelo (Nyssa sylvatica), lovely in colour in autumn; but the summer-leafing trees of the American woods have been much neglected since the vogue for planting Conifers came in, so that we can point to but few examples of good results in our country. The Hemlock Spruce thrives in wet ground, also the Norway Spruce and the Sitka Spruce. We resort to trees of the Pine tribe to clothe sandy or stony hills, but it is as well to know that for low and wet land we are not obliged to confine ourselves to Willows, Alders and Poplars if for any reason we prefer evergreen trees. In southern parts of Britain, where (after its first youth is past) the Norway Spruce is often a failure, it will yet grow well beside streams and in wet bottoms. The Sitka Spruce—a valuable tree—is good also, and the Douglas Fir thrives in the shelter of the woods.

The worst evil of all is the mixed muddle planting which is so common in England and does more to destroy all good effect in our gardens than anything else. Very often the trees are planted to a level face, without any thought of the natural habits or ways of the things planted. The evil arises from trusting to people to plant who have never given a thought to the work from the artistic point of view.

A not infrequent feature is the ugly, formless pool that no skill can make tolerable. Made without any pretence of grace of outline, they are disfigurements, sometimes dangers. The best way is often to drain and turn them into ferneries or Azalea gardens. Water is no good if hideous in outline and not large enough to reflect light and to allow of graceful planting of Willow, Dogwood and Reed.

CHAPTER XXIV

The Bog Garden

The bog garden is a home for the numerous children of the wild that will not thrive on our harsh, bare, and dry garden borders, but thrive cushioned on moss or in moist peat soil. Many beautiful plants, like the Wind Gentian and Creeping Hairbell, grow on our bogs and marshes. In North America, even by the margins of the railways, one sees, day after day, the vivid blooms of the Cardinal-flower springing erect from the wet peaty hollows; and far under the shady woods stretch the black bog pools, the ground between being so shaky that you move a few steps with difficulty. And where the woody vegetation disappears the Pitcher-plant (Sarracenia), Golden Club (Orontium), Water Arum (Calla palustris), and a host of other handsome bog plants cover the ground for hundreds of acres, with perhaps an occasional slender bush of Virginian Magnolia among them.

Southwards and seawards, the bog flowers, like the splendid kinds of herbaceous Hibiscus, become tropical in size and brilliancy, while far north and west and south along the mountains grows the queen of the peat bog—the beautiful and showy Mocassin-flower (Cypripedium spectabile). Then in California, all along the Sierras, a number of delicate little annual plants continue to grow in small mountain bogs long after the plains are quite parched, and annual vegetation has quite disappeared from them. But who shall record the beauty and interest of the flowers of the wide-spreading marshlands of this globe of ours, from those in the vast wet woods of America, dark and brown, hidden from the sunbeams, to the little bogs of the high Alps, far above the woods, where the ground often teems with Nature's most brilliant flowers? One thing however, we may gather from our small experience—that many plants commonly termed "alpine," and found on high mountains are true bog plants. This must be clear to anyone who has seen our pretty Bird's-eye Primrose in the wet mountain-side bogs of Westmorland, or the Bavarian Gentian in the spongy soil by alpine rivulets.

Perhaps the most charming plants to commence with are our own native bog plants—Pinguicula, Drosera, Parnassia, Menyanthes, Viola palustris, Anagallis tenella, Nartheciu, Osmunda, Lastrea Oreopteris, Thelypteris spinulosa, and other Ferns; Sibthorpia europæa, Linnæa borealis, Primula farinosa, Campanula hederacea, Chrysosplenium alternifolium and oppositifolium; Saxifraga Hirculus, aizoides, stellaris, Caltha, and Marsh Orchises. These, and a host of plants from our marshes and the summits of our higher mountains, will flourish as freely as in their native habitats, and may all be grown in a few square feet of bog; while Rhododendrons, Kalmias, dwarf Ferns, and Sedges will serve for the bolder features.

One of the great charms of the bog garden is that everything thrives and multiplies in it, and nothing droops or dies, but the real difficulty is to prevent the stronger plants from overgrowing, and eventually destroying, the weaker. A small pool of water filled with water plants is a charming addition to the bog garden.

In the bog garden many of our most beautiful plants, which in a summer like that of 1895 have been languishing for moisture in the borders, may be grown to perfection surpassing in beauty all our former impressions of them. Of primary importance, of course, is the position, and where this is naturally of a moist, boggy or swampy character, matters will be much simplified. We will assume there is such a spot at disposal, a swampy, treacherous, and, as we are wont to regard it, useless piece of land, under water the greater part of the year. Such a spot will be sure of its crop of naturally water-loving plants, such as Rushes, Sedges, or the like, and the first care must be to root them out one and all. In doing so, be careful that 12 inches or so of the margin be overhauled, as in all probability there will be here roots and seeds of all these wildlings. According to the nature of the boggy piece and also the depth of the water, it may be necessary for cleansing the ground to cut a deep trench and allow the water to pass away, as, without the moisture, the whole is much more convenient for preparation, and roots are more readily eradicated. The ground thoroughly cleansed at the outset, attention should next be directed to the soil. This may be variable, according to the variety of plants it is intended to introduce. For instance, strong-growing plants like the Meadow Sweets are all at home in a fairly stiff and moist soil. On the other hand, Iris Kæmpferi Trillium, Cypripedium, Lilium pardalinum, L. superbum, and other such things have a decided preference for soil of a vegetable character, such as peat, leaves, and the like. These latter, again, have a preference for the drier parts of the bed, while such as the Calthas and Menyanthes trifoliata revel in wet mud. To meet the varied degrees of moisture which the plants prefer will be quite an easy matter in an artificially constructed bog by the adoption of an undulating surface throughout. Slightly raised mounds are by far the most convenient, and certainly the most economical, way of providing for the greatest number of plants.

The shape, of course, should be picturesque, and, unless a depression of the whole exists, let this receive the next attention, and in such a way that the highest part will be 9 inches below the average surrounding soil. The paths should next be dealt with, excavating these nearly a foot deep in the central parts and gradually rising at the entrances. The soil taken from the paths may, if good, be used to form the raised beds for the planting of moisture-loving plants, such as are content if their roots only reach water. The sides of these beds may need rough support, such as rude sandstone blocks, to keep the soil in its place. These, or similar things, may also form stepping-stones in the wetter parts, as by this means the plants may be viewed without inconvenience. Beds of various sizes will be needed in proportion to the kind of plants that shall hereafter occupy them. For instance, the sloping banks at the edge, which may also take the form of a slightly projecting mound, would constitute excellent positions for some of the hardy Bamboos. Similar opportunities may occur at intervals throughout the margin for planting with such things as Acanthus, Yucca, Eulalia, Astilbe rivularis, Spiræa Aruncus, Bocconia cordata, and others of similar proportions, while the lower slopes and depressions between these would make excellent places for Osmunda regalis, Lilium giganteum, L. pardalinum, L. canadense, and L. superbum in peaty beds. The latter three of these are really swamp-loving by nature, and it is scarcely possible to see them in anything approaching perfection elsewhere. In the moisture so close at hand such things simply revel, and the owner of them may for years see them towering far above his head in their day of flowering—a picture of health and beauty. With such things it should always be borne in mind that constant saturation is not absolutely essential, though, indeed, they receive it more or less in their native habitats. Where space for bog gardens is limited, a very charming carpet to the Lilies just named would be the Wood

Lily of North America (Trillium grandiflorum). The two things may be planted or replanted at the same season when necessity arises. The Trillium, moreover, would come in spring-time and would protect the growth of the Lilium against our late spring frosts. For the Liliums a foot deep of peat, leaf-soil, and turf, with sharp river grit, would form a good bed, and with a mulch each year of leaf-soil and a little very rotten manure would serve them for many years. It may surprise many to know that under such conditions these Trilliums would in a few years, if left alone, attain to nearly 2 feet and be lovely in the size and purity of their flowers. In another of these depressions Cypripedium spectabile could easily be established, or a bed may be devoted to the more showy hardy species, giving 6 inches of peat or more, with leaf-soil added. The species named is rather late in sending up its growth, and affords plenty of time for a carpet of Trillium to flower before much headway is made. Other beautiful carpeting plants for these would be found in the American Mayflower (Epigæa repens or Pratia angulata), and if the position be shaded, as it should be for the Cypripediums, a charming, yet delicate, fringe may be found in Adiantum pedatum. Besides C. spectabile, C. pubescens and C. parviflorum are well deserving attention, together with Orchis foliosa, the beautiful "Madeira Orchis," and the Habenarias, especially H. ciliaris and fimbriata; all delight in moisture and require but little root room. Then if a glow of rich colour was needed in such places it could be supplied in Spiræa venusta or S. palmata, both delighting in moist soil. Another fine effect may be had by grouping Lobelia fulgens, or indeed any of the scarlet Lobelias and Sikkim Primrose. In wet parts may be planted Osmunda regalis, Onoclea sensibilis, Struthiopteris germanica, and Astilbe rivularis, allowing room for each. Groups of the herbaceous Phloxes in their best and most distinct shades, particularly of salmon scarlet and the purest white, would find their natural wants completely satisfied in the bog garden and give fine colour. In English gardens it is only in a moist season that we see the Phlox in even fair condition, for the reason that the original species is a native of wet meadows. This condition we can best imitate by deep digging and heavy manuring, and so much the better if the beds of these be saturated with water. Only in the constant cooling moisture of the bog can Primula japonica be seen in perfection, for here will it produce rosettes of leaves 2½ feet across, and giant whorls of its crimson flowers, attaining to nearly the same height. Another charming Primrose is that from the swampy mountain meadows of the Himalayas, P. sikkimensis, essentially moisture-loving; but to get the best results this must be treated as a biennial, grown on quickly, and planted in the bog as soon as large enough to handle. Other species of Primula suited to the higher and drier parts of the bog would be found in P. cashmeriana, capitata, denticulata, rosea, farinosa, involucrata, viscosa, and others, all alike beautiful in their way, and attaining greater vigour with the abundant moisture. Some of the smaller kinds of the viscosa type are better for slight shade, such as may be provided by Dielytra spectabilis (a really delightful plant in boggy ground) and various Spiræas. It should be noted that many shade-loving plants delight in full sun when given abundant moisture at the root. Particularly noticeable is this with the Liliums I have noted previously. In the early part of the year the bog garden should be aglow with such things as Marsh Marigolds, in single and double forms. In the wet mud in the lower parts and about the stepping-stones these would appear quite natural, and in like places Ficaria grandiflora, a plant too rarely seen, with its blossoms of shining gold; then Senecio Doronicum, with golden orange flowers, Dielytra eximia, Trollius: any of the Dentarias and Dodecatheons likewise are all well suited for the raised parts where the roots will touch the moisture. The Dodecatheons in peat, loam, and leaf-soil in equal parts, particularly D. Jeffreyanum, grow to a large size: Hepaticas, too, are greatly improved in company with these last, while the charming effects that may be produced are almost without end. Corydalis nobilis in peat and loam, C. lutea, together with the Water Mimulus (M. luteus), all provide rich masses of yellow. Gentiana asclepiadea, G. Andrewsi as well as G. verna, grow charmingly in the bog.

Nor is the list of plants exhausted; indeed, they are far too numerous to give in detail, but yet to be mentioned as among the grandest are many Irises, I. Kæmpferi in particular. Meconopsis Wallichiana (the blue Poppy of the Himalayas) produces quite a unique effect in the moisture parts. Saxifraga peltata, S. Fortunei, S. Hirculus, S. granulata plena, Soldanellas, Senecio pulcher, Sisyrinchium grandiflorum and many more are all benefited by the varying degrees of moisture to be found in the bog garden.

In gardens where no moist piece of ground exists, such as those with gravel or sandy subsoils, it will be necessary to select a low part and mark out an irregular outline. Next dig out the soil 18 inches or 2 feet in depth, so as to allow of at least 6 inches of clay being puddled in the bottom to retain the moisture. For bog plants clay is far better than concrete, because it supplies food for many moisture-loving plants. To keep the clay in position, sloping sides will be best, and for the soils named it will scarcely be necessary to have more than a small outlet for excessive moisture, and this at about 12 inches high from the deepest part. For this a narrow clinker or rough brick drain will suffice, so placed that the outlet may be blocked, if necessary, for affording greater moisture. By digging a shallow trench around the upper margin of the bog-bed, and using Bamboos or Bocconia cordata—these valuable for their rapid annual growth—such things would give the needful shade in summer.

In large gardens and cool, hilly districts the bog garden should always be found. Some years ago I had charge of just such a garden: in the flower garden was a fountain basin wherein water plants were grown; the overflow from this went tumbling in many ways over a series of rocks into the rock garden pond containing Orontium aquaticum, Nymphæas, and Sagittarias. In turn the overflow from the rock garden was conducted to the bog garden proper, where many masses of Cypripedium spectabile, with fully a score of spikes of its beautiful flowers to each tuft, grew in luxuriance in peat and leaves under a welcome shade. Here, too, Osmundas were rampant together with Primula japonica and a variety of plants already mentioned, and Ourisia coccinea, tightly pressing the surface of a stone, flowered splendidly.—E. J.

In some of the southern counties there is not much marsh land that we can deal with, but in many parts of our islands, especially Ireland north and south, and also in mountain country everywhere, there are many natural bog gardens which only need a little development, climate, soil and everything else being all we can desire for our bog garden. The peat soil which we seek for in vain in some southern counties is there, and even many of the welcome sorts of plants, such as Heaths and the Sweet Gale, are to be found there if we are shy of attempting the more delicate plants of other countries.

CHAPTER XXV

The Hardy Fern Garden

The marriage of the fern and flower garden is worth effecting, our many hardy evergreen Ferns being so good for association with hardy flowers. In my garden we have planted hardy ferns with British, North American and others, with good effect, both in summer and winter, using them mainly beneath Clematis and in the cooler part of the garden. There are many varieties of our native Ferns which would be excellent companions to plants suited for sheltered, half-shady nooks, and there are hardy and vigorous exotic kinds. Graceful effects may be had in foregrounds, in drives through glades, through the bold use of the larger hardy Ferns, whether evergreen or not. The Bracken is everywhere; but there are Ferns of graceful form which delight in the partial shade of open woods and drives, and succeed even in the sun. Ferns have, as a rule, been stowed away in obscure corners, and have rarely come into the garden landscape, though they may give us beautiful aspects of vegetation not only in the garden, but by grassy glades, paths, and drives.

In the home counties there is probably not a better fernery than that at Danesbury. It is on a sloping bank in a rather deep dell, overhung with trees and Ivy, in the shade of which the Ferns delight. As regards the planting, the various families are arranged in distinct groups, and each group has a position and a soil favourable to its requirements. The best way to grow Ferns, however, is with flowers, as in Nature, and a hardy fernery may be very beautiful. At Danesbury the most sheltered, moist spot is given to the evergreen Blechnums, which delight in a damp atmosphere, and to the delicate forms of Asplenium. Osmunda, which thrives amazingly, is in a low swamp. The soil used for these Royal Ferns is a mixture of good loam and fibrous peat. The better deciduous kinds of Polypodium, such as P. Phegopteris and P. Dryopteris, have sheltered positions; and in quiet nooks may be found charming groups of the Parsley Fern, and Cystopteris fragilis, a most delicate and graceful Fern. Lastrea Filix-mas and its varieties occupy the more exposed positions in company with fine colonies of the evergreen kinds, comprising some unique varieties of the Polystichums, Scolopendriums, Polypodiums, etc. A plentiful supply of water is available.

The Fern-lover will remember that not only have we our own beautiful native Ferns for adorning our gardens, but also the hardy Ferns of America, Asia, and the continent of Europe. As to the hardiness of exotic Ferns, Mr Milne-Redhead writes from Clitheroe:—

> Is it not strange that we so seldom see, even in good gardens, any well-grown plants of exotic Osmundas, Struthiopteris, &c.? Here, after a long spell of hot, dry weather, we had on May 20, 1896, a sharp snap of frost which completely cut off the more than usually beautiful flowers of Azalea mollis, and seriously injured the young growths of some Japanese Pines, such as Abies firma, A. sachalinensis, and others. This frost turned the young fronds of our English Filix-mas and Filix-fœmina quite black. Close by these plants, and under similar conditions of soil and exposure, the American Adiantum pedatum, 1 foot high, and the tender-looking Onoclea sensibilis were quite unhurt, and Osmunda interrupta and O. cinnamomea entirely escaped and are now very fine. Our English O. regalis was slightly touched, but the Brazilian O. spectabilis brought by myself from dry banks in the Organ Mountains was not even browned in its early and delicate fronds. All the Ferns I have named are great ornaments to any moist and rather shady place in the shrubbery. In a sheltered nook in the rock garden I find, to my surprise, that Gymnogramma triangularis has survived the perils not only of a frosty spring, but the still greater ones of a wet autumn and winter, and is now throwing up healthily its pretty triangular fronds, whose under-surface is quite white with the powder peculiar to the genus—in fact a hardy silver Fern.

A visit to Mr Sclater's Fern garden at Newick shows us the good effects that may be had by using the nobler hardy Ferns—both native and foreign—in a bolder way, and often in the open sun. The idea that a fernery is best in a dark corner has had unfortunate results in keeping the grace of such plants out of the garden picture. Hardy Ferns are being used in bold and simple ways at Kew, where at one time they were in an obscure fernery, and even if some Ferns require shade, many do not in our cool climate. Shade is, moreover, an elastic term; the bold hardy Ferns one sees in the American woodlands would not have too much sun in the open in Britain, provided they were in the right soil.

Many hardy Ferns are excellent for association with hardy flowers, and many may be grouped with evergreen rock and hill plants in forming borders and groups of evergreen plants. Though we have enough native Ferns in these islands to give us very fine effects, as we see at Penrhyn, or wherever Ferns are boldly grouped, some of the finest Ferns we see at Newick, and also at Rhianva and other gardens are natives of North America. Foremost among the strong-growing hardy exotic kinds, there are the handsome North American Osmunda cinnamomea, and O. Claytoniana, O. gracilis, a very pretty species of particularly slender habit; the Sensitive Fern (Onoclea), Dicksonia punctiloba, the beautiful Canadian Maiden-hair, the American Ostrich Feather Fern, Lastrea Goldiana, Woodwardia virginica, all of North American origin and attaining between 2 feet and 3 feet in height. Among the smaller Ferns are Aspidium nevadense, novaboracense and thelypteroides, Asplenium angustifolium, Athyrium Michauxi and Woodwardia angustifolia, all of which grow from 18 inches to 24 inches. Allosorus acrostichoides, the handsome Polypodium hexagonopterum, Woodsia obtusa, oregana and scopulina, and also two pretty Selaginellas, viz., oregana and Douglasi. All these are of small dimensions, varying as they do from 6 inches to 12 inches in height. The pretty Hypolepis anthriscifolia of South Africa; the robust Lastrea atrata, from India; the Japanese Lastrea decurrens, the massive Struthiopteris orientalis, also a native of Japan, and the pretty Davallia Mariesi are all equal in hardiness to any of our British deciduous Ferns.

Some of the evergreen Ferns, whether British or exotic, which stand the severity of our climate, are as hardy as those which lose their leaves in winter, and no Fern could be hardier than the various small-growing Aspleniums, which grow in old walls exposed to severe frosts, such as the black stemmed Spleenwort (several), and its pretty crested and notched forms, the little Wall Rue or Rue Fern, the forked and other native Spleenworts. All these are small, seldom exceeding 8 inches in height, while the black Maiden-hair Spleenwort Blechnum and its several beautiful forms usually average from 9 inches to 12 inches in height. Polypodium also contains some handsome evergreen plants;

even the common Polypody is a fine plant in its way, and is seen at its best when growing on a wall, on the branches of a tree, or on the roof of a low house. But by far the handsomest of its numerous forms are the Welsh Polypody, the Irish and the Cornish, and its handsome, finely-cut varieties in which the fronds are of a light and feathery nature. Then there are the more or less heavily crested forms, all of larger dimensions than the species from which they are issue. The common Hart's-tongue supplies us with many forms giving fine effect and free growth.

As regards strong-growing evergreen hardy Ferns, however, none can compare with the Prickly Shield Fern and the soft Prickly Shield Fern, and its beautiful varieties which produce massive fronds 18 inches to 24 inches long. Then there is an extensive section of varieties in which the fronds in many instances are as finely cut as those of the Lace Fern, and infinitely finer in effect. The soft Prickly Shield Fern has also produced some remarkably crested forms, all of which are equal in vigour and in dimensions to the typical species. The Holly Fern is also hardy, and is one of those plants which are usually killed with kindness, through being grown in a temperature higher than is required.

Not less effective and quite as interesting as the above, though of smaller dimensions, are the North American Asplenium ebenum, Phegopteris alpestris, Pellæa atropurpurea, Woodsia alpina and W. glabella, varying in height from 6 inches to 12 inches. There are also some remarkably handsome strong-growing sorts, native of Japan, the most decorative as also the most distinct among these being Lastrea Standishi, with fronds 24 inches to 30 inches long, and of a lovely and cheerful green colour; Lastrea erythrosora, with fronds 18 inches to 24 inches long, of a beautiful bronzy red colour when young, and of a deep dark green hue when mature. Lastrea opaca is another handsome Japanese form, broad and massive, of a fine metallic colour when young, and of a deep velvety green when mature. In Lastrea Sieboldi we have a totally distinct plant, having the general aspect of a somewhat dwarf Polypodium aureum and of the same bluish colour. This and Dictyogramma japonica, which have somewhat bold and broad fronds, are also quite hardy, and so are the Japanese Lastrea prolifica, a species with finely-cut fronds, bearing numerous small plants; the handsome Polystichum setosum, with beautiful dark green, shining foliage; Polystichum tsus-simense, Lastrea corusca and L. aristata. Lomaria chilensis is a large-growing

Fern with fronds 24 inches to 30 inches long and of a particularly deep green colour. Niphobolus Lingua is a very distinct Fern with entire fronds of a very leathery nature, dark green above and silvery beneath, having somewhat the general appearance of our common Hart's-tongue, but in this case the fronds, instead of starting from a single crown, are produced along a slender rhizome of a wiry nature. Perhaps one of the prettiest of the hardy evergreen Ferns is the violet-scented Lastrea fragrans.

It is a mistake to consider all Ferns as plants requiring shade and moisture. There are, on the contrary, Ferns which like full sunshine and bright light. Without counting Cystopteris alpina and fragilis, which grow in our walls as well in sun as in shade, there is one class of Ferns which actually requires sunshine. Cheilanthes from the Old World, as well as those from the New, only do well in a sunny aspect. I could not succeed at Geneva in cultivating Cheilanthes odora, lanuginosa and vestita. In spite of every care given to them, they suffered from general weakness, ending in decay. At last I one day saw Woodsia hyperborea, that delicate and fragile plant, in full sun along an alpine road in Italy, and on returning I planted all my Cheilanthes in sunshine on a south wall. The result was good, and I recommend the plan to Fern growers. But it was necessary also to change the soil in which these plants were cultivated, and I set them in soft porous mould composed of Sphagnum Moss, peat and sand; good drainage and frequent watering ensured an immediate and excellent result. That which proved satisfactory for Cheilanthes I then tried for Woodsia hyperborea and ilvensis (the treatment did not do for W. obtusa); then for Scolopendrium Hemionitis, that pretty and curious Fern from the south so rarely met with in gardens, where it is considered difficult to grow. Then I gave the same treatment to Nothochlena Marantæ; and this lovely Fern, which formerly did not do with me, turned out marvellously well. It is, then, certain that many species of Ferns require sun and plenty of air.—H. CORREVON, in *Gardeners' Chronicle*.

The flower garden should be in the sun, but there may be a chance now and then of growing Ferns in shady corners. In my garden I took advantage of the cool side of a summer-house to plant the Feather Ferns, which have done very well there, and with other things are a graceful foil to the bright flowers. In the same place the Maiden-hair Fern of the American woods thrives and is most welcome. On the cool side of a wall I put some graceful native Ferns of recent years, and they are as pretty as any Fern in the tropics, thriving not perhaps as well as in a deep gully; but we are glad to have them. Some of the little Ferns of the district came of themselves on the cool side of a wall. Polypody grows there very well and the Maiden-hair Spleenwort also.

The following exotic Ferns may be grown in the open air if the more tender are covered with old fronds or soft hay over the crowns in winter. These would be better in sheltered nooks in the rock garden in good peaty earth. Those kinds marked with an asterisk should receive protection in this form.

Exotic Hardy Ferns

Adiantum pedatum
Allosorus
  acrostichoides
Aspidium cristatum
  Clintonianum
  fragrans
  nevadense
  novaboracense
  rigidum argutum
  spinulosum
  thelypteroides
Asplenium
  angustifolium
  ebenum
  *fontanum (Europe)
  thelypteroides
  Michauxi

Cotrychium
  virginicum
*Cvrtomium
  caryotideum
  (E. Indies)
  *falcatum (Japan)
  *Fortunei (Japan)
Dennstædtia
  punctilobula
Hypolepsis millefolium
  (N. Zealand)
  anthriscifolia
  (S. Africa)
Lastrea
  *atrata (India)
  *decurrens (Japan)
  fragrans
  Goldiana

intermedia
marginalis
*opaca (China)
Lastrea—*continued*.
  prolifica (Jamaica)
  *Sieboldi (Japan)
  varia (China)
Lomaria alpina (N. Zealand)
  chilensis (Chili)
  crenulata (Chili)
Onoclea sensibilis
Osmunda cinnamomea
Osmunda Claytoniana
  gracilis
  japonica
*Pellæa atropurpurea
  *gracilis

Phegopteris alpestris
Dryopteris
  hexagonoptera
  polypodioides
Polystichum
  acrostichoides
  a. grandiceps
  a. incisum
  Brauni
  concavum (Japan)
  munitum
  (California)
  m. imbricans
  polyblepharum
  (Japan)
  *proliferum
  (Australia)
  *setosum (Japan)

Struthiopteris ger-
  manica (Europe)
*orientalis (Japan)
  pennsylvanica
  p. recurva
Woodsia
  glabella
  obtusa
  oregana
  scopulina
Woodwardia
  angustifolia
  *japonica (Japan)
  orientalis (Japan)
  radicans (S. Europe)
  r. americana
  virginica

CHAPTER XXVI

Fragrance

A man who makes a garden should have a heart for plants that have the gift of sweetness as well as beauty of form or colour. And what a mystery as well as charm—wild Roses sweet as the breath of heaven, and wild Roses of repulsive odour all born of the earth-mother and, it may be, springing from the same spot. Flowers sweet at night and scentless in the day; flowers of evil odour at one hour and fragrant at another; plants sweet in breath of blossom, but deadly in leaf and sap; Lilies sweet as they are fair, and Lilies that must not be let into the house; bushes in which all that is delightful in odour permeates to every March-daring bud. The Grant Allens of the day, who tell us how the Dandelion sprang from the Primrose some millions of years ago, would no doubt explain all these things to us, by what Sir Richard Owen used to call "conjectural biology," but we need not care, for to us is given this precious fragrance, happily almost without effort, and as free as the clouds from man's power to spoil.

Every fertile country has its fragrant flowers and trees; alpine meadows with Orchids and mountain Violets; the Primrose-scented woods, Honeysuckle-wreathed and May-frosted hedgerows of Britain; the Cedars of India and of the mountains of Asia Minor, with Lebanon; trees of the same stately order, perhaps still more fragrant in the warmer Pacific breezes of the Rocky Mountains and Oregon, where the many great Pines often spring from a carpet of fragrant Evergreens, and a thousand flowers which fade away after their early bloom, and stand withered in the heat, while the tall Pines over-head distil for ever their grateful odour in the sunny air. Myrtle, Rosemary, and Lavender, and all the aromatic bushes and herbs clothing the little capes that jut into the great sea which washes the shores of Greece, Italy, Sicily, and

Corsica; garden islands scattered through vast Pacific seas, as stars are scattered in the heavens; enormous tropical forests, little entered by man; great island gardens like Java and Ceylon and Borneo, rich in spices and lovely plant life; Australian bush, with plants strange as if from another world, but often most delicate in odour even in the distorted fragments of them we see in our gardens.

It is not only from the fragile flower-vases these sweet odours flow; they breathe through leaf and stem, and the whole being of many trees and bushes, from the stately Gum trees of Australia to the Sweet Verbena of Chili. Many must have felt the charm of the strange scent of the Box bush before Oliver Wendell Holmes told us of its "breathing the fragrance of eternity." The scent of flowers is often cloying, as of the Tuberose, while that of leaves is often delicate and refreshing, as in the budding Larch, and in the leaves of Balm and Rosemary, while fragrance is often stored in the wood, as in the Cedar of Lebanon and many other trees, and even down through the roots.

It is given to few to see many of these sweet plants in their native lands, but we who love our gardens may enjoy many of them about us, not merely in drawings or descriptions, but the living, breathing things themselves. The Geraniums in the cottage window bring us the spicy fragrance of the South African hills: the Lavender bush of the sunny hills of Provence, where it is at home; the Roses in the garden bring near us the breath of the wild Roses on a thousand hills; the sweet or pot herbs of our gardens are a gift of the shore-lands of France and Italy and Greece. The Sweet Bay bush in the farmer's or cottage garden comes with its story from the streams of Greece, where it seeks moisture in a thirsty land along with the wild Olive and the Arbutus. And this Sweet Bay is the Laurel of the poets, of the first and greatest of all poet and artist nations of the earth—the Laurel sacred to Apollo, and used in many ways in his worship, as we may see on coins, and in many other things that remain to us of the great peoples of the past. The Myrtle, of less fame, but also a sacred plant beloved for its leaves and blossoms, was, like the Laurel, seen near the temples of the race who built their temples as the Lily is built, whose song is deathless, and the fragments of whose art are despair to the artist of our time. And thus the fragrant bushes of our gardens may entwine for us, apart from their gift of beauty, living associations and beautiful thoughts for ever famous in human story.

It is not only odours of trees and flowers known to all we have to think of, but also many delicate ones, less known, perhaps, by reason of the blossoms that give them being without showy colour, as the wild Vine, the Sweet Vernal, Lemon, and other grasses. And among these modest flowers there are none more delicate in odour than the blossoms of the common white Willow, the yellow-twigged and the other Willows of Britain and Northern Europe, which are all the more grateful in air coming to us

O'er the northern moorland, o'er the northern foam.

What is the lesson these sweet flowers have for us? They tell us—if there were no other flowers to tell us—that a garden should be a living thing; its life not only fair in form and lovely in colour, but in its breath and essence coming from the Divine. They tell us that the very common attempt to conform their fair lives into tile or other patterns, to clip or set them out as so much mere colour of the paper-stainer or carpet-maker, is to degrade them and make our gardens ugly and ridiculous, from the point of view of Nature and of true art. Yet many of these treasures for the open garden have been shut out of our thoughts owing to the exclusion of almost everything that did not make showy colour and lend itself to crude ways of setting out flowers.

Of the many things that should be thought of in the making of a garden to live in, this of fragrance is one of the first. And, happily among every class of flowers which may adorn our open-air gardens there are fragrant things to be found. Apart from the groups of plants in which all, or nearly all, are fragrant, as in Roses, the annual and biennial flowers of our gardens are rich in fragrance—Stocks, Mignonette, Sweet Peas, Sweet Sultan, Wallflowers, double Rockets, Sweet Scabious, and many others. These, among the most easily raised of plants, may be enjoyed by the poorest cottage gardeners. The garden borders of hardy flowers bear for us odours as precious as any breath of tropical Orchid, from the Lily-of-the-Valley to the Carnation, this last yielding, perhaps, the most grateful fragrance of all the flowering host in our garden land. In these borders are things sweeter than words may tell of—Woodruff, Balm, Pinks, Violets, garden Primroses, Polyanthuses, Day and other Lilies, early Iris, Narcissus, Evening Primroses, Mezereon, and Pansies delicate in their sweetness.

No one may be richer in fragrance than the wise man who plants hardy shrubs and flowering trees—Magnolia, May, Daphne, Lilac, Wild Rose, Azalea, Honeysuckle—names each telling of whole families of fragrant things. From the same regions whence come the Laurel and the Myrtle we have the Laurustinus, beautiful in our sea-coast and warmer districts, and many other lovely bushes happy in our climate; one, the Winter Sweet, pouring out delicious fragrance in mid-winter; Sweet Gale, Allspice, and the delightful little May-flower that creeps about in the woodland shade in North America. So, though we cannot boast of Lemon or Orange groves, our climate is kind to many lovely and fragrant shrubs.

Even our ugly walls may be sweet gardens with Magnolia, Honeysuckle, Clematis, Sweet Verbena, and the delightful old Jasmine, still clothing many a house in London. Most precious of all, however, are the noble climbing Tea Roses raised in our own time. Among the abortions of this century these are a real gain—the loveliest flowers ever raised by man. Noble in form and colour, and scented as delicately as a June morn in alpine pastures, with these most precious of garden Roses we could cover all the ugly walls in England and Ireland, and Heaven knows many of them are in want of a veil.

Some Fragrant Plants for British Gardens

Abelia	Crinum	Lupins	Pondflower	Sweet Scabious
Abronia	Cyclamen	Magnolias	Plaintain Lily	Sweet Sultan
Allspice	Datura	Marvel of Peru	Primroses	Sweet Verbena
Almond	Day Lily	May-flower	Rhododendrons	Sweet-William
Alyssum	Deutzia	Meadow Sweet	Rock Rose	Thyme
Apples	Evening Primrose	Mexican Orange	Rockets	Tuberose
Auricula	Forsythia	Flower	Rose	Tulip Tree
Azalea	Grape Hyacinth	Mezereon	Rosemary	Tulips
Balm	Hawthorns	Mignonette	Scilla	Twinflower
Balm of Gilead	Heartsease	Mock Orange	Stocks	Vine
Bee Balm	Heliotrope	Musk	St. Bruno's Lily	Violets
Belladonna Lily	Honeysuckles	Myrtle	Snowflake	Wallflowers
Blue Bells	Horse Chestnut	Narcissus	Southernwood	Water-Lilies
Brugmansia	Hyacinths	Night-scented Stocks	Styrax	Willows
Burning Bush	Iris	Pæony (some)	Sweet Bay	Winter Green
Carnation	Jasmine	Pancratium	Sweet Cicely	Winter Heliotrope
Clematis	Lavender	Pansy	Sweet Fern Bush	Winter-Sweet
Cethra	Lilac	Pelargonium	Sweet Flag	Wistaria
Columbine	Lily	Phlox	Sweet Gale	Woodruff
Cowslips	Lily-of-the-Valley	Polyanthus	Sweet Pea	Yarrow

CHAPTER XXVII

Simpler Flower Garden Plans and
the Relation of the Flower Garden to the House

A great waste is owing to frivolous and thoughtless "design" as to plan and shapes of the beds in the flower garden. What a vision opens out to any one who considers the design of the flower garden when he thinks of the curiosities and vexations in the forms of beds in almost every land where a flower garden exists! The gardener is the heir—to his great misfortune—of much useless complexity and frivolous design, born of applying conventional designs to the ground. These designs come to us from a remote epoch, and the designing of gardens being from very early times in the hands of the decorative "artist," the garden was subjected to their will, and in our own days we even see gardens laid without the slightest relation to garden use, difficult to plant, and costly to form and to keep in order. At South Kensington the elaborate tracery of sand and gravel was attractive to some when first set out, but it soon turned to dust and ashes. It was, indeed, to a great extent formed of broken brickdust, in a vain attempt to get rid of the gardener and his flowers. The colours were supplied from the building sheds, where boys were seen pounding up bricks and slates, and beds were made of silver sand, so that no gardener could disfigure them. The Box edgings of beds a foot wide or smaller soon got out of order, and after a few years the whole thing was painful to see, while good gardeners were wasting precious time trying to plant paltry beds in almost every frivolous device known to the art of conventional design.

Even where such extravagances were never attempted we see the evil of the same order of ideas, and in many gardens the idea of adapting the beds to the ground never occurs to the designer, but a design has been taken out of some old book. If the ground does not suit the plan, so much the worse for the ground and all who have to work on it. From the results of this style of forming beds the cottage gardens escaped, the space being small and the cottage gardener content with the paths about his door. Now there are bold spirits who do not mind setting their houses among rocks and heather, but we must cultivate a flower garden, and simplicity as to the form of the beds should be the rule in it. Our object should be to see the flowers and not the beds, so that while we have all the advantage of mass and depth of soil, and all the good a bed can give for convenience of working or excellence of growth, we should take little pride in its form, and plant it so that we may see the picturesque effects of the plants and flowers, and forget the form of the bed in the picture.

The relation of the beds to each other is often much too complex and there is little freedom. Designs that were well enough for furniture or walls or panels when applied to the garden gave us a new set of difficulties. Carried out in panel or in the carpet they answer their purpose, if we like them; but a flower-bed is a thing for much work in cultivating, arranging and keeping it, and it is best to see that we are not hindered by needless complexities in dealing with the beds. In good plans there is no difficulty of access, no small points to be cut in grass or other material, no vexatious obstruction to work, but beds as airy and simple as possible and giving us much more room for flowers than beds of the ordinary type.

The plan of the gardener's house of Uffington, near Stamford, an example of the older-fashioned garden not once uncommon. At one end of the little garden is the gardener's house, and high walls surround the rest of the garden, so that there is shelter and every comfort for the plants. The garden is simply laid out to suit the ground, the plants—Roses and hardy flowers in great variety, a plan which admits of delightful effect in such walled gardens. Picturesque masses of Wistaria covered one side of the wall and part of the house—the whole was a picture; and it would be difficult to find in garden enclosures anything more delightful during more than half the year.

The main drawback in gardens of this sort in the old days was the absence of grouping or any attempt to hold "things together"—a fault which is easily got over. It is easy to avoid scattering things one likes all over the beds at equal distances, and, without "squaring" them in any stupid way, to keep them rather more together in natural groups, in which they are more effective, and in winter it is much easier to remember where they are. In this way, too, it is easy to give a somewhat distinct look to each part of the garden. Box edgings may be used in such a garden, and where they thrive and are well kept they are very pretty in effect, but always distinctly inferior to a stone edging because more troublesome, and also because dwarf plants cannot grow over them here and there as they can over a rough edging of natural stone, the best of all edgings.

This garden shows two essential things in the art of garden design: First, that it is by studying the ground itself, rather than bringing in any conventional plans, that we arrive at the best results.

Gardening is so pleasant in many ways that almost any plan may pass for pretty and yet be far from being the most artistic result that could be got among a given set of conditions or difficulties it may be of ground. If in such a case we adopt such plans as are sent out from offices both in France and England, it is possible that (with considerable cost) we may adapt them to the situation, but assuredly that way cannot give us the most artistic result.

The new flower garden at Shrubland Park is situated exactly in front of the house and tells its own story. The plan shows the simple form of beds adopted, planned to suit their places, in lieu of the complex pattern beds for carpet bedding, sand, coloured brick, and also the change from such gardening to true flower gardening. The names of the plants used are printed in position, but the actual way of grouping cannot well be shown in such a plan—the plants are not in little dots, but in easy, bold groups here and there running together. The flower gardening adopted is permanent, *i.e.*, there is no moving of things in the usual wholesale way in spring and autumn. The beds are planted to stay, and that excludes spring gardening of the ordinary kind. But many early spring flowers are used in the garden, the mainstay of which is summer and autumn flowers, the period chosen for beauty being that when the house is occupied, and all beautiful hardy flowers from Roses to Pansies that flower from May to November are those preferred. There is no formality or repetition in the flower planting, but picturesque groups, here and there running together, and sometimes softened by dwarf plants running below the taller ones. The beds are set in a pleasant lawn, and there is easy access to them in all directions from the grass.

CHAPTER XXVIII

Walks and Edgings

Our gardens are often laid out with so many needless walks, edgings, and impediments of many kinds that work cannot be done in a simple way, and half the time is lost in taking care of or avoiding useless or frivolous things. In many large places there is no true flower gardening; wretched plants are stuck out in the parterre every year, a few stunted things are scratched in round the choke-muddle shrubbery, and but little labour or love is bestowed on the growth of flowers, or there are miles of walks bordered by bare stretches of earth, as cheerful as Woking cemetery in its early years. The gardener is helpless to turn such a waste into a paradise; his time and his thoughts are often taken up by the keeping in order of needless and often ugly walks, leaving him little time for true flower gardening, that is, forming a real garden of Roses, or groups of choice shrubs, or beds of Lilies, or of other noble hardy plants, so that the beds may fairly nourish their tenants for a dozen years. Instead of the never-ending and wearisome hen-scratchings of autumn and spring, we ought to prepare one portion of the flower garden or pleasure ground each year, so that it will yield beauty for many years. But this cannot be done while half the gardener's time is taken up with barber's work.

Our own landscape gardeners are a little more sparing of these hideous walks than the French; but we very often have twice too many walks, which torment the poor gardener by needless and stupid labour. The planning of these walks in various elaborate ways has been supposed to have some relation to landscape gardening; but one needless walk often bars all good effect in its vicinity. Flower-beds are often best set in grass, and those who care to see them will approach them quite as readily on grass as on hard walks. For the three or four months of our winter season there is little need of frequent resort to flower-beds, and for much of the rest of the year the turf is better than any walk. I do not mean that there should be no walk to the flower garden, but that every walk not necessary for use should be turfed over. Few have any idea how much they would gain, not merely in labour, but in the beauty and repose of their gardens, by doing away with needless walks.

For hard work and general use the gravel walk is the best of all for garden and pleasure grounds. The colour of walks is important; that of the yellow gravels being by far the best. Of this we have examples in the country around London, in the gravels of Croydon, Farnham, and also those of Middlesex. These walks are not only good in colour but also excellent in texture. It is a relief to see these brownish-yellow walks after the purple pebble walks of the neighbourhoods of Dublin and Edinburgh. After the sound formation of these walks the main point is to keep them to the essential needs of the place, and when this is done their effect is usually right. Even this excellent gravel is sometimes improved about London by the addition of sea shells, cockle shells mostly gathered from the coasts of Kent; and, after the walk is formed and hardened, this is lightly scattered over the surface and rapidly breaks down and gives to the walk a clean smooth surface.

In public gardens and parks large areas of gravel are sometimes necessary, and in some ways of "laying out," such as those round French châteaux, wide arid areas of gravel are supposed to have a *raison d'être*; but in English gardens they are better avoided. English roads, lanes, and pathways are often pictures, because consecrated by use and often beautiful in line, following as they often do lines of easiest grade or gentle curves round hills; but in gardens, roads and paths are often ugly because overdone, and nothing can be worse than hot areas of gravel, not only without any relation to the needs of the place, but wasting precious ground that might be made grateful to the eye with turf, or of some human interest with plants.

A walk which is much liked is the stone walk, suggested by the little stone paths to cottages. In large open gardens such walks would not be so good, but in small enclosed spaces and flower gardens where we have to plant very closely in beds, stone walks are a gain. In some districts a pretty rough flat stone is found, of which there is a good example at Sedgwick Park. In cities, when renewing the side-walks, it is sometimes easy to get old flagstones, which are excellent for the purpose. I use such old stones and mostly set them at random, or in any way they come best. The advantages are that we get rid of the sticky surface of gravel in wet weather or after frost, avoid rolling and weeding, for the most part the stones are pleasant to walk on at all times, and we can work at the beds or borders freely in all weathers without fear of soiling gravel. The colour of the stones is good and in sunny gardens in hot summers they help to keep the ground moist, while the broken and varied incidents of the surface get rid of the hard unyielding lines of the gravel walk and help the picture. They should never be set in mortar or cement of any kind, but in sand or fine sandy soil, and the work can be done by a careful man with a little practice. If in newly formed ground there is a little sinking of the stone, it can be corrected afterwards. Small rock plants, like Thyme, the Fairy Mint, and little Hairbells, may be grown between the divisions of the stone, and, indeed, they often come of themselves, and their effect is very pretty in a small garden. Another point in favour of the stone walk is that it forms its own edging, and we do not need any living edging; and if for any purpose, in a wet country or otherwise, we wish to somewhat raise the flower-beds, we can use the same kind of stone for edging the beds.

Once free of all necessary walks about the house of gravel or stone, which constant work and use make essential, it is often easy in country gardens to soon break into grass walks which are pleasantest of all ways of getting about the country garden or pleasure ground. Not only can we take them into the wild garden and rough places, but they lead us to flowering shrubs and beds of hardy plants and to the rock garden, or through the pleasure ground anywhere, as easily and more pleasantly than any regularly set out walks. There is much saving of labour in their formation because, given sound, drained ground, which is to be found around most country houses, we have little to do except mark out and keep the walks regularly mown. When this work is compared with the labour of carting, the knowledge and the annual care which are necessary to form and keep hard walks in order, the gain in favour of the grass walk is enormous. It is perhaps only in our country that the climate enables us to have the privilege of these verdant walks, which are impossible in warmer lands, owing to the great heat destroying the herbage, and, therefore, in Britain we should make good use of what our climate aids us so much in doing.

We have, of course, to think of the fall of the grass walk for the sake of ease in mowing and in walking too, as very much of their comfort will depend, at least in hilly ground, on the careful way these walks are studied as regards their gradation. There is really not much difference in the degree of moisture in such walks and gravel walks, and, besides, so little use is made of walks of any kind in wet weather, that, taking them all the year round, they serve as well as any other.

Apart from the grass walks which can be formed in so large an area of Britain we may have walks through Heath and the short vegetation that grows in heathy districts, and these walks will be no less pleasant than the grass walks. The short turf of the Heath, and often the mown Heather itself, forms an excellent springy walk, as in parts of Surrey. Such walks want little making, only some care in laying down their lines so as to take them into the prettiest spots and letting them edge themselves with Heather, Ferns, and Whortleberry. But no more than any other should such walks be multiplied beyond what is necessary, and they ought to be broad enough and airy enough to take us in the pleasantest way to the most interesting parts of the garden or pleasure ground or woods. In woody or half shady places we may enjoy the mossy walks as in very sandy or light soils we may have a turf almost of Thyme.

There are also well-made walks to be had from concrete and true asphalt. These walks have distinct advantages for courtyards and small spaces, or even small gardens in certain places; they are better in colour than the tarred walk, and more enduring if well made. They are clean, but they have certain disadvantages as compared with stone walks. They require a much more expensive and careful setting, and they are certainly not more enduring. Also, they do not allow us the privilege of putting plants between the joints, one of the great charms of the stone walk, which can be easily set to allow Thyme and dwarf-rock plants to come up between them; and therefore in all districts in which a warm-coloured stone is procurable or rough flagstone from quarries, it is very much better to use it as we can always have gravel for any roads that have to be traversed by carriages or carts; the space for concrete, asphalt, or stone walks is not considerable, and the natural material should be used wherever it be possible.

Even small things may mar the effect of a flower garden, however rich in its plants, and among the things that do so are cast edgings of tiles or iron, often very ugly, and as costly as ugly, some of the earthenware edgings perishing rapidly in frost. But if they never perished, and were as cheap as pebbles by the shore, they would be none the less offensive from the point of view of effect, with their hard patterned shapes, often bad colour, and the necessity of setting them with precision in cement or mortar; whereas the enduring and beautiful edging wants none of these costly attentions. The seeming advantage of these patterned and beaded tile edgings is that they appear permanent, and get rid of the labour of clipping and keeping box edgings in good order; but these ends are met quite as well by perfectly inoffensive edgings.

The true way in all gardens of any good and simple design is to get edgings which, while quite unobtrusive in form or colour, may remain for many years without attention. In all good gardens there is so much to be done and thought of every day in the year, that it is important to get rid of all mere routine work with edgings of Box and other things that want frequent trimming or re-making, in which work much of the labour of gardeners has been wasted in the past.

Natural stone is the best of all materials for permanent edgings for the flower garden, or any garden where an edging is required, and no effort should be spared to get it. In many districts it is quite easy to do so, as in some of the home counties the refuse of quarries (in Surrey Bargate stone, and in Oxfordshire and Gloucestershire the flaky stone used for the roofs of old time) is excellent for edgings. Much difference will occur in stone in various districts, and some will not be so good in colour and shape as the stone just mentioned, but the advantage of natural stone in various ways is so great that even inferior forms of it should be chosen before any other material. In undressed, or very roughly dressed natural stone, it does not matter in the least if the stones vary in size, as we have not to set them rigidly like the cast tiles. Sunk half-way firmly in the earth, after a little time they soon assume a good colour; green mosses stain them in the winter, and if we wish to grace them with rock flowers they are very friendly to them, and Rockfoil, or Stonecrop, or Thyme may creep over them, and make them prettier than any edging made wholly of plants, like Box or Thrift, or Ivy. Unlike the tile, stones are none the worse if they fall a little out of line, as they are easily reset, and also easily removed by handy garden men without expensive workmen, or any aid from mortar or trowel. In large and stately gardens dressed stone may be used to frame a grass plot or handsome straight border, but in most cases this expense would be thrown away, as we get so good a result with the undressed stone. But in a flower garden like that at Shrubland Park, the dressed stone of good and simple form, and properly set as it should be in such a position near the house, is quite rightly used. Near cities and towns the removal of old or half-worn stone pavements, like the York stone used in London, often gives us opportunities of securing it for forming edging; and being often got in large pieces it requires rough dressing to allow of its being firmly and evenly set in the ground. I have used this largely for edgings, which will last as long as they are allowed to remain. The beautiful green stone of Cumberland would make as good an edging as one could desire, and many kinds of stone may be used.

In districts where there is no stone to be had, and we have to use any kind of artificial stone or terra cotta, these should never have any pattern or beading, but be cast in quite simple forms, never following the patterns usually adopted by the makers of garden tiles. Certain inferior forms of dead edgings should be avoided, such as boards, that soon rot, and are wholly unfit in all ways as edgings. Iron, too, as used in continental gardens or in any shape, should never be used as an edging, ordinary bricks half set in the ground being far better than any of these.

Grass edgings sometimes are used to flower borders, but are always full of labour and trouble. And they have various drawbacks apart from the mowing and edge-cutting, chief among these being that the border flowers within cannot ramble over them as they do over the stone edgings in such pretty ways. These narrow grass margins are often used as edgings to flower borders in the kitchen garden in places where very little labour is to spare for the garden, but, little as it is, it has to be given throughout the season to these grass edgings, which are worse than useless as a finish to a flower border. By these I do not mean the grass margins to the garden lawns, or a carpet of turf, as these are easily attended to when the lawn is being mown, but the foot-wide grass edgings which require attention when time can be badly spared for them, and are often so narrow that it is not easy to use a machine for mowing them.

Of all the living things useful as edgings in gardens, the first place belongs to Box, for ages used and deservedly liked from its neat habit and good colour. When there were many fewer plants to look after than we have now, to tend some miles of Box edging was often the pride of the gardener, and even now we see it sometimes done, though the hand often fails through the labour required to keep the Box in good order, and the edging gets spotty and in some soils worn out and diseased. A Box edging must be clipped with much care and regularity every May after the danger of hard frosts is past, as these sometimes touch the young growth. If cut in May the young growth soon hides the hard mark of the shears. Pretty as it is in certain gardens, the drawbacks to

Box as a flower-garden edging are serious; it requires much labour to keep it in order, and not every garden workman can clip it well. It is a harbour for slugs and weeds, drying and starving the soil near, whereas the stone edging keeps the soil moist and comforts the rock flowers that crawl over it. We cannot allow dwarf and creeping plants to crawl over the Box, or they will scald and injure it, but with the stone, we are free in all ways, and get a pretty effect when Pinks and other dwarf plants, crossing the stone edging here and there, push out into the walk itself. I like Box best as a tall, stout edging or low hedge, used in a bold way as high Rosemary edgings are used in southern gardens about 18 inches high, or even a little higher, to enclose playgrounds or separate gardens or to mark an interesting site as that of the old house at Castlewellan. Sometimes old and neglected Box edgings grown into low hedges are pretty in a garden, as in George Washington's old home at Mount Vernon in Virginia. And low hedges of Box are now and then a good aid near the flower garden, as at Panshanger.

Among other edgings made of woody or shrubby things, we have the Yew, which bears clipping into edgings a foot high, and which might be worth using in some positions, though much clipping of this sort causes much labour and to me sorrow. Ivy is more precious for its shoots, which garland the earth as well as wall or tree. It is more used abroad than in Britain, the freshness of its green being more valued where good turf is less common, and Ivy is of the highest value as an edging in various ways, but better as a garland round a plot or belt of shrubs than near flower beds, and as graceful edgings near and under trees. Like the Box, it may also be used as a bold hedge-like garland to frame a little garden or other spot which we wish to separate from the surrounding ground. The Tree Ivy is best for this, but the common Ivy, if planted as an edging in any open place, will in time assume the shrubby or tree form, and make a handsome and bold garland. Where, for any reason, we desire Ivy edgings, it is better not to slavishly follow the French way of always using the Irish Ivy for edgings. The dark masses of this in the public gardens of London, Paris, and German cities are very wearisome, and help to obscure rather than demonstrate the value of the Ivy as the best of all climbers of the northern world. The common Ivy, of which the Irish form is a variety, is a plant of wide distribution throughout Europe, North Africa, and Asia, and varies very much in form, there being in Britain over fifty cultivated forms of it. The Irish variety seems to have taken the fancy of continental European gardeners, and is much more cultivated by them than any

other, but many of the varieties though less known are more graceful
and varied in form, and even colour, some of them having in winter a
bronzy hue, instead of the dark look of the Irish Ivy. Some, too, are fine
in form, from the great Persian Ivy to the little cut-leaved Ivy. Even the
common Ivy of our woods is prettier than the one so much used.

Among the bold edging one sees enclosing the "careless" and
broad borders of Spanish or Algerian or other southern gardens,
overshaded by orange or other fruit trees, is the Rosemary, clipped
into square-topped bushy edges, about 15 inches high. Though tender
in many parts with us, it may be used in the same way on warm soils
and in mild districts, and the Lavender may be used in the same way,
though in its case it is best not to clip it, and there is a dwarf form,
which is best for edgings to bold borders.

Among various evergreen shrubs which may be used as edgings are
the dwarf Cotoneasters, Periwinkles, smaller Vacciniums, Partridge
Berry, the alpine forest Heath, and some of the smaller kinds of our
native Heaths, varying them after the nature of the soil and the kind
of plants or shrubs we are arranging; Heaths and shrubs of a like
nature being best for association with peat-loving evergreen shrubs,
though they need not all be confined to these or to such soils. Such
evergreen edgings of low shrubs are often very useful where we plant
masses of select evergreen flowering shrubs, and they may be used
in free belts or groups as well as in hard set lines, the last being in
many cases a sure way to mar the effect of otherwise good planting
in pleasure grounds.

TRIALS OF EDGING PLANTS

These are only well done where there is stone edging of some kind. In
my youth I saw many miles of Box edgings being clipped, and endless
labour bestowed upon such wasteful work done at a season when
essential work was pressing. With a garden of my own I made up
my mind to stop all such waste, and got some old York stone paving,
which, broken up, made edgings to last for hundreds of years; also,
rough sandstone rock gave bolder edgings for shrubs. Given these stone
edgings, I enjoyed much beautiful life of alpine and rock plants, which
liked the edging stone as much as any rock garden. In this way may be
grown numbers of beautiful plants to give an added grace of colour
and flower. To give an idea of the result of this plan and of the plants
that have given me the most pleasure is the aim of this chapter.

The Wall Harebell (*Campanula muralis*).—Of all the plants used, this is the most long-lived and useful. Other Hairbells of the mountains are difficult to grow, and even in careful hands are lost, but this lovely Harebell creeps up rocks, and even penetrates walls, flowering for years; and so densely that the number of bells in one foot of the line could not be counted. Flowering in early summer, if we cut off the flowers with the shears the plants bloom again right into November.

The Lancaster Geranium (*Geranium Lancastriense*).—This plant, native of an island on the coast of Lancashire, has given as much pleasure as any plant of the alpine rocks. It is dwarf, flowers all the summer, is beautiful in colour and habit.

Alpine Forest Heath (*Erica carnea*).—This is not in the flower garden, but bordering beds and walks in the Heath garden, where it is the best early Heath. Beginning to flower early in the spring, it gives way when the sun gets strong. It is from a calcareous country, so it may be used in districts where other Heaths will not grow.

Australian Everlasting (*Helichrysum bellidioides*).—A newly come plant, this surprises me by its fitness for the work, being dwarf, abundant in bloom, and free-growing too anywhere on dry walls and as an edging.

Gentianella (*Gentiana acaulis*).—This is the most precious of all edging plants in the calcareous soils of Ireland and Scotland. In the south of England in ordinary soils it gives way in dry weather and is difficult to establish. One gets over that by placing it behind a stone edging, when flowers may be expected, but never quite so fine as in the soils it loves.

Rocky Mountain Phloxes (*P. subulata* and other dwarf kinds).—We have had these for many years now on the top of a dry-stone wall dividing the flower garden from the rising ground, and their fine colours and other qualities have pleased me well in groups, which last for years in good health. Quick to grow, they are among the good edging plants that help to keep down the weeds.

Gauze plant (*Gypsophila repens*).—This has been the best as to endurance, good in colour and long in bloom. It has been more than ten years in one edging without it ever showing a sign of weakness, flowering all the summer and right into the autumn. The pink variety is as useful as the white. Sometimes other rock plants stray into it, and that is an added charm.

The Dwarf Lavender.—No edging meets with more approval than the Dwarf Lavender. It is more compact than the usual forms, and the flowers are of a deeper colour. Lavender, growing over a vast area on the warmer slopes of the Alps and in many lands around the great sea, varies much, and to that habit we owe this and other forms. The Dwarf Lavender makes a neat edging in the fruit or kitchen garden where the large forms might be in the way.

Turban Hairbell (*Campanula turbinata*).—This, the true plant, is a handsome Hairbell, better for the rock garden than as an edging. I tried it in ordinary cool soil just within the stone edging, where it did well, and in flower the effect was fine. It does not, however, meet my wants as a good edging to a flower-bed; it should bloom throughout the summer.

Mountain Sandwort (*Arenaria montana*).—This fine rock plant makes the loveliest edging of the bolder sort that one could desire. Behind a line of sandstone blocks it flowered beautifully, and is, so planted, very well fitted as a frame for shrubs, hardy and long-enduring.

The Blue Bindweed (*Convolvulus mauritanicus*).—This is the one plant I cannot do without as an edging—most graceful of all in the way it arranges itself, and also on dry walls, which it drapes as no other Bindweed could. A native of the mountains of N. Africa, where I had the pleasure of seeing it in flower in a rocky waste. I generally in autumn take up the plants that have formed an edging in summer, housing some and planting others on a sunny ledge of a retaining wall, in the hope they may live and flower thereon. It seeds freely.

The Pasque Flower (*Anemone Pulsatilla*).—This beautiful plant was, in the carpet-gardening craze, lost to gardens, as all the good things that did not fall in with the false taste of the day were thrown on the rubbish-heap. Some seedlings were planted in the cool loam of the district, and gave a charming variety of colour. This, the finest edging I ever had, was by a fruit garden walk, as in the flower garden I seek things that grace the summer with their flower and even last well into autumn.

Dwarf Tufted Pansies (hybrids of Viola).—A host of these, of often good colours, makes lovely margins to flower-beds of Roses. Easy of increase and culture in cool soils, and best in the cool northern hill land, many fine kinds, like John Quarton and Lady Knox, are well known. This should not prevent us raising seedlings as in that way we get vigorous plants to form edgings or carpets.

Indian Cinquefoil (*Potentilla dubia*).—In its large family there must be plants of value for our purpose, but the one named above is the only one that keeps with me as if it liked its task of forming a neat edging studded with clear yellow flowers. Of easy culture in any soil, it never looks as if it wanted to go back to the Himalayas. Some charming silvery-leaved Cinquefoils should make beautiful margins, but so far they are not easy to increase.

An alpine Toadflax (*Linaria pallida*).—A modest, patient, and delightful little creeper running in and out of the stone edging, always increasing and always in flower bordering the Carnation bed or other bed; not a robust plant, but easy of increase, and grows as if it enjoyed the garden.

Pinks (*Dianthus plumarius*).—The welcome fragrance and grey colour of these make them welcome as edgings, and they often give us good effects. In my soil they are not so enduring as on calcareous or free, sandy soil. The Maiden Pink (Dianthus deltoides) is a hardy and bright-flowering plant used with some effect, but the season of bloom is not long. In its vast family in northern and alpine lands there may be some free and hardy enough to make an edging in the choicest flower-bed.

The Siberian Stonecrop, (*Sedum Ewerst*).—A stout, grey plant forming a bold edging, quite hardy and easy of culture and increase in any soil. The Japanese Stonecrop (S. Sieboldi) is even more graceful, but in my soil not so free, and a victim to slugs. So it gets some comfort in a frame, and in spring is promoted to a vase, in which it is happy and quite pleasant to see, even well into autumn.

Purple Rock-Cress (*Aubrietia*).—Of the multitude of rock and alpine plants that come to these islands, this is the most useful, growing on walls, rocks, and wherever a few grains of it are sown. Edgings formed with it are beautiful in every way, those best made of rich purple kinds. At one time different Latin names were given to the forms of the plant, but they are all varieties of one mother plant, though varying much in lovely colour, and all as hardy as the Dock. Their flowering season is early, and usually three months long. The growth is so dense that the plants are able to keep free of weeds.

Rockfoils (*Saxifraga*).—The mossy kinds grow freely in cool soil, but are apt to perish in a dry one, and are only useful in shade. The Silvery Rockfoils I used with good result, but these are apt to get patchy in time, and the flowers are rather in the way. Yet I am grateful to them, for silvery leaves of the Aizoon group often carried me through before getting so keen on the plants that grace the beds with their flowers all the summer.

Great Indian Rockfoils (*Megasea*).—These I make extensive use of in margining large groups of flowering trees. Bold, free, and taking on often a good colour, they are excellent rightly used, and have the good quality of keeping off weeds. They are among my friends for that reason, and are valued not for narrow edgings, but may well spread into effective belts here and there about the shrubbery. In very hard winters the leaves may be injured, but they soon recover, and have kept many a corner at peace for years in the poorest soils.

Barrenworts (*Epimedium*).—Having plenty of these, they were tried as a stout edging, framing, so to say, large masses of shrubs and fruit trees in the orchard, and the way they have done it deserves a word. Hardy, strong growers, and with a fine classic form of leaf, good as winter colour, they formed a noble frame to the groups, and did not allow a weed to come near.

The Japanese Stonecrop (*Sedum spectabile*).—Long an admirer of this tall Stonecrop, I tried it around a mass of Rhododendrons and other bold shrubs, and there it throve and made a lovely belt of colour every autumn for over twenty years. But in war-time the shrubs began to encroach, and the unmown Grass to come in, and so we had to change it.

Thymes (*Thymus*).—These fragrant turfy plants tempt one to make edgings of them, and they charm so used on warm or calcareous soils, not so good on cold soils except on raised banks or rock garden. T. micans I use as a modest green edge. Some of my Thymes puzzle me, stubby little cushions in flower, and there must be good hardy edgings among the many species known on the northern hills.

The Carpathian Harebell (*C. carpatica*).—There are several good forms of this fine plant, a white and delicate intermediate colour, between white and blue. All mixed formed an attractive edging to a bed of Rose Zephirin on its own roots. A good perennial, may it remain long at its post.

Hepatica (*Anemone Hepatica*).—Often too scarce for edgings, and barely seen as poor forgotten dots, I have at last taken courage and made some edgings of it in the past fine October days. But as it has a poor chance in the open sun, it is used to border the paths under the pergola, where the shade will be right for its health. The plants are all of the wild blue kind, never having seen any of the variations so good.

The Silvery Speedwell (*Veronica incana*).—This, an old friend of the rock garden, has proved a good edging plant in leaf, effective at all seasons and with rich purple flowers in early summer, growing in any soil and of easy increase. Among the many New Zealand Speedwells there may be one or more good edging plants, but I never found one, save V. Lyalli, which is hardy, but not very effective in leaf or flower.

The Forget-me-nots.—Of these, the best is the true Forget-me-not and its forms, which make a pretty, broad edging to a mass of shrubs in cool soils and have been sometimes charming and free in bloom, but a little wayward and apt to get longing for the streamside, and then to get "seedy." Also as soon as the aphides find them in the garden out they swarm so as to make them no longer look like a Forget-me-not. On the waterside this does not happen, as the aphides have no love for the water. The Swiss Forget-me-not makes a pretty blue edging, but to keep it in health it wants frequent replanting.

The Dwarf Partridge Berry (*Gaultheria procumbens*).—This dwarf evergreen makes an admirable edging for beds of choice evergreens. It is not fit for the flower garden, which should be in the full sun. It is easy to grow and increase in any free soil. The larger Partridge Berry (G. Shallon) of N.W. America is too strong for edgings, but is a fine evergreen in the wood and a fine low foreground shrub.

The hardy Leadwort (*Plumbago Larpentæ*).—An old Chinese plant of our gardens, often neglected, this forms a beautiful edging on the brow of a low wall, and now, as I write, in mid-November, is fine in colour. Of easy culture and facile increase by division, it has also the added advantage of keeping the weeds off. A close grower even the Goutweed does not infringe on its ground. An excellent border for a large bed in an open sunny spot in any poor soil.

Sand Pink (*Tunica Saxifraga*).—This little plant is always in flower during summer and autumn, and is a favourite of mine. It is common on the sand-heaps in N. Italy; is freely raised from seed and hardy.

Blue Gromwell (*Lithospermum*).—This makes a beautiful edging where it has room to spread out over the stone or where it will. In free soils it is quite hardy and lasting, and exquisite in colour, but not so good on cold soil.

A rock Knotwort (*Polygonum vaccinifolium*).—This free and hardy plant is useful for edging groups of the larger shrubs, for which it answers well. Is easy to increase and hardy.

CHAPTER XXIX

The Flower Garden in the House

One of the real gains in any flower garden worthy of the name is that we have in it lovely forms and delicate colours for the house, from the dawn of spring with its noble Lenten Roses on sheltered borders, until autumn goes into winter in a mantle of Starworts. Many English and all German and French flower gardens in parterres offer us only Lobelias, and various plant rubbish of purplish or variegated hues, very few of them worth cutting, whereas our real flower garden is a store of Narcissus, Azalea, Rose, Lily, Tulip, and Carnation, and all the fairest things of earth. All we have to care about is placing them in simple ways to show their form as well as colour. Apart from the good plan of having a plot for the culture of any flowers we wish to cut for the house, a true flower garden will yield many flowers worthy of a place on an artist's or any other table for their forms, colour, or fragrance. Many of these, from the Narcissus to the Tea Rose, give flowers so freely that we need not be afraid to cut; indeed, in many cases, careful cutting prolongs the bloom (as of Roses). Many shrubs we may improve as we cut their branches for the house, for example Winter Sweet, Forsythia, and Lilac.

It is not merely the first impression of flowers, good as it may be, that we have to think of, but the charms which intimacy gives to many of the nobler flowers—some opening and closing before our eyes, and showing beauties of form in doing so that we never suspected when passing them in the open air. In the changing and varied lights of a house we have many opportunities of showing flowers in a more interesting way, particularly to those who do not see them much out of doors. We have in gardens many new flowers of great beauty of form—Californian, Central Asiatic, Japanese, even the mountains of

China and India giving precious things, as well as the rich flora of North America as yet not as much seen in our gardens as it deserves to be. So that it will be seen how good is the reason why care should be given to show the flowers in the house when we have them to spare out of doors.

At first sight there may not seem much against our doing justice to flowers in the house, but our flower vases have shared the fate of most manufactured things within the past generation, and suffer from the mania for overdoing with designs called "decorative," which is supposed to have some connection with "art." Every article in many houses being overcharged with these wearisome patterns, it was not to be expected that the opportunity of "adorning" our flower-pots would be lost, and so we may have ugly forms and glaring patterns, where all should be simple in form, and modest and good in colour. The coal-scuttle, with its "decoration," does not stand in our way so much as the flower vase, as in this we have to put living things in their delicate natural colours and shapes, and to look at these, stuck in vases with hard colours and designs, is impossible to the artistic mind.

And when we have seen the ugliness of much of this work, what is to be done in the way of remedy, as the shops are so much against us? The first need is a great variety of pots, basins, and jars or vases; so that no flower that garden, wood, or hedgerow can give us, need be without a fitting vessel the moment it is brought into the house. What are known as the Munstead glasses are a great help, because their shapes are carefully made to suit various flowers, and they are very useful and good in form—made, too, of plain glass; but, however good this series is, it is well to use a variety of other things in any simple ware that comes in our way, very often things on the way to the rubbish heap, such as Devonshire cream jars in brown ware. Nassau seltzer bottles, in the brown ware too, may well take a single flower or branch, while old ginger pots, quite simple shallow basins in yellow ware, and other articles made for use in trade, come in very well.

There is no need to exclude finer or more costly things than these if good in shape and not outrageous in colour, but various reasons lead us to prefer the simpler wares, in which the flowers look often quite as well as in any others. A mass of Edith Gifford Rose looks very well in a good old silver bowl, and good china, silver, or bronze vases or basins may be used for choice positions or occasions, though it will generally be best not to submit fine or fragile vessels of this kind to the risks of constant use. Among the finest things ever made in the shape of vases for cut flowers is the old Japanese work, which is often as lovely in form and as beautiful with true ornaments as anything made by the old Greeks; but the Japanese, like others, have taken to "potboiling" in bronze, and many of the things now seen at sales in London are coarse in workmanship. It might be worth while to have good and avowed reproductions of some of the more useful old forms—the slender, uprising ones are so good for many tall flowers; Italian bronze bowls are often useful too; and the darkness within the bronze vessels tends to keep the flowers longer than when they are in glass vessels exposed to the light.

Japanese ways of arranging flowers are extremely interesting and may sometimes be practised with advantage; but, with a great variety and good shape of vessels, the Japanese way is not so necessary as a system, for the reason that, given a variety of good shapes and different materials, we can place any single flower, branch, or bunch in a way that it will look well with very slight effort and in very little time. Any way involving much labour over the arrangement of flowers is not the best for us or for the result—far from it.

Having got a good and constant supply of flowers, and variety of vessels, the question of arrangement is the only serious one that remains to be thought of, and it is not nearly so difficult if we seek unity, harmony, and simplicity of effect, rather than the complexities which we have all seen at flower shows and in "table decorations," many of them involving much wearisome labour, while a shoot of a wild rose growing out of a hedge, or a wreath of Honeysuckle, would put the whole thing to shame from the point of view of beauty. In all such matters laying down rules leads to monotony, and yet there is much to be said for ways distinctly apart from the old nosegay masses and the modern jumble, and generally it is best to show one flower at a time, especially if a noble one like the Carnation, which varies finely in colour. The baskets and basins of Carnations arranged by the late Lady Henry Grosvenor, at Bulwick, were lovely to see, and the best of them were of one Carnation of good colour. These were the flowers from her fine collection of outdoor Carnations, so useful for cutting in summer and autumn, when people are enjoying their gardens. But the improved culture of the Carnation as a plant for winter and spring bloom under glass gives us quantities of this precious flower for six months more when the outdoor supply is over. These are among the best flowers for the dinner table as well as the house generally, and on the dinner table the effect by artificial or by natural light of one or two flowers of the season is often better than that given by a variety of flowers. What is just said of the Carnation applies to various noble groups of hardy flowers, such as the Tulip, Narcissus, and Lily.

It is not only in vases we see the good of showing one flower or group at a time; a good result will often come through a single spray or branch of a shrub. The Japanese have taught us to see the beauty of form and line in a single twig or branch, with its natural habit shown, apart from any beauty and form or colour its flowers may have. This is important, in view of the many shrubs that flower in our climate in spring, and of which if flowering shoots are cut when in bud the flowers open slowly and well in the house. They are best placed in Japanese bronze or other opaque jars. The taller Japanese bronze jars with narrow necks are very useful for these, and it is an excellent practice to cut the bud-laden shoots of Sloe, Plum, Apple, Crab, and like plants, and put them in jars to bloom in the house. By this means we advance their blooming time; and, in the case of severe weather, the beauty of early shrubs may be lost to us unless we adopt this plan. We see how well the French practice of growing Lilac in the dwelling-house prolongs the beauty of this shrub, and it is not difficult to do something of the kind for the hardy shrubs and early trees that come with the Daffodils, but are not so well able to brave the climate. These shoots of early shrubs are also usually best arranged each by itself, though some go well together, and graceful leaves of evergreens may be used with them. One advantage of dealing with one flower at a time is that we show and do not conceal the variety of beauty we have. For, if all are thrown together, that variety will be much less evident than if we make clear the colour and form of each kind. Some proof of this may be seen in the work of the best flower-painters. In the work of M. Fantin-Latour, for example, his nosegays of many flowers, evidently bought at some country market stand, are painted as well as his simple subjects, but these last are far the best pictures. There is such a wide range of plants, shrubs, and woodland and hedgerow flowers, that we must not hesitate to depart from any general idea if it tends to keep us from making the best of things in simple and ready ways.

Often the water and the water-side will give us fine things for the house, and the new Water-Lilies of rare distinction if cut in the freshly expanded state will keep very well for some days and give us quite a new order of beauty. For them we want bold and simple basins, as, if we can put some of their handsome leaves in with them, the effect is all the better. Although very fine in the open water, where they do admirably, the effect of the flower near at hand in the house is quite different and very beautiful, and as these plants increase their value as cut flowers for the house will be found to be great. There are also plants of the water-side which may help with foliage or flower; one of the best being the Forget-me-not, which flowers so well in the house, and the great Buttercup.

Many as are the flowers of the open air excellent for house, the leaves of the open-air tree or shrub or plant are hardly of less use for the same end: notably the foliage of evergreen shrubs in warm and sea-coast districts, from evergreen Magnolia, Poet's Laurel Cypress, Juniper and Thuja, Cherry Laurel, and Bamboo; even in the coldest districts we have the evergreen Barberry, and more than fifty forms of the best of all evergreen climbers, the Ivy, and the Holly with its scarlet, yellow, or orange berries. The trees in autumn give us leaves rich in colour—Maple, Medlar, Mespilus, Parrotia, Tulip-tree, and many others. The shrubs and climbers, too, help—Bramble, Wild Roses, Water Elder (Viburnum), Common Barberry, with its graceful rain of red berries; Vines in many forms; hardy flowers, too, help with Acanthus, Alexandrian Laurel, Solomon's Seal, Iris, Plantain Lily. Rock plants are rich in good leaves: Cyclamen, Heuchera, Christmas and Lenten Roses, the large Indian Rockfoils and the Barrenworts; and then there are the hardy Ferns of our own country and Europe, and also those of North America as hardy as our own.

A great help in a house is a handy water supply in a little room, near the flower garden or usual entrance for flowers, where vessels may be stored and flowers quickly arranged, used water and flowers got rid of, and so planned that the mistress of the house, or whoever arranges the flowers, may use it at all times without other aid. This greatly helps in every way, and makes the arrangement of flowers for the house more than ever a pleasure.

CHAPTER XXX

Evergreen Trees and Shrubs

"Oh the oak and the ash and the bonny ivy tree,
They flourish at home in my own country."—*Old Ballad.*

The above lines might be worth thinking of by those bent on planting evergreens, as if it were borne in mind that the evergreens we plant have to face winters in an Oak and Ash land, we should have less of rampant but not hardy evergreens which perish in numbers after hard winters.

There are no background hues prettier than those afforded by some evergreens like the Yew, Box, and Ilex; but their use requires care; we may have too many of them, and they should not take the place of flowering shrubs and flowers of many kinds. It is outside the flower garden that evergreens are most useful, and in a cold country like ours, especially on the eastern coasts and in wind-swept districts, Holly banks and hedges of other hardy evergreens are often a necessity. In our country we have the privilege of growing more evergreen shrubs and trees than continental countries, species resisting winter here which have not the slightest chance of doing so in Central Europe.

Into our brown and frozen northern woods come a few adventurers from southern lands that do not lose their green in winter but take a deeper verdure—Ivy, Holly, and Yew enduring all but the very hardest frosts that visit our isles, some bright with berries as well as verdure—giving welcome shelter to northern and wind-swept gardens, and in our own time each varying into many noble varieties. These native evergreens and their varieties are, and for ever must be, the most precious of all for the British Isles.

When after a very hard winter we see the evergreen trees of the garden in mourning, and many of them dead, as happens to Laurels, Laurustinuses, and often even the Bay, it is a good time to consider the hardiness and other good qualities of our British evergreens and the many forms raised from them. If we are fortunate enough to have old Yew trees near us, we do not find that a hard winter makes much difference to them, even winters that brown the evergreen Oak. We have collected within the past two hundred years evergreen trees from all parts of the northern world, but it is doubtful if any of them are better than the common Yew, which when old is often picturesque, and which lives for over a thousand years. Of this great tree we have many varieties, but none of them quite so good as the wild kind when old. In the garden little thought is given to it, and it is crowded among shrubs, or in graveyards, where the roots are cut by digging, so that one seldom sees it in its true character when old, which is very beautiful.

After the Yew, the best of our evergreen shrubs is the Holly, which in no other country attains the beauty it does in our own; certainly no evergreen brought over the sea is so valuable not only in its native form, often attaining 40 ft. even on the hills. Not merely as a garden tree is it precious, but as a most delightful shelter around fields for stock in paddocks and places which want shelter. A big wreath of old unclipped Holly on the cold sides of fields is the best protection, and a grove of Holly north of any garden ground is the best evergreen we can plant for shelter; the only thing we have to fear being rabbits, which when numerous make Holly difficult to establish by barking the newly-planted trees, and in hard winters even barking and killing many old trees. As to the garden, we may make beautiful evergreen gardens of the forms of Holly alone.

Notwithstanding the many conifers brought from other countries within the past few generations, as regards beauty it is very doubtful if more than one or two equal our native Fir. In any case few things in our country are more picturesque than old groups and groves of the Scotch Fir; few indeed of the conifers we treasure from other countries will ever give us anything so good as its ruddy stems and frost-proof crests.

The best of evergreen climbers is our native Ivy, and the many beautiful forms that have arisen from it. This in our woods arranges its own beautiful effects, but in gardens it might be made more use of, and no other evergreen climber comes near it in value. The form most commonly planted in gardens—the Irish Ivy—is not so graceful as some others, and there are many forms varying even in colour. These for edgings, banks, screens covering old trees, and rocks might be made far more use of. In many northern countries our Ivy will not live in the open air, and we rarely take enough advantage of such a possession in making both shelters, wreaths, and screens. Care is required to keep it off our houses and off cottage roofs or it will damage them; but there are many pretty things to make of it away from buildings, and among them Ivy-clad and Ivy-covered wigwams, summer-houses, and covered ways, the Ivy.

Box, which is a true native in certain dry hills in the south of England, is so crowded in gardens that one seldom sees its beauty as one may on the hills full in the sun, where the branches take a plumy toss. To wander among natural groves of Box is pleasant and we should plant it in colonies by itself full in the sun, so that it might show the same grace of form that it shows wild on the chalk hills. It is the best of our native evergreens for garden use, making pretty low hedges as at Panshanger, and for dividing lines near the flower garden it is better than Yew or Holly.

The Arbutus, which borders nearly all the streams in Greece, ventures into Ireland, and is abundant there in certain parts in the south. This beautiful shrub, though tender in midland counties, is very precious for the seashore and mild districts not only as an evergreen, but for the beauty of its flowers and fruit. Still, it is the one British evergreen which must not be planted where the winters are severe in inland districts, and usually perishes on the London clay. It is the best of our native evergreens that deserve the preference, instead of the heavy Cherry Laurels and various evergreens not even hardy, so that after a hard frost we often see the suburbs of country towns black with their dead.

One of the most baneful things in our gardens has been the introduction of distorted and ugly conifers which often disfigure the foregrounds of beautiful houses. These are often sports and variations raised in modern days, as is the case with the too common Irish Yew. It is not only that we have to deplore the tender trees of California, which in their own country are beautiful, though, unhappily, not so in ours, but it is the mass of distorted, unnatural, and ugly forms, the names of which disfigure even the best catalogues, that is most confusing and dangerous. In one foreign catalogue there are no less than twenty-eight varieties of the Norway Spruce, in all sorts of dwarf and monstrous shapes—some of them, indeed, dignified with the name monstrosa—not one of which should ever be seen in a garden. The true beauty of the Pine comes from its form and dignity, as we see it in old Firs that clothe the hills of Scotland, California, or Switzerland. It is not in distortion or in little green pincushions we must look for the charm of the Pine, but rather in storm-tossed head and often naked stems; and hence all these ridiculous forms should be excluded from gardens of any pretence to beauty.

Another most unfortunate tree in this way, as helping to fill out gardens with graceless things, is the western Arbor vitæ (Thuja occidentalis). This, which is a very hardy tree but never a dignified one, even where it grows in the north about Lake Superior and through the Canadas, is, unhappily, also hardy in our gardens, and we may see in one catalogue no less than twenty-three forms of this tree all dignified with Latin names. There are plenty of beautiful things, new and old, worthy of the name, without filling our gardens with such monstrosities, many of which are variegated. Of all ugly things, nothing is worse than the variegated Conifer, which usually perishes as soon as its variegated parts die, the half-dead tree often seeming a bush full of wisps of hay.

In many once well-planted pleasure grounds the Pontic Rhododendron almost runs over and destroys every other shrub, and hides out the most beautiful tree effects, growing often a little above the line of sight. Even where people have taken the greatest trouble to plant a good collection of trees, the monotony of it, always the same in colour, winter or summer, except when dashed by its ill-coloured flowers, is depressing. The walk from the ruins at Cowdray to the new house is an example that might be mentioned amongst a thousand others of a noble bank of trees, varied and full of beauty, but, in consequence of this shrub spreading beneath them all along the walk, showing nothing but a dank wall of evergreen. This ugliness and monotony come about through the use of the Pontic as a covert plant, and also owing to its facility of growth the beautiful sorts of Rhododendron being usually grafted on it. In a garden where there are men to look after plants so grafted and pull away the suckers, this plan may do, but when planting is done in a bold way about woods, or even pleasure grounds, this is not nor can it always be attended to, so that the suckers come up and in time destroy the valuable sorts. The final result is never half so pretty as in the most ill-kept natural wood, with Bracken and Brier in fine colour and some little variety of form below the trees; therefore everybody who cares for the beauty of undergrowth should cease this covering of the ground with this poor shrub, not so hardy as the splendid kinds of American origin often grafted on it to die. With the Cherry Laurel and the Portugal Laurel it is the main cause of the monotony and cheerless air of so many pleasure grounds.

The nurseryman who grows rare trees or shrubs very often finds them left on his hands, so that many nurseries only grow a few stereotyped things, mainly those that grow freely, and, owing to the over-use of weed-evergreens like Privet, are without beauty, and offensive in odour when in flower. The presence of such things is one of the causes of the miserable aspect of the shrubberies in many gardens, which might be very beautiful and interesting with a varied life. Many shrubs of little or no beauty in themselves very often destroy by their vigour the rare and beautiful garden vegetation, so that we have not only the ugliness of a brake of Laurel, or half-evergreen Privet, or Pontic Rhododendron to survey, but often the fact that these shrubs have overrun and killed far more precious things. And this nursery rubbish having killed every good thing begins to eat up itself, and hence we see so many shrubberies worn out.

It is not only the ill-effect of these all-devouring evergreens we have to consider, but that they shut out the evergreen flowering shrubs and trees of the highest beauty of colour as well as of foliage, and the many hardy Rhododendrons of finest colour. If we would only cease to graft them, and instead get them from layers on their own roots, we should not be overcrowded with the R. ponticum of the present system. They are not only hardy, in the sense that many of our popular evergreens are hardy in favoured districts or by the sea, so kind as it is to evergreens, but they are hardy everywhere in England. I mean the many broad-leaved Rhododendrons which have mostly come to us from the wild American species, and are hardy in North and Eastern America. Apart from the use of such things, by carefully selecting their colours we may have not merely an evergreen background of fine and varied green, but also the most precious flowering shrubs ever raised by man and in their natural forms, often varying in fine colour and form too, if we will only cease to compel them to live on one mean and too vigorous shrub.

As to the kinds of Rhododendron that are raised from the Pontic kind, or even from the Indian Rhododendrons, so far as tried they are not in any way so good as the varieties raised from the North American kinds, which have the fine constitution of R. Catawbiense in them, and of which many are hardy not merely in Old England but in the much more severe winters of New England. Apart from plants of these kinds from layers we may also have them as seedlings, though the named kinds from layers give us the means of grouping a finely coloured kind which may often be desirable. It is also very probable that we shall, as various regions of the northern world are opened up, introduce to cultivation other fine wild species, and get precious races from them, so for many reasons the sooner we get out of the common routine of the nurseries in grafting every fine kind we already have on R. ponticum, the better.

Apart from trees of poor forms, there are others which are stately in their own country but a doubtful gain to ours, like the Wellingtonia and other Californian trees and the Chili Pine. Sometimes the foregrounds of even fine old houses are marred by such trees, and unfortunately people use them in the idea that they are by their use doing something old-fashioned and "Elizabethan," whereas they are marring the beauty of the landscape and of our native trees, often so fine, beyond the bounds of the garden. We ought not to spoil the beauty of our home landscapes by using such things, which are so abundant in many places that the nobler exotic evergreen trees like the evergreen Oak are forgotten. This European tree from Holkham in Norfolk to the west of England and in many gardens round the coasts of our islands, is a great evergreen tree and a fine background and shelter.

The Cedar of Lebanon is perhaps the finest evergreen tree ever brought to our country and as hardy as our own trees. If we use ever-green trees they ought to be the noblest and hardiest. The loss of this tree by storms could not happen to anything like the same extent if peo-ple went on planting young trees. The many catalogues issued help to-wards the neglect of the really precious trees by bringing out novelties from all parts of the world—absolutely unproved trees; whilst the plant-ing of such grand trees as the Cedar of Lebanon and the Ilex of Europe are often forgotten. A mistake made in Cedar planting is that of only planting isolated trees with great branches on all sides, an enormous surface exposed to strong wind. In their own country, where Cedars are naturally massed together, although the gales are severe, the trees are not destroyed by wind in anything like the same degree. The Cedar of Lebanon is beautiful in the "specimen" way, but it is at least equally beautiful massed in groups. In their own countries, in addition to being massed and grouped together, the soil is often stony and rocky, the growth is slower, and the trees take a firmer hold, whereas in our river valleys, where the Lebanon Cedar is often planted in an isolated way, the growth is softer and the resistance to wind less, and a more artistic and natural way of planting would lessen the accidents to which this noblest of evergreen trees is exposed.

Few countries are so rich in the means of shelter as our own, owing to the evergreens that grow freely with us and thrive in seashore and wind-swept districts. Shelter may be near flower-beds and distant or wind-breaks, across the line of prevailing winds, and the north and east winds, and may be of Yew, Holly, Cedar of Lebanon (never Deodar), native Fir, a few other hardy Firs, and the Ilex.

Among the kinds of shelter, walls, thickly clad with climbers, evergreens and others, are often the best for close garden work, because they do not rob the ground, as almost any evergreen tree will; and in doing their work, they themselves may bear many of our most beautiful flowers. Half-hardy evergreens, like the common Cherry Laurel and Portugal Laurel, should never be planted to shelter the garden, because they may get cut down in hard winters. Happily, even in the most exposed places, a good many hardy flowers may be grown with success, such as Carnations, Pinks, and many rock plants which lie close to the ground, and are therefore little exposed to wind, and thrive in exposed places where soil and cultivation are not against them.

Some are doubtful of planting near the sea, considering the bleak look of things and the cutting winds. Yet even in places where the few trees that are planted are cut sharp off by the sea wind above the walls, as in Anglesea, we may see how soon good planting will get over difficulties that seem insurmountable. By the use near the sea of small-leaved trees like the Tamarisks, Sea Buckthorn, and small Willows, we very soon get a bit of shelter, and by backing these with the close-growing conifers like our common Juniper and some of the sea-loving Pines, like Pinaster, and in mild southern and western districts the Californian Cypress and the Monterey Pine, we soon get shelter and companionship for our trees, and fifty yards away we may soon walk in woods as stately as in any part of the country. Having got our shelter in this way the growth of the hardy Pines of the northern world seems as easy by the sea as anywhere; indeed, more so, because if there is any one place where the rather tender Pines are grown well it is near the sea in places around our coast, where if the soil is good, one has not to be so careful about the hardiness of trees we select as we have to be in inland places.

The Evergreen Oak takes a lead among the trees near the sea, and it ought to be largely used; but as it is not very easily transplanted from nursery-bought plants, it is just as well to raise it on the place and plant it young. Seed may be scattered with some advantage in places we wish it to grow in, as it grows freely from seed.

The Evergreen Oak withstood the great gales of 1897 in the south and west of England better than any other tree. At Killerton and Knightshayes, and many other places where the destruction was greatest, the Evergreen Oak was not among the many victims. It is a precious tree for the south and west and all seashore districts, and should never be forgotten among the crowd of novelties. As with so many trees, it suffers from indiscriminate planting with other and sometimes coarser things, and is rarely grouped in any effective way, although here and there, as at Ham House, at Killerton, and at St Ann's, we may see the effect of holding this tree together.

In addition to the common evergreen trees of Europe, Scotch Fir, Spruce and Silver Firs, we have the noble Corsican Pine, which, from its habitat in Calabria and in Corsica, can have no objection to the sea. The Pines of the Pacific coast, too, are well used to its influences, and we see in our country good results from planting them near the sea, as, for example, Menzies' Spruce at Hunstanton, the Monterey Pine at Bicton, the Redwood in many places near the sea. One good result of planting in such places is that we may use so many evergreen trees, from the Holly to the Cedar, and so get a certain amount of warmth as well as shelter.

Though our country generally is not perhaps fitted for the growth of the Cork Oak, a fine evergreen tree, it is here and there seen in southern and sheltered parts on warm soils, as in certain parts of Devonshire and on the warm side of the Sussex Downs, even in good condition. Of this fact we have an example in the Cork Oaks at Goodwood, all that could be desired in health and beauty. This Oak naturally inhabits the southern parts of Europe and the northern parts of Africa, and it is interesting to see that it can attain the size of a stately tree in our own country in some favoured places, but the Evergreen Oak for our islands is the Ilex and its various forms.

Some Genera of Evergreen Trees and Shrubs Hardy in the British Isles[1]

Abies	Azara	Cedrus	Cryptomeria	Elæagnus
Aralia	Bambusa	Chamœrops	Cupressus	*Embothrium
Araucaria	*Benthamia	Choisya	Daphne	Ephedra
*Arbutus	Berberis	*Cistus	Daphniphyllum	Erica
Arundinaria	Buxus	Cotoneaster	*Desfontainea	Escallonia
Aucuba	Camellia	Cratægus	Diplopappus	Euonymus

*Fabiana	Leiophyllum	Pernettya	Retinospora	Taxus
Garrya	Leucothoe	Phillyrea	Rhamnus	Thuja
Gaultheria	Libocedrus	Phlomis	Rhododendron	Thujopsis
Hedera	Ligustrum	Phyllostachys	Rosmarinus	Ulex
Ilex	Magnolia	Pieris	Ruscus	Veronica
Juniperus	Myrica	Pinus	Sequoia	Viburnum
Kalmia	Olearia	Quercus	Skimmia	Vinca
Laurus	Osmanthus	Raphiolepis	Smilax	Yucca
Ledum				

¹ Some of those marked * are hardy only in seashore districts or warm soils, and in some genera named few species are evergreen.

CHAPTER XXXI

Clipping Evergreen and Other Trees

"Vous travaillez pour ainsi dire à côté de Dieu, vous n'êtes que les collaborateurs de la loi divine de la végétation. Dieu, dans ses œuvres immuable, ne se prête pas à nos chimères; la nature n'a pas de complaisance pour nos faux systèmes. Elle est souveraine, absolue comme son Auteur. Elle résiste à nos tentatives folles; elle déjoue, et quelquefois rudement, nos illusions. Elle nous seconde, elle nous aide, elle nous recompense, si nous touchons juste et si nous travaillons dans son sens vrai; mais si nous nous trompons, si nous voulons la violenter, la contraindre, la fausser, elle nous donne à l'instant même des dementis éclatants en faits par la stérilité, par le dépérissement, par la mort de tout ce que nous avons voulu créer en dépit d'elle et à l'inverse de ses lois."—LAMARTINE, DISCOURS AUX JARDINIERS.

The Yew in its natural form is the most beautiful evergreen of our western world—finer than the Cedar in its feathery branching, and more beautiful than any Cedar in the colour of its stem. In our own day we see trees of the same great order as the Yew gathered from a thousand hills—from British Columbia, through North America and Europe to the Atlas Mountains, and not one of them has yet proved to be so beautiful as our native Yew when unclipped root or branch. But in gardens the quest for the exotic is so active that few give a fair chance to the Yew as a tree, while in graveyards, where it is so often seen in a very old state, the cutting of the roots hurts the growth, though there are Yews in our churchyards that have seen a thousand winters. It is not my own idea only that I urge here, but that of all who have ever thought of the beauty of trees, foremost among whom we must place artists who have the happiness of always drawing natural forms. Let anyone stand near the Cedar-like Yews by the Pilgrim's Way on the North Downs, and, comparing them with trees cut into fantastic shapes, consider what the difference means to the artist who seeks beauty of tree form!

What right have we to deform things so lovely in form? No cramming of Chinese feet into impossible shoes is half so foolish as the wilful and brutal distortion of the beautiful forms of trees. The cost of this mutilation alone is one reason against it, as we see where miles of trees cut into walls have to be clipped, as at Versailles and Schönbrunn. This shearing is a mere "survival" of the day when we had very few trees, and they were clipped to fit the crude notion of "garden design" of the day. The fact that men when they had few trees made them into walls to make them serve their ways of "design" is no reason why we, rich in the trees of all the hills of the north, should go on mutilating them.

While it may be right to clip a tree to form a dividing-line or hedge, it is never so to clip trees grown for their own sakes, as by shaving such we only get ugly, unnatural forms. Men who trim with shears or knife so fine a *tree* as the Holly are dead to beauty of form and cannot surely have seen how fine in form old Holly trees are. To give us such ugly forms in gardens is to show one's self callous to beauty of tree form, and to prove that one cannot even see ugliness. The Cherry Laurel in its natural shape in the woods is often fine in form; but it is planted everywhere in gardens without thought of its fitness for each place, and as it grows apace, the shears are called in, and its shoots are cut into ugly banks and formless masses. There is no place in which it is clipped for which we could not get shrubs of the desired size that would not need the shears.

Now and then we see attempts on the part of those with more knowledge of some half-mechanical grade of decorative "design" than of beautiful form to galvanise the corpse of the topiary art. Such an idea would not occur to anyone knowing the many beautiful things now within our reach, nor to any landscape-painter who studies beautiful forms of earth or trees or flowers, nor to any lover of Nature in tree or flower. Sometimes these puerilities are set into book form. For one author there is no art in gardening, but cutting a tree into the shape of a cocked hat is "art," and he says:—

> I have no more scruple in using the scissors upon tree or shrub, where trimness is desirable, than I have in mowing the turf of the lawn that once represented a virgin world ... and in the formal part of the garden my Yews should take the shape of pyramids, or peacocks, or cocked hats, or ramping lions in Lincoln green, or any other conceit I had a mind to, which vegetable sculpture can take.

After reading this I thought of some of the true "vegetable sculpture" that I had seen; Reed and Lily, models in stem and leaf; the Grey Willows of Britain as lovely against our British skies as Olives are in the south; many-columned Oak groves set in seas of Primroses, Cuckoo flowers, and Violets; Silver Birch woods of Northern Europe beyond all grace possible in stone; the eternal garland of beauty that one kind of Palm waves for hundreds of miles throughout the land of Egypt—a vein of summer in a lifeless world; the noble Pine woods of California and Oregon, like fleets of colossal masts on mountain waves—these and many other lovely forms in garden and wood, and then wondered that anyone could be so blind to the beauty of the natural forms of plants and trees as to write as this author does.

From the days of the Greeks to our own time, the delight of all great artists has been to get as near this divine beauty as what they work in permits. But this deplorable *vegetable sculptor's* delight is in distorting beautiful forms; and this in the one art in which we have the happiness of possessing the living things themselves, and not merely representations of them. The old people from whom he takes his ideas were not so foolish, as when the Yew was used as a hedge or was put at a garden gate it was necessary to clip it to keep it in bounds. Apart from the ugliness of the cocked-hat tree, or other pantomimic trees the want of life and change in a garden made up of such trees should open the eyes of any one to its drawbacks, as in it there is none of the joy of spring, or summer's crown of flowers, or winter's rest.

In old days, whether in a manor house or castle garden, the use of Yew hedges had some clear motive of shelter or division, or clothing against massive walls as at Berkeley, or at a cottage door as a living shelter. But when we use Yew hedges from the mere desire for them, and without much thought of the ground or other reasons, we may find ourselves in trouble. At a place where Roses were earnestly sought, the Rose borders were backed up close by Yew hedges; the Yews were not very troublesome the first year or two, but, as they grew, they became merciless robbers. There are many ways of growing Roses, but it would be difficult to invent any worse way than this, which leaves the gardener always "between the devil and the deep sea," trying to keep back the hungry Yew roots all the while, it being quite easy to secure a background which, instead of eating up the Roses, would support and shelter them beautifully, walls, Oak palings, other trellises, or espaliers of bushy climbers, like Honeysuckle and Clematis.

Another bad way is to place lines of Yew hedges so close together that the sun can hardly sweeten the ground between them, this being generally the result of carrying out some book plan, without thought of the ground or its use. More stupid still is cutting up level lawns with Yew hedges across them, or sometimes projected into them a little way, with flower-beds in between, within a couple of feet of the all-devouring Yew, all this very costly Yew planting working for ugliness, and against the health, and even life, of all the flowers near.

It is not only the needs of our own greatly increased garden flora—new races of plants never known to the old people, such as our Tea Roses and the rich collections of shrubs from Japan and other countries, that will not bear mutilation or robbing at the root—that should make us pause, as, even in what remains to us of old flower gardens on ancient tapestries and pictures, we may see some evidence that the lady had room in her flower garden to look around and work among her flowers, unencumbered by a maze of robbing hedges. Some, perhaps, of these close lines of Yews, set with such little thought, owe their origin to the maze idea; but the maze was for a wholly different end, and in it we have only to grow its trees and the paths are free for the roots. In the Rose and flower garden the cost and care to get an artistic and beautiful result are too heavy to have them eaten up before our eyes by the hungriest of tree roots.

A gardener with shears in his hand is generally doing fool's work, but there is much difference between his clipping old or sheltering lines of Yews, or even the peacocks in Box, and the clipping which goes on in some gardens where beds are filled with small evergreen bushes instead of flowers. Some effect may be obtained in a way, but the bushes usually get far too thick, and then the shears are used to keep them in bounds, and what ought to be graceful groups of flowers or shrubs of good form becomes flat, hard, and ugly. The clipping may have been designed at first, but oftener it is done to repress overgrowth. A more stupid way of filling the beds of a flower garden could hardly be imagined, because we lose all the grace and form of the shrubs, and also the chance of seeing flowers growing among them. It is one of the prettiest phases of flower gardening when Lilies, Gladioli, and other graceful plants spring from groups of choice evergreens. The end of all this laborious mutilation is to cause disease and overcrowding, and the best thing is to clear the deformed things away and plant in more natural ways. If we want flower-beds, let us have them; by doing so we can have varied life for more than half the year. If we want beds of choice evergreens we can have them without destroying their forms by the shears.

Recently magazines and illustrated journals, in the great chase after subjects, have dealt with the clipped gardens of England, and some of the most ridiculous work ever perpetrated in this way has been chosen for illustration. Of English counties, Derbyshire is the most notorious for examples of disfigured trees. The Dutch, who painted like nature, and built like sane men, left their plantations to the shears, but they always cut to lines or had some kind of plan judging from their old engraved books. British clipping has one phase which has no relation to any plan, and in so far exceeds in extravagance the methods of the Dutch, Austrian, and French, and that is the clipping single, and often forest, trees into the shape of green bolsters. A false idea runs through all growers of trees of the Pine tribe, the most frequent victims of the practice, that these trees should be kept in a conical shape, the truth being that all the Pine trees in the world in their state of highest beauty lose their lower branches, and show the beauty of their stem and form when growing in their natural way. With a few exceptions, it is the way of these trees to shed their lower branches as other trees shed their leaves. In countries where Pines often stand alone, as on the foothills of California, I have seen them with 100 feet or more of clean stem.

We are told that Elvaston is not remarkable for natural beauty and that the grounds there are so flat that landscape-gardeners, in despair of any other planting, are compelled to have recourse to topiary work; that "even that man of fame, 'Capability' Brown, seems to have shrunk from the work of laying out the grounds. Whereupon the earl demanded his reason, and Brown replied, 'Because the place is so flat,' &c."

Now, level ground has a great deal in it that is favourable to artistic ways of planting. With such ground we may more easily secure breadth, simplicity, and dignity, get dividing lines in the easiest way, richer soil and finer and more stately growth and nobler shelter. Many of the most beautiful gardens of Europe are on level ground, as Laxenberg in Vienna, the English garden in Munich, not to speak of many in our own river valleys and in counties like Lincolnshire. What would be said of planting in all the flat countries of Northern Europe if the assertion were true that we cannot make level ground beautiful by planting in natural ways, to say nothing of the absurdity of assuming that the only way out of the difficulty is in the stupid disfigurement of trees?

First of all is the loss of tree form—a wonderful and beautiful gift, so beautiful, indeed, that the marvel is that we should have to allude to it at all, as in nearly every parish in England one has only to walk one hundred yards or so to come face to face with fine examples of good tree form. There is more strength and beauty of line in many an Ash tree by a farmhouse yard than in all the clipped trees in Britain. Some protest against the cropping and docking of animals' ears and tails, but, when the worst is done in that way, the dog or the horse remains in full beauty of form in all essential parts, but if we clip a noble tree, which in natural conditions is a lesson in lovely form in all its parts, we reduce it at once to a shapeless absurdity.

The second great loss is that of light and shade, which are very important elements of beauty. These are entirely neutralised by shaving trees to a level surface, whether the trees take the form of a line, or we clip them singly, as in the British phase of tree clipping. If we see old examples of the natural Yew, a forest tree, and the commonest victim of the shears among evergreen forest trees, and if we look at them in almost any light, we may soon see how much we lose by destroying light and shade, as the play of these enhances the force and beauty of all the rest.

The third objection is the loss of refined colour. In gardens we are so much concerned with garish colour that we often fail to consider the more delicate colours of nature, and such fine tone as we see in a grove of old Yews, bronzed by the winter, or in Ilex with the beautiful silver of the leaf, or a grove of coral-bearing Hollies. All the favourite trees used for clipping are far more beautiful in colour in a natural state; the loss of the stem colour alone is a great one, as we may see wherever old Yews show their stems.

In the movement of these trees stirred by the wind, and the gentle sighing of their branches, we have some most welcome aspects of tree life. In groves of Ilex, as at Ham House, and masses of the same tree, as at St Ann's, the effect of the motion of the branches is to many a beautiful one. This movement is also of great beauty in groves of old Yew trees, and is seen in every Cedar and Pine that pillars the hills. The voice of the wind in these trees is one of the most grateful sounds in nature, and has often inspired the poet.

> "I see the branches downward bent,
>   Like keys of some great instrument."

And even when the storm is past we hear delicate music in the free Pine tips.

> "What noise is this? what low and solemn tone,
>   Which, though all wings of all the winds seem furled,
> Nor even the zephyr's fairy flute is blown,
> Makes thus for ever its mysterious moan
>   From out the whispering Pine-tops' shadowy world?
>
> Ah, can it be the antique tales are true?
>   Doth some lone Dryad haunt the breezeless air,
> Fronting yon bright immitigable blue,
> And wildly breathing all her wild soul through
>   That strange unearthly music of despair?
>
> Or, can it be that ages since, storm-tossed,
>   And driven far inland from the roaring lea,
> Some baffled ocean spirit, worn and lost,
> Here, through dry summer's dearth and winter's frost,
>   Yearns for the sharp sweet kisses of the sea?"

The fifth objection is that the constant mutilation of trees leads to disease not unfrequently, as may be seen at Versailles. In the Derbyshire examples the stems of dead Pines are shown in the pictures! It is simply an end one might expect from the annual mutilation of a forest tree, which the Yew certainly is, as we see it among the Cedars on the mountains of North Africa, as well as in our own country and in Western Europe. Other trees of the same great Pine order are yet more impatient of the shears, and some of them, like the Cedar, escape solely because of their dignity. However, we distort the Yew, which is in nature sometimes as fine as a Cedar.

The maze is an inheritance from a past time, but not a precious one, being one of the notions about gardening which arose when people had very little idea of the infinite beauty of the garden flora as we now know it. Some people may be wealthy enough to show us all the beauty of a garden and at the same time such ugly frivolities as this, but they must be few. The maze is not pretty as part of a home landscape or garden, and should be left for the most part to places of the public tea-garden kind. One of its drawbacks is the death and distortion of the evergreens that go to form its close lines, owing to the frequent clipping; if clipping be neglected the end is still worse, and the whole thing is soon ready for the fire.

CHAPTER XXXII

Lawns and Playgrounds

The lawn is the heart of the true British garden, and of all forms of garden the freest and, may be, the most varied and charming, adapted as it is to all sorts of areas from that around the smallest house. It is above all things the English form of garden made best in the rich level valley land, and, with the least amount of trouble and labour to make or keep it, certainly gives the best result in effect. The terrace garden we have seen, in its origin and best meaning, arises from wholly different sort of ground from that on which we make a lawn. If the Italians and others who built on hills to avoid malaria had had healthy and level ground they would have been very glad of it, and thought it beautiful. With the lawn there is little or no trouble in securing fine background effects, variety, pretty dividing lines, recesses for any favourites we may have in the way of flowers, freedom, relief, air, and breadth. There is room on the lawn for every flower and tree, from the Cedar, and the group of fruit trees planted for the beauty of their flowers and fruit, down to rich beds of Lilies.

One of the most foolish dogmas ever laid down about a garden is that made in a recent book by an architect, in which we are told emphatically that there is no such thing as a garden to be made except within four walls. Many of the most beautiful gardens in the British Isles are without any other aid than a background of trees and evergreens, with no trace of walls, which are absolutely needless in many situations to get the most artistic results in a garden. And lovely gardens may be made around lawns without marring the breadth and airiness which is the charm of a lawn, or in the least interfering with the use of its open parts as a playground.

Where there is space enough there are reasons in country places for cutting off by a hedge a playground from the garden or pleasure ground, as is done at Madresfield and Campsey Ash and many of the older gardens; and what is used generally is the Yew or Holly, but clipped hedges give little shade and no flowers. Now, in the like position, if we adopt the pergola, we get shade, and many graceful flowers. Clematis, tall Roses, Wistaria, and almost every beautiful climber could be grown thereon, some better than on walls, because we can allow for more *abandon* than on walls, and it is not at all so easy to crucify Vine or climber on a pergola. We can have evergreens, too, if we wish, with garlands of handsome Ivies among them, and players might rest in the shade and lookers on sit there to see the play. Various bold openings should be made on the play lawn side, and the whole so arranged as to be a sort of living cloister. Well done, the structure might be, apart from its shade and coolness and use as a dividing line, a garden of a very graceful kind, while the recent hot seasons lead one to think that the Italian way of putting a roof of Vine leaves between one's self and the sun is worth carrying out in our own country.

Pergolas have various uses in covering paths which are too much exposed to the sun, and are a great aid in the garden, and there is no better way of growing beautiful climbing plants than a green covered way, whether supported by Oak posts, or brick or stone pillars as in Italy. The covered ways made in England are often too narrow. In forming all such things a certain amount of freedom is essential; and we cannot enjoy the air in the usual narrow covered way, which, apart from its own error as to size, is also soon narrowed by growth. Where Oak is not distinctly preferred, 14-in. brick pillars are best, and the plants take to them very soon. Common brown or rough stock bricks are far better for this use than showy red bricks. In stone districts stone would do better, and it needs no fine dressing or designing after any pattern. It is better in fact done in the free way the Italians do it; but then in Italy every man is a mason, or knows what to do with stone, and also the stone there comes out in long posts or flakes, which serve as posts. This is also the case in the north of England, where beautiful posts of the green stone may be seen in use on the farms.

The beautiful climbing shrubs and other plants that would find a good congenial home on such a pergola are a good reason for its use. Among them various graceful forms of our Grape Vine, as well as the Japanese and American wild Vines, a group which now includes the Virginian creepers of our gardens, which are also useful, but not so good as the true Vines; the lovely Wistaria, and not only the old Chinese kind, the best of all, but the beautiful Japanese long-racemed kind (*W. multijuga*); and various others too, though we think none comes near to these in beauty; the brilliant Flame Nasturtium in cool districts; the Green Briar (Smilax) of America and also the South of Europe, for warm soils; handsome double and white-stemmed Brambles; wild and single Roses; Box Thorn, with its brilliant showers of berries; European, American and Japanese Honeysuckles; Jasmines; over fifty kinds of Ivy, the noblest of northern and evergreen climbers; evergreen Thorn, with its bright berries; Cotoneasters of graceful habit; Clematises, especially the graceful wild kinds of America, Europe, and North Africa. In mild districts particularly, the winter-blooming Clematis of North Africa and the Mediterranean Islands, which flowers in winter or early spring, would be very pretty and give light shade. The showy trumpet flowers (*Bignonia*), quite hardy in southern and midland counties; and the Dutchman's pipe (*Aristolochia*), with its large leaves, would also be useful. The fine-leaved Lardizabala of Chili, the brilliant coral Barberry of the same country (*Berberidopsis*); the graceful, if not showy silk Vine (*Periploca*) of Southern Europe; the Chinese Akebia, the use of the rarer climbers depending much on the climate, elevation, soil, and nearness to the sea.

An alternative to the Yew hedge and the covered way is the plashed alley, but in some Elizabethan gardens it was often planted with trees of too vigorous growth, such as the Lime, which led to excessive mutilation and eventual distortion of the tree. Now, with our present great variety of trees, some of them very graceful and light in foliage, it is by no means necessary to resort to such ugly mutilation; and it would be easy, as an alternative to the pergola, the clipped hedge or the plashed alley, to have a shaded walk of medium-sized or low trees only. These might even be fruit trees; but the best would be such elegant-leaved trees as the Acacias, which preserve their leaves for a long time in summer. One drawback of the Lime, in addition to its excessive vigour, is the fact that it sheds its leaves very early in the autumn, and, indeed, we have often seen the leaves tumble off in St James's Park at the end of July, and in Paris also. It is most unpleasant to have in an alley a tree which is liable to such an early loss of its leaves. The common Lime is a tree of the mountains and cool hills of Europe, and it cannot endure great heats and hot autumns; whereas some of the trees of North America and other countries are quite fresh in the hottest days. Among these none is better than the Acacia, of which, in France especially, a number of elegant varieties have been raised, as hardy as the parent species which charmed William Cobbett, but more graceful in foliage. Among the best of these is the Mimosa-leaved Acacia, an elegant tree, which gives us a pleasantly shaded walk, and yet is not likely ever to become too coarse in habit.

Fine turf is essential in and near the house and garden—turf wholly apart from the open park or playground. Flower-beds are often set in turf, or there are small grassy spaces near the house or the garden on the good effect of which depends very much the beauty of the home landscape, as coming so much into the foreground of what should be pictures. One reason why we should take care to get the best turf which the conditions of soil or climate allow is that no other country but ours can have such good turf. In many countries, even in Europe, they cannot have it at all, but grass seed has to be sown every year to get some semblance of turf. Where, however, our natural advantages are so great, our care should be to get the full benefit of them; and though in many places the turf, through the goodness of the soil, is all that could be desired even in Britain, in others a very poor turf is often seen, and much effort is often given in vain attempts to get a turf worthy of a flower garden.

Many people think that any rough preparation will secure them a good sward, and merely trench and turf the ground; even experienced ground workmen fail to get a fine turf for the flower garden, though they may lay turf well enough for a cricket ground. Others think that turf will come of itself, but are often rudely disappointed; and therefore some instructions as to the best way of laying down turf, where the work has to be done from the beginning, and also for repairing it when out of order, may be useful to some readers. The following is written by Mr James Burnham, who has made for me some of the most beautiful garden lawns I have seen, some of them laid in hot spring weather.

"Should the spot chosen be on heavy soil, such as clay, take the levels and fix them 16 feet apart around the outside of the piece intended for a lawn. Take some levels across the piece, then take 12 inches of earth out below the levels. Should any of these 12 inches contain good soil, wheel that on to the outside of the piece, removing all the clay to a place near and burning it into ballast, using slack coal. Find the natural fall of the ground, and place pegs 16 feet apart in lines from top to bottom the way it falls, then dig out the soil in line of pegs with a draining tool, 12 inches deep at top end, bottom end 18 inches deep. This will give a fall of 6 inches. Then lay in 2-inch drain pipes, with a 3-inch pipe at the bottom end for a main to take the water that drains from the sub-soil. See that this main is taken to some outlet. Cover the pipes with 3 inches of burnt ballast, and spread 3 inches of burnt ballast all over the piece of ground. Dig the ground over 12 inches deep, at the same time mixing the 3 inches of burnt ballast with the clay, taking care not to disturb the pipes or dig below them. After treading all over firmly, place on the surface 2 inches of burnt ballast, filling to the level with loam mixed with the good soil you have laid on one side from the surface. If you have no good soil, fill up with loam mixed with coarse gravel, brick rubbish, and burnt ballast. Tread all over again as before, making it level with a spade, pressing in any lump or stone that appears level with the ground. No rake should be used. You have now 2 feet of trenched earth. Do not dig down deeper in one place than another. A stick cut 2 feet long by the worker's side is the best. He can, with the stick, test his depth from time to time.

"In laying the turf keep the joints of each piece half-an-inch apart. When it is all laid down pat it gently all over with a turf-beater. It is better to take up the turf that is a little higher than the rest and take out a little of the soil than to beat it down to the level. Then spread some burnt ballast, ashes from the burnt refuse of the garden, and the top 2 inches of soil from the wood sifted through a half-inch mesh sieve, mixed well together, all over the grass. Move it about until all the joints in the turf are level. Wait for rain, then go over the lawn and take out all weeds. Give another dressing of the soil as before, adding to this a little road grit and old mortar. If no old mortar is available, slaked lime will answer. Move this about until all is level again. In the month of March or the first week in April, if the weather is fine, sow all over the lawn some of the best lawn grass seed. Get some fine Thorn bushes and lace them together in the shape of a fan heavy enough for two men to drag about the lawn in various ways. Roll with a light roller, and keep off the lawn until the grass has grown 3 inches, then cut it with a scythe. Roll with a light roller the first season, and when mowing with the machine see that the knives are not set too close to the ground.

"Should the ground selected for turf not contain clay, so much the better. Dig holes here and there 2 feet deep in the winter months. If no water lies at the bottom of the holes, this shows it will not want artificial draining; if there is water drain as on heavy soil. In trenching the ground, if the sub-soil be bad, take 3 inches of this away, filling up to the level with good soil, to which have been added half-inch crushed bones in the proportion of four tons to the acre, fire-brick rubbish and burnt ballast in the same proportions as for the heavy soil. Turf and treat as on heavy soil. If you have a good grass field, take the turf for your lawn, also top spit away, replace with rough soil, and place 3 inches of the loam that has been dug out upon the rough soil you have put in, then sow, bush harrow, and lightly roll.

"Weeds, moss, and bare places on lawns show that they are worn out. To remedy this, take off the turf in rolls 3 feet long, 1 foot wide, and 1 inch thick. If the turf cannot be rolled, take 6 inches of the surface away, then trench 2 feet deep, keeping the good soil on the top as you proceed. Tread firmly all over and fill up to the level with good soil; mix with the loam, burnt ballast, old brick rubbish, half-inch crushed bones, and road sidings or sweepings. Then turf and treat as in the case of new lawns. On old lawns there are very often handsome deciduous trees too close to which it would be dangerous to trench. To get grass to grow under these, take away 2 inches of the exhausted soil, replace with good, and sow thereon grass seed thickly. Rake the seed in gently, roll it lightly, and water when necessary. This may be repeated in the same way as often as the soil under the trees becomes bare.

"In some cases where turf is scarce, a roll of turf 3 feet long and 1 foot wide may be taken and cut in half lengthways. With this form the outlines of the beds, which have been staked out previously, beat down to the level required, and bring up the intervening spaces to the level of the turf with good soil. Make this firm, rake it level, and on this sow some good grass seed. Bush harrow it over, roll lightly, and protect from birds where these are troublesome. Cut the grass when 6 inches high with a scythe, and keep it well watered during the summer if the weather is dry. In this way a beautiful lawn may be had at little expense as compared with turfing it completely over.

"In some parts of Hampshire and Surrey, where peat and sand abound, seeds are by far the best to use to form a good turf. Remove all peat from the site you wish for a lawn, pile it on the outside of the work and cast plenty of water upon it. Then take out 2 or 3 inches of the dark sand that lies under the peat, and cast this also over the pile of peat. Take out 12 inches of the sand, dig all over 12 inches deep and tread it firmly. Get all the road scrapings and road trimmings to be had with a little clay and stiff loam, and cast upon the peat pile. Having got together the quantity you think will fill up to your level, cut up small the peat you have in the pile and mix all well together with this, fill up to the level, tread firmly all over, then give everywhere a good coating of cow manure, turned 3 inches under the surface, and tread firmly all over. In the month of March sow thickly. Do not let the surface get dry the first summer, and cut the grass when 6 inches high with a scythe.

"Attention should be paid to keeping all lawns free from weeds. Dress lawns once a year with one bushel of salt mixed with fourteen bushels of wood ashes not too much burnt, using for this purpose refuse, underwood, waste faggots, old Laurels or other condemned shrubs. When you see the wood is consumed spread the ashes abroad and cover them with good soil. Break the charred wood small, mix all well together, do not sift, spread upon the lawn, and roll it in."

CHAPTER XXXIII

Garden Houses, Bridges, Gates, Fences, and Roads

Isolated building in a garden is difficult to do with any good result. At one period the building of temples was very common in pleasure gardens, and many of them are still to be seen. It is best, when these are of good form and structure, to keep them with care and make some simple use of them, by removing at once all suggestion of the grotto and having simple Oak benches or other good seats. The interior also should be made simple in colour and free from covert for wood-lice or earwigs. It is in connection with the house, or part of its lower storeys, that garden shelters, loggias, and the like may be best made; of this we see examples at North Mymms and Bramshill, and where they give shade or a "garden room" as part of the house they are a real gain.

Few things about country houses and gardens are worse in effect and construction than the so-called "rustic work." It is complex and ugly, its merit being that it rots away in a few years. It is probably at its worst in garden chairs, summer-houses, and rustic bridges. An important rule for bridges is never to make them where they are not really needed, though the opposite course is followed almost in every place of any size where there is water. On rustic bridges over streams, natural or otherwise, there is much wasted labour.

Some of the worst work ever done in gardens has been in the construction of needless bridges, often over wretched duck-ponds of small extent. Even people who have some knowledge of country life, and who ought to possess taste, come to grief over bridge building, and sheets of water are disfigured by bridges ugly in form and material. For the most frivolous reasons these ugly things are constructed, though often by going ten yards further one could have crept round the head of the pond by a path.

But there are many cases where some kind of bridge is necessary in pleasure grounds or woodlands. The difficulty of the woodwork bridge is that it begins to rot as soon as it is put up, that rot and decay are all we get out of it, and very often such bridges fall into such a dangerous state before we have time to repair them, that animals may get into danger.

A much better way is the earth-bank, with a drain pipe through, and this suffices where there is a slight flow of water, and also to cross gorges. We can find the earth to make it on the spot, and by punning, and in the case of larger work of this kind, carting over it, we can get it to settle down in one winter to the level we want it, and soon have a permanent way across. Such banks will support any weight, and are as free from decay as the best stone bridge. One of their best points is that the sides and approaches and slope of the earth-bank can be made pretty at once by planting with Honeysuckle, Broom, Sweet Brier, or any other hardy things. The materials being on the spot, it is needless to cart things a long way. By making a culvert of bricks, the earth-bank is equally good to cross constantly running streamlets. The drain should be large enough to carry any spate and let it pass. For a large drain crossing the road to house, the concrete (reinforced) tubes we get from Northampton are excellent.

The summer-house is generally a failure and often a heap of decay. To make such a structure of wood that soon decays is labour wasted. It may be possible, by using the best woods and good Oak slabs, to make a summer-house which will be picturesque and enduring, but it is better to build it of stone or some lasting material.

One can make an enduring and charming summer-house out of living trees. An old Yew or a group of old Yews, or a low-spreading Oak (there is a fine example of this kind of living summer-house at Shrubland), an old Beech or a group of evergreen Oaks will make a pleasant summer-house, and with a little care for effect, and by pruning away old and worn-out branches, so as to get air and room without injuring the beauty of the trees, it is easy to form cool tents for hot days.

The iron fence destroys the beauty of half the country seats in England, and the evil is growing every day. There are various serious objections to iron fencing, but we will only deal here with its effect on the landscape. Any picture is out of the question with an iron fence in the foreground. Where an open fence is wanted, nothing is so fine in form and colour as a split Oak fence and rails made of heart of Oak with stout posts. A sawn wood fence is not so good. As Oak is so plentiful on many estates, good examples of split Oak post and rail fences should be more often seen. Oak palings are often used, and sometimes where a good live fence of Holly, Quick and wild Rose on a good bank would be far better; but Oak paling is often a precious aid in a garden as a dividing line where the colour of brick or other walls would be against their use or where for various reasons walls would not do.

Sunk fences of stone or brick are often of the highest value in the pleasure ground, and sometimes near the flower garden, as they help us to avoid the hideous mechanical fences of our day, and are often the best way of keeping open views, especially if planted with a garland of creeping plants or wild roses above. They should be strongly if roughly built, without mortar, and they may be a home for beautiful plants. They should be made on a "batter" or slightly sloping back, the stones packed close together, *i.e.* without much earth, and layers of rock plants should be put between them. Retaining walls could be made in this way, and where they permit of it may be made into beautiful alpine gardens. Apart from the sunk fence, there is often need for low retaining walls, especially in places of diversified surface. These walls also may be made the home of delightful plant beauty in the simplest way.

It is rare to see a garden seat that is not an eyesore. Few make them well and simply in wood, and there is always decay to be considered. Of our own woods Oak is the best. Oak is best without paint and in the natural colour of the Oak wood. No seat is so good as one of good stone simply designed and strongly made, and in our country one objection to stone is met by the use of a mat or a light trellis of Bamboo or split laths of Oak held together by cross pieces and placed on top of the stone. Stone seats should always be set on stone supports bedded in concrete. A good Oak seat is one with strong stone supports, the top being a slab of Oak laid with two bars across its lower side to keep it in place. The top in this form being so easily removed, may be stowed away for the winter, as wooden seats should always be. Sometimes old tree stumps help to make useful seats, and the bole of the tree, if cut, makes a very good rustic seat. Where stone is plentiful, as in many hill and other parts, it is often easy to make useful seats out of blocks of stone in rocky places.

The covered way may be a charming thing in a garden and make a home for climbers, as well as a shady way, and also form a valuable screen. Shade is more essential in other countries than in ours, and the Italian covered way is often a very picturesque object. The best material to make the supports of is rough stone or brick. On an enduring support like this the woodwork is more easily constructed afterwards. Simple rough stone posts may be had in certain quarries in the north of England, in the lake country, but in the absence of these it will be better to build columns of brick or stone than to trust to any wood. In all open-air work the enduring way is true economy, and though we cannot all readily get the hard green stone gate posts stained with yellow Lichen of the farms about Keswick, or the everlasting granite fence posts that one sees in Italy, we should make a stand against work which has to be done over and over again. Of woods, Oak free of sap-wood makes the best supports. By using Oak with stone or brick supports, a covered way may be made which will last for years without falling into decay as is the case with this kind of work when done with woods and without lasting supports.

A pretty way of supporting plants and forming covered ways is to use certain trees of a light and graceful character for supporting climbers, just as the Italians often support their Vines on living trees kept within bounds. Such trees as the Weeping Aspen, Weeping Birch, and fruit trees of graceful, drooping forms, would do well and would be worth having for their own sakes, while through the trees hardy climbers could freely run.

Among the things which are least beautiful in many gardens and pleasure grounds is the boathouse. Our builders are not simple in their ways, and are seldom satisfied with any one, good colour or material to make a house with, or even a boathouse, but every kind of ugly variegation is tried, so that harshness in effect is the usual result, where all should be simple and quiet in colour, as it is in boathouses on the Norfolk Broads made of reeds and rough posts. The simpler the better in all such work, using local material like Oak, which comes in so well for the posts, and reeds for the roof; but the simplest brickwork and brown tiles would be far better than the contrast of ugly colours which the modern builder both in France and England delights in. The place, too, should be carefully chosen and the building not conspicuous. To avoid the cost of railway carriage in the making of simple structures like boathouses, and also carting, which is such a costly matter in many districts, it is best to use materials of the estate or country. Little shelters for mowing machines, tools, and the like can be made with wood covered with Larch bark, as at Coolhurst, and a very pretty effect they have, besides being less troublesome to make than the heather or thatched roofs, especially in districts where the good thatcher is getting rare. And on the whole the best roof for any structure that has to last is of tiles of good colour: tiles made and tested in the locality being often the best.

I tried the shingle roof on boathouse and summer-house with disastrous result, much cost and no last! So I had to go to the stone roof done by the Colly Weston men.

Ill-made roads are often a cause of great expense and discomfort. In up and down country they need more care than level land, but in all cases they deserve thought if to last. The drive here was planned and made as well as we knew, but on one field above it a heavy rain broke through and swept off much of the surface, and several like accidents made us think more of the roads. It is best to have no roads more than are really needed for use. Give them a good stone base, and drain so that heaviest spates may get away harmless.

CHAPTER XXXIV

The Orchard Beautiful

The spirit of beauty was at the birth of the trees that give us the hardy fruits of the northern world—Crab, wild Plum, Pear, and Cherry—yielding back for us in their bloom the delicate colours of the clouds, and lovelier far in their flowers than Fig or Vine of the south. The old way of having an orchard near the house was a good one. Planted for use, it was precious for its beauty, and not only when the spring winds bore the breath of the blossoms of Cherry, Plum, Apple, and Pear, as there were the fruit odours too, and the early Daffodils and Snowdrops, and overhead the lovely trees that bear our orchard fruits—Apples, Pears, Cherries, Plums, Medlars, Damsons, Bullaces, and Quinces. To make pictures to last round the year, I should ask for many of these orchard trees on a few acres of ground, none the worse if too hilly for the plough; a belt of Hollies, Yew, and Fir on the cold sides to comfort trees and men; with careless garlands of Honeysuckle, Rose, and fragrant Clematis among them here and there, and in the fence bank plenty of Sweet Brier and Hawthorn. If we see fine effects where orchards are poorly planted with one kind of tree, as the Apple (in many country places in our islands there are no orchards worthy the name), what might not be looked for of an orchard in which the beauty of all our hardy fruit trees would be visible? If we consider the number of distinct kinds of fruit trees and the many varieties of each, we may get some idea of the pictures one might have in an orchard, beginning with the bloom of the Bullaces in the fence. The various Plums and Damsons are beautiful in bloom, as in the Thames valley and about Evesham. The Apple varies much in bloom, as may be seen in Kentish and Normandy orchards, where the flowers of some are of extraordinary beauty. The Pear, less showy in colour, the Medlar, so beautiful in flower and in foliage, and the Quince, so pretty in bloom in Tulip time, must not be forgotten. The Cherry is often a beautiful tree in its cultivated as well as wild forms, and the Cherry orchards in parts of Kent, as near Sittingbourne, are pictures when in bloom. There is no better work in a country place than choosing a piece of good ground to form an orchard; and a dozen acres are not too much in a country place where there is land to spare.

Some may be deterred by the fear that their soil is too poor, and planting is more successful on the fruit tree soils of Devon, Hereford, and Kent than in some other districts; but the difference in soils is no reason why some counties and districts should be bare of orchards. In many the soil is as good as need be, and indeed, in the country south of London, where much of the land is taken up with orchards, we may see the trees suffering more from drought in dry years than they do on the sandstone soils of Cheshire or in Ireland and Scotland, where there is a heavier rainfall. Few of our orchard trees require a special soil, and where chalky or warm soil occurs, the best way is to keep to the kinds of fruit it favours most. But though the orchard beautiful must be of trees in all their natural vigour, and of forms lovely in winter as in spring and summer, the trees must not be neglected, allowed to perish from drought, or become decayed from bug, scale or other pests, and it should be the care of those who enjoy their beauty to protect them from all such dangers. The idea that certain counties only are suited for fruit growing is erroneous, and need not deter us from planting orchards of the hardier trees and of good local kinds. Much of Ireland is as bare of orchards as the back of a stranded whale, but who could say this was the fault of the country?

Owing to the use of dwarfing stocks, fruit gardens and orchards are now beginning to show shapes of trees that are poor compared with the tall orchard tree. However much these dwarf and pinched shapes may appeal to the gardener in his own domain, in the orchard beautiful they have no place. For the natural form of all our fruit trees is good indeed, winter or summer. We know what the effect in flower-time is in the orchard pictures of such painters as Mark Fisher and Alfred Parsons, if we have not taken the trouble to see the finer pictures of the orchard themselves, seen best, perhaps, on dark and wet days in flower-time. Lastly, the effect of finely-coloured fruit on high trees is one of the best in our gardens. Therefore, in every case, whatever thinning of the branches we do, let the tree take its natural form, not only for its own sake or the greater beauty of natural form generally, but also for the interesting variety of form we get even among varieties sprung from the same species.

Clearly if we prune to any one ideal type of tree we can never see the interesting variety of form shown by the varieties of one species, as the Apple and Pear. Keeping to the natural form of each tree, moreover, does not in the least prevent thinning of the branches where overcrowded—the best way of pruning.

Never in the orchard, where the true way is to let the tree take its natural and mature form, should the practice of root pruning be allowed. Our orchard trees—especially the trees native of Britain like the Apple and the Pear—are almost forest trees in nature, and take some years first of all to make their growth and then mature it. In gardens for various reasons men try to get in artificial ways the fruit that Nature gives best at the time of maturity, so root pruning was invented, and it may have some use in certain soils and in limited gardens, but one would hardly think it would enter into people's heads to practise root pruning in the orchard; though the word is a catching one and leads people astray. I have several times had the question seriously put to me as to how to root prune forest trees—a case where all pruning is absurd in any proper sense save in the way effected by the forest itself. The trees in the orchard should be allowed to come freely to maturity, and in the way the years fly this is not a long wait. By planting well-chosen young trees every year the whole gradually comes into noble bearing, and the difference between the naturally grown and laden tree and one of the pinched root-pruned ones is great.

Cider orchards are picturesque in the west of England and in Normandy, and so long as men think any kind of fermented stuff good enough for their blood, cider has on northern men the first claim from the beauty of the trees in flower and fruit, and indeed throughout the year. The cider orchard also will allow us to grow naturally-grown trees and those raised from seed. Cider orchards are extremely beautiful, and the trees in them take fine natural forms. They have a charm, too, in the brightness of the fruit, and also one in the lateness of the blooms of some, many of the cider Apples flowering later than the orchard Apples. In some cider orchards near Rouen (Lyons-la-Forêt) I saw the finest, tallest, and cleanest trees were raised from seed; the owner, a far-famed cider grower, told me they were his best trees, and raised from seed of good cider Apples. If he found on their fruiting that they were what he wanted as cider Apples he was glad to keep them; if not, he cut their heads off and regrafted them with good cider sorts. These were free and handsome trees with good grass below them, just like the Cherry orchards in the best parts of Kent, where the lambs pick the early grass. But however beautiful such an orchard, clearly it will not give us the variety of form and beauty found in the mixed orchard, in which Cherry, Apple, Plum, Pear, Medlar, Quince, Walnut, and Mulberry take a place; there also the various interesting trees allied to our fruit trees might come in, such as the true and common Service tree, Almond, Cornelian Cherry, and Crab.

Where we made use of grafted trees—and generally there is no choice in the matter—we should always in the orchard use the most natural stock. It is much better to graft Pear trees on the wild Pear than on the Quince, a union harmful to the Pear on many soils. If we could get the trees on their own roots without any grafting it would often be much better, but we are slaves to the routine of the trade. The history of grafting is as old as the oldest civilisations—its best reason, the rapid increase of a given variety. In every country one or two fruit trees predominate, and are usually natives of the country, like the Apple in Northern Europe and the Olive in the South. When men found a good variety of a native fruit they sought to increase it in the quickest way, and so having learned the art of grafting, they put the best varieties on wild stems in hedgerows, or dug up young trees and grafted them in their gardens. The practice eventually became stereotyped into the production of the nursery practice of grafting many varieties of fruit trees on the same stock, often without the least regard to the lasting health and duration of the trees so grafted. In some cases when we use the wild form of the tree as a stock for the orchard tree we succeed; but grafting is the cause of a great deal of the disease and barrenness of our orchards. Where we graft, it is well to graft low; that is to say, in the case of cider Apples, for example, it is much safer and better to take a tree grafted close to the ground than grafted standard high, as the high graft is more liable to accident and does not make so fine a tree. In the orchard the good old practice of sowing the stone or pip of a fine fruit now and then may also be followed with interest.

Even in the good fruit counties like Kent one may see in dry years orchards starved from want of water, and the turf beneath almost brown as the desert. Where manure is plentiful it is well to use it as a mulch for such trees, but where it is not, we may employ various other materials for keeping the roots safe from the effects of drought.

Not only the tree roots want the water, but the roots of the competing grass suck the moisture out of the soil. The competition of the grass could be put an end to at once, and the trees very much nourished, by the use of any easily found mulching from materials which are often abundant in a country place. Among the best of these, where plentiful, is the common Furze, if cut down in spring and placed over the ground round the base of young or poor orchard trees. Next to furze, or even better, is the bracken, an excellent mulch for fruit and flower garden. It prevents the grass from robbing the trees and lets the water fall through to the ground, helping to keep it there, too, by preventing direct evaporation; moreover, the small leaves falling off nourish the ground. So, again, the sweepings of drives and of farm or garden yards are useful, and also any small faggots—often allowed to rot in the woods after the underwood is cleared. Then also there are the weeds and refuse of gardens of all kinds which form detestable rubbish heaps that would be much better abolished, and all cleanings from the garden placed directly over the roots of young orchard trees.

Even rank weeds, which swarm about yard and shrubberies would help, and one of the best ways to weaken them and help towards their destruction is by mowing them down in the pride of their growth in the middle of summer—nettles and docks, as the case may be—and instead of burning them or taking them to the rubbish heap use them over the tree roots. Even the weeds and long grass growing round the base of the trees, if mown and left on the ground, will make a difference in the growth and health of fruit trees. Such care is all the more needed if our orchard is upon poor or shaly soils in the drier counties; in naturally rich and deep soil we need it less.

For fences, living things are at once the most enduring, effective, and in the end the best. We see the hideous result of the ironmonger's fence in marring the foregrounds of many landscape pictures. Holly, Quick, or Cockspur Thorn, with a sprinkling of Sloe or Bullace here and there, give us the best orchard fence; once well made, far easier to keep up than the iron fence. Yew is a danger, and a hedge of it should never be planted where animals come near as they usually do the orchard, and if the Yew comes by itself, as it often will, it should be cut clean out and burnt as soon as cut down. Holly is the best evergreen orchard fence for our country, and we should be careful about getting the plants direct from a good nursery—clean seedling plants not much over a yard high. The best time to plant Hollies is in May if growing in the place, but on light soil plant in autumn; all the more need to do this if we bring the plants by rail. Unless the soil is very light I should make the fence on a bank, because a turf bank is itself such a good fence to begin with, and a free Holly hedge on a good bank with, perhaps, a Sloe here and there through it, is one of the prettiest sights of the land, and forms the best of shelters for an orchard in our country. Where shelter is much sought the hedge should not be clipped, and is much handsomer if free-grown. The orchard fence should not be cut in every year to a hard line, but Sloe, and May and Sweet Brier, and wild Rose left to bloom and berry, the hedge to be a shelter as well as a fence, and not trimmed oftener than every ten years or so. Then it should be cut down and woven together in the strong way seen in parts of Kent on the hills.

The English fruit garden is often a museum of varieties, many of them worthless and not even known to the owner. This is wrong in the garden, and doubly so in the orchard, where the fruit trees should be trees in stature and none of poor quality. Too many varieties is partly the result of the seeking after new kinds in the nurseries. In orchard culture we should be chary of planting any new kind, and with the immense number of Apples grown in our own country already, we may choose kinds of enduring fame. It is the more necessary to do this now when good Apples are coming from various countries, where men do not plant a collection when they want a crop of a few first-rate kinds. So we should in our orchards never plant single trees, but always, having chosen a good kind, plant enough to make it worth gathering. Local kinds and local circumstances often deserve the first attention, and some local kinds of fruit are among the best. When in doubt always end it by choosing kinds of proved quality rather than any novelties that may be offered. Any fruit requiring the protection of walls or in the least tender should never be put in the orchard. It is probable that some of the fruit trees of Northern and Central Europe, and Russia, would be well suited for our climate, but as yet little is known of these except that they are interesting and many of them distinct. The vigour of the tree should be considered and its fertility. Kinds rarely fertile are not worth having, always bearing in mind, however, that a good kind is often spoiled by a bad stock or by conditions unsuited to it.

The beauty of flower of certain varieties may well influence in their choice. Once when talking with Mr Ruskin of the beauty of the fruit as compared with the flower of our northern fruit trees, he said in reply to some praise of the fruit beauty: "Give me the flower and spare me the stomach-ache!"

In view of the confusion brought about by fat catalogues, new varieties of doubtful value, the number of early kinds worthless for winter and spring use, and the planting of untried kinds, a good rule would be to put any kind we propose to plant under separate study as to its merits in all ways, and only plant one kind a year. The kind chosen for orchard culture should be of undoubted merit and distinction, and of high quality when cooked, without which Apples to keep are worthless. In fixing but one kind a year, the first consideration should be its quality, and the second its constancy in bearing, as to which there is a great difference in Apples. Hardiness and vigour are essential, and our judgment as regards orchard planting should never be influenced by the produce of trees grafted on the paradise or other stocks which limit the natural growth of the tree.

Apples known for many years, like the *Blenheim, Kentish Filbasket, Wellington, French Crab, Sussex Forge, Warner's King, Yorkshire Greening, Tom Putt, Reinette Grise, Bramley's* and *Alfriston* should never be left out of our consideration in this respect, as, however they may be affected by situation or soil, their value has been proved, and that is a great point, as in the case of new varieties chosen for some one minor quality, such as colour, it is only after they have been grown for years we begin to find out their bad qualities.

Some of the most beautiful things in our garden or home landscapes are the orchards of the west of England, more often planted with the Apple than with the Pear. The Pear tree in this country should be much more grown as an orchard tree, for its beauty even if not for its fruit, which yearly grows in value. Some Pears of our own time, like *Doyenné du Comice* and *Beurré Hardy*, are worth a score of the old kinds. The Pear tree is finer in form and stature than the Apple, and it is not rare to see trees in Worcestershire of the size of forest trees. Such trees, with their varied and picturesque form, are worth thinking of when planting for beauty.

The use of the Quince as a dwarfing stock for many years past in England has been against the Pear as an orchard tree. No Pear grafted on this stock ever succeeds as a standard tree. In our fertile valleys and the rich soil of gardens the Quince is for some kinds often a good stock, but over a large area of poor sandy and chalky land it is worthless; and its use has done much harm to Pear cultivation. In using the Pear, or natural stock, we may hope that it will do well on any land, be it heavy Wealden clay or on upland soils. It is true we must wait for results; the standard Pear is a forest tree in its way, and

must be allowed time to mature, but it is surely better to let the years
run by than to plant trees which may never succeed as standards. For
trees so planted to endure we should choose good kinds that ripen in
our country, and see, in every case, that they are grafted on the wild
Pear—their natural stock—since we cannot easily get them on their
own roots. The most important point is that of varieties. We should
never plant any but good Pears, which, as standards, will ripen in
our country under any fair conditions, such Pears as *Beurré Giffard,
Beurré Goubault, Beurré Dumont, Beurré Hardy, Fondante des Bois,
Rousselet de Reims, Doyenné du Comice, Marie Louise, Urbaniste,
Soldat Laboureur, Triomphe de Jodoigne, Comtesse de Paris, Nouvelle
Fulvie, Bergamotte Saumier, Charles Cognée, Doyenné d'Alençon,
Josephine de Malines, Suzette de Bavay.*

Fruit trees grown in any way are fair to see in the time of flower
and fruit, but our orchard must be in turf if we are to have the best
expression of its beauty. In fruit gardens where the whole surface is
cultivated with small fruits below and taller trees overhead we may
get as good, or, it may be, better fruit, but we miss the finer light
and shade and verdure of the orchard in turf, the pretty incidents of
the ground, and the animal life among the trees in spring, as sheep in
Kent, and the interest of wild gardening in the grass. Also the orchard
turf, by its shade or shelter, or in some way, becomes most welcome
nibbling for lambs and calves in the spring. A gain of the orchard in
turf is that we can plant it on any ground, however broken or steep,
and in many parts of the country there is much ground of this sort to
be planted. Now, while we may in the garden or the fruit garden plant
trees without stakes, we cannot do so in the grass orchard, because
of the incursions of animals; therefore staking is needed, not only to
support the tall and strong young trees which we ought to plant, but
also to guard against various injuries. The best is to use very strong
stakes and make them protect and support the trees, and also carry
the wire netting which is essential wherever rabbits, hares, goats, or
other browsing animals exist. The way to do this is to have a very
stout stake—Larch or Old Oak. Sometimes in the repairing of old
sheds a number of old Oak rafters are rejected—excellent for staking
young trees in orchards, first digging the hole and putting the stake
firmly into a depth of 3 feet below the surface. Cradles of Oak and
iron are much in use; the first is very well in an Oak country where
labour is plentiful; iron is costly and ugly, and not so good as the single
stout stake, which is easy to get of Larch or stub Oak in many country

places. The common way of tying a faggot of Quicks or any thorny shrub is often good when done by a good fencer. The trees should be tied with care with soft ropes of straw or jute, and when planted be loosely but carefully wired with netting well out of the reach of browsing animals. This wiring is supported well by the strong stake, and, well done, it keeps rabbits and hares, as well as cattle, at bay, and worse than all for trees, young horses. A usual way in Kent is to drive in three stout stakes, 6 feet or more in height, round the tree, and fasten cross-bars to them. This can be done at a total cost of about 1od. a tree, and should last twelve to fifteen years.

One of the reasons for a good orchard, from the point of view of all who care for beauty, is its value for wild gardening. It is so well fitted for this, that many times Narcissi and other bulbs from the garden have even established themselves in its turf, so that long years after the culture of the flowers has been given up in the garden, owing to changes of fashion, people have been able in old orchards to find naturalised some of the most beautiful kinds of Narcissi. Where the soil is cool and deep, these flowers are easily grown, and in warm soils many of our hardiest and most beautiful spring flowers might easily be naturalised. On the cool side of the orchard bank, Primrose and Oxlip would bloom long and well, and on all sides of it Daffodils, Snowflakes, Snowdrops, wild Tulips, or any like bulbs to spare from the garden; and from the garden trimmings, too, tufts of Balm and Myrrh to live for ever among the grass of the bank. The robin would build in the moss of the bank, the goldfinch in the silvery lichen of the trees, and the thrush, near the winter's end, herald the buds with noble song.

Bold planters need not hesitate to adorn some of their orchard trees with graceful climbing plants. A few of these climbers would be too vigorous eventually for the fruit tree, but a good many are never so on vigorous orchard trees. The autumn-flowering Clematis (flammula) is such a light grower that it would not make much difference to the tree, and there are a number of wild Clematis with the same light character that would not hurt an orchard tree. Some of the fine-leaved Vines, too, would give a dash of rich colour in the autumn, and do little harm, and some of the more fragile Honeysuckles might also be tried.

CHAPTER XXXV

Labours for Good or Evil; Draining;
Rotation; Monotony; Glass; Moving Earth

The cost of the making and keeping of the gardens and pleasure grounds of the British Isles is too vast to realise. No other people in the world spend so generously on their gardens and plantations—not a selfish end either, as all noble planting and gardening add to the beauty of the land. In every case it is therefore worth while asking, does the labour so freely given work for good ends—for ugliness or beauty, waste in stereotyped monotony, or days well spent in adding to the treasures of our gardens and plantings, both in enduring variety and in picturesque effects; pictures, in fact, all round the year? There is immense and hideous waste in misapplied labour and bad art, and therefore some of these enemies of good work deserve a little thought.

Most garden lovers strive for an ideal soil, but this does not always lead to happy results, and, even if we could have it, would only lead to monotony in vegetation. No doubt many will seek at all costs for the soil called the best, but the wisest way is rather to rejoice in and improve the soil fate has planted us on. A good deep and free loam is best for many things, and for high cultivation or market work, deep valley soils are almost essential, but we often see poor peats giving excellent results from a flower gardening point of view, in enabling us to grow with ease many more kinds of plants than could be grown on heavy soil. How fertile sand may become with good cultivation is shown by the fact that some of the very best soils for hardy plants are those that have been poor sea sand, but improved by cultivation, and sometimes such soils are drought-resisting, as on reclaimed seashore lands. Yet now and then we see certain sandy soils absolutely refuse to grow Roses and Carnations, and in such cases it is often better to give up the struggle. Chalky hills are wretched for trees and some shrubs, but there are few soils more congenial to garden vegetation than some chalky soils, and chalk tumbling into a valley soil is often excellent.

The most hopeless soils are the true clays, but the word "clay" is used in a loose way by many who have never seen a real clay. In the east of England and in Ireland, for example, the term is often used for dark, free soil. The true clay which occurs in the northern suburbs of London and near Horsham is not a soil on which a man could get a living, or if he does so he will get one anywhere! With such a soil our only hope is to cart good earth on to the ground. Whatever the nature of the soil in a given garden, it should to a large extent govern what we grow. If happy enough to have a sandy peat, how easy it is to grow all the lovely evergreens of the northern mountains, which rejoice in such soil—things which, if they live on loamy and heavy soils, are never really happy thereon. On such soil, too, all the most beautiful kinds of hardy shrubs may be grown without trouble, and planted among these shrubs the Lilies and hardy bulbous flowers of Japan and America. If a deep and at the same time poor sea sand comes in our way, we can make perfect bulb gardens on it, and also grow trees and flowering shrubs very well after a time.

Soil must not always be blamed for failure, because rainfall, elevation, and, very often, nearness to the sea will affect certain plants very much. Thus shrubs that do well near the sea will, on the same kind of soil, perish far inland. It is essential to study the secret of the soil and find out the plants that thrive best on it. Once free from the limits and needs of the flower garden proper, the best way will often be to use any local peculiarities of soil instead of doing away with them: A bog? Instead of draining it keep it and adorn it with some of the often beautiful things that grow in bogs. A sandy knoll? Plant with Rosemary or Rock Roses. A peaty, sheltered hollow? Make it into a beautiful Rhododendron glade, and so get variety of plant life in various conditions.

Then as regards the soil and the natural habitats of plants, there is no doubt that it is useful to know where they come from, whether plains, valleys, or rocks, and what soil they grow on; but it is a knowledge that may sometimes mislead, because rainfall and elevation and other causes may lead us to suppose results due to soil which are really so to accident of position. Many of the beautiful plants of the mountains of the East, such as Aubrietia, and a number of rock plants which grow in any soil,

would do no better if we tried to imitate their actual conditions of life
in their native habitats, which are often absolutely different from the
soils of our lowland gardens in which many rock plants thrive and
endure for years.

Many think that heavy watering is necessary in seasons of drought,
and it may be worth while showing how such heavy labour may be
avoided. There are soils which are so thirsty, like the hot sandy soils
of Surrey, that watering is essential, and some chalky soils, too,
are almost hopeless without heavy watering, while water is often
extremely difficult to get enough of on dry hills. But under general
conditions there is not much trouble in getting rid of this labour and
its attendant ugliness. The essential thing is to make the beds deep
enough. Even with the best intentions, many people fail to do this,
and workmen in forming gardens are sometimes misled as to the depth
of soil in beds made when gardens are being laid out, the soil when
it settles being really much less than it seems in the making. The best
way for those who care for their flowers is to dig the beds right out
to a depth of 30 inches below the surface before any of the good soil
is put in. Then, if for general garden use such beds are filled in with
good, rich, loamy soil and are gently raised, as all beds should be in
wet countries, 4 inches or 6 inches above the surface, they will rarely
be found to fail in any drought. Much depends on the size of the bed;
the little, angular, frivolous beds which have too often been the rule
in gardens cannot resist drought so long as broad simple beds. With
these precautions, and also autumn and winter planting, we ought,
in the British Isles, to free ourselves from much of the heavy labour
and cost of watering, and it would be better to have half the space
we give to flowers well prepared, than always be at work with the
water barrel.

To be busy planting in autumn and early winter is a great gain too,
because the plants get rooted before the hot time comes, and the kind
of plants we grow is important as regards the water question. Where
we have deep beds of Roses, Lilies, Carnations, Irises, Delphiniums,
and all the noble flowers that can be planted in autumn or winter,
we may save ourselves the labour of watering often. Well-prepared
beds of choice evergreen or other flowering shrubs, with Lilies and
the choicest hardy flowers among them, also resist drought well. Thus
it will be seen how much we gain in this way alone by the use of right
open-air gardening.

What is here said, although true of the south of England and dry soils generally, is not so as to soil on cool hills, and in the west country where the rainfall is heavier. In such cases it is not nearly so important to have the soil so deep, and a good fertile soil half the depth, with copious rain, may do. But, taking the country generally, there is no doubt that such deep culture well repays the doing. The farmer is often unable to alter the staple of his ground owing to its extent, but the flower gardener, dealing with a much smaller area, should never rest until he has got a deep as well as a good soil. This is given to many by Nature in rich valley lands, and on such happy soil the flower gardener's main work as regards the labours of the soil is changing the crop now and then, with some modification of the soil to suit certain plants.

Where, owing to the dryness of the soil or subsoil, or to shortness of the rainfall, we have to resort to much artificial watering, it is a great point to save the rain water as the best of all water, not only for household uses but for plants. Next to it comes river water, but to the gardens that want most water, rivers, unfortunately, do not come, so that for garden use it would often be very wise to do what people do more in other countries than ours, and that is, save all the rain water we can instead of letting it run to waste as it does so often.

In our country, too, much thought and labour are given to drainage in the flower garden, to the neglect of change of plants and deep cultivation. During our hot summers some way to keep water in the beds is more important than getting rid of it. Some soils are in little need of artificial drainage, such as free sands, sandy loams, chalky and limestone soils, and much ground lying high, and much alluvial land. Houses are not usually built on bogs or marshy land, and in the course of years the ground round most houses has been made dry enough for use, and hence elaborate work in drains, bottoming with brick-rubbish or concrete, is often wasted labour. In some years even in the west country we may see plants lying half-dead on the ground for want of water, and the same plants in deep soil, and where no thought was given to drainage, in perfect health at the same time. There are places where, owing to excessive rainfall and the wet nature of the soil, we may have to drain, but it is often overdone.

Apart from the over-draining for ordinary garden things, it may be well to remember that flower-garden plants in our country are often half starved through drainage, like Phlox and scarlet Lobelia, which in their own country are marsh plants, or inhabit the edges of pools. In the southern country they simply refuse to show their true character where the ground is drained in the usual way.

Gardeners' land and farmers' land are usually wholly different. Drainage is often the simplest and best way for the farmer to alter the tilth and texture of saturated and cold or sour land, whereas the flower gardener, dealing with a small space for his beds, has the power of altering the tilth and texture of his land in a thorough way, and so making it open to the influence of rain and air. The position of the flower garden is usually wholly different from that of agricultural land. The flower garden itself is frequently raised, and in a terraced or at all events often dry position, where the main drainage is long settled, and gently raising the surfaces of flower-beds, to a height say of 4 inches to 6 inches, enables us to get rid of the surface water. By raising our beds slightly—not in the ugly way practised in the London parks—we free the surface of any water lying on it, and this is a good plan to follow, except in hot and shallow soils, where it would be better not to raise the surface above the level.

A cause of the poor growth of hardy flowers is want of change of soil, and, in addition, the soils in which they grow are often robbed by a network of hungry tree roots. There are botanic gardens in Europe where the same wretched plants have been starving in the same soil for fifty years, and little ever done to help them. So, again, there are favourite borders in gardens which are almost as much in want of a change, but, owing to their position sometimes being a favourite one, people hesitate to give it to them. In such cases we should prepare a new border for the plants and remove them, and trench, renew and improve the soil of the old beds or borders, afterwards taking a crop as different as possible for a year or two. If we take a crop of annual flowers, the annuals rejoice in the fresh ground, and they might be followed by a year of Carnations, after which a return might be made to a good mixed border. When, however, we do change a border or bed, the staple of the soil ought to be made deep enough and changed if need be. In dealing with a soil which is too rich in humus, an addition of lime will improve it, but generally the soils are too poor, and require renewing and deepening. Bedding plants have the advantage of fresh soil and often a total change every year, and hence the bright vigour they often show when the seasons are fair. A little of the same generous change would help Roses, Lilies, and all the finer things in an equal degree, though many of these will be quite happy in the same soil for years if it be well prepared at first.

Many people fidget at the sight of beautiful leaves in autumn, instead of enjoying them, as Shelley did, and gardeners are often sweeping them up when they would be much better employed planting good plants or shrubs. What are we to do with the garden leaves? We cannot, it is true, have them in drifts in the flower garden, but it is better to let them all fall before we take much trouble in removing them. In gathering them up we may best add them to a place set apart for leaf mould. But in every case where they may be let alone it is much better to let them stay on the surface of wood, grove, shrubbery, or group of shrubs, for protection and nourishment for the ground. If anyone during the hot years that we have had—as in 1893—had stood on a height in a woody country, he would have seen that, while the fields were brown and bare, and cattle and crops distressed for want of water, the wood retained its verdure, and the growth of the year was as good as usual. Why was this? It is explained by the beautiful function of the leaf, which not only does the vital work of the tree, but also shields the ground from the direct action of the sun. When the leaf has fallen its work is not half done, as it protects and nourishes the roots throughout the year, so that in the hottest years the fibres of the trees find nourishment in decaying leaves. This surely is a reason that leaves should not be scraped out from beneath every shrub or tree, and there is no reason whatever why they should form part of the rubbish heap.

It is not only the better use of the waste as a fertiliser that is a gain, it is the saving of very troublesome labour, often occurring in the warmest part of the year, when every hour is precious over the really important work of the garden—getting in crops of all kinds at the right time and in the best way. Also we save the disfigurement of the rubbish yard itself, and get rid of the smoke of the fires kept going to consume it—another nuisance about a country house or garden. The ash, the one result of all the waste of labour and filth of the rubbish heap, is certainly of some use, but not one-sixth of the good of the stuff used in the direct way. It is not only the summer aid we gain, but all we put on in this way settles down in winter to a nice little coat of humus, which nourishes the roots and protects them from frost as well as heat.

The destruction of the seeds of weeds is the only shadow of reason for the rubbish heap, but it is bad gardening to let weeds go to seed. And though certain areas of town gardens have no neighbours from which seeds can be blown, this is not so in the country, where weed seeds from woods and fields and young plantations abound in the air. There is no good remedy for weeds except early and regular hoeing.

There are many conditions in which, even if we do allow weeds to go to seed, they can be used as a mulch; as, for example, in young orchard and turf and other planting in or near turf where weed seeds can do no harm. Burning, therefore, should be kept to a few essential uses. The source of success in flower gardening is to be always busy sowing or planting; there is scarcely a day or a week when some things have not been planted or attended to if we want a succession of beauty; but when the men are from morn to night busy hoeing and watering and with other routine work, it is difficult to get time for securing the successions of plants of various kinds on which the lasting beauty of a garden at all seasons depends.

The old labour of grubbing up walks, which was so constant and dreadful in the very heat of summer, is got rid of by weed-killers, of which one dressing a year will sometimes suffice to keep the walks clean, and, better still, prevent us from having to rip up the surfaces of the walks, which was common in every garden until quite recently, and is carried on still in many places. By abolishing ignoble routine work, in this and all ways we can, we have time for the real work of the garden, in adding to its beauty with new or beautiful things and improved ways of growing and arranging them.

A fire on the spot is a great aid in the garden when active changes have to be made, and foul borders or shrubberies renovated or replanted. Where, in stiff soils, Twitch and other bad weeds take possession, with perhaps a number of worn-out shrubs, the simplest way is often to burn all, not trying to disentangle weeds from the soil in the usual way, but simply skinning the surface 2 inches, or more if need be, and burning it and the vital parts of the weeds, first removing any plants that are worth saving. In light soils the labour of cleaning foul ground is less than in heavy, adhesive soils, but fire is a great aid in all such cases. If we are removing ugly and heavy masses of Laurels, or other evergreens which have never given grace or flower to the scene, we should burn them root and branch at the same time. The result will be that we get rid of our worst weeds, and turn enemies like Goutweed into ashes. This weedy surface of garden ground is often some of the best of the soil, and it is much better to keep it where it is, but purified. Regular cleaning will keep down all young weeds, but it is a struggle to get the old and bad weeds out of the soil, owing to the broken roots of Bindweed, Twitch and Goutweed, which escape the closest forking and sharpest eyes. There is no barrowing or carting to take the weeds to some rotting heap, while, on the other hand, the friendly fire eats up and kills at once the whole of them and converts them and the burnt surface they infested into good earth. Whatever we may think of cremation for ourselves, it is a good friend in fighting weeds and in helping us to thoroughly cleanse foul garden ground. We have not even the trouble they had with Don Quixote's books, which was to carry them into the yard to burn them.

Mulching or covering the surface with various kinds of light materials, such as leaf mould, cocoa fibre, manure, and sand, or anything, in fact, which gives an inch or two of loose surface to the earth and prevents evaporation, is a great aid on many soils, but not so important where the beds have been thoroughly prepared, at least not for Roses, Carnations, and many of the best flowers, because, if the roots can go down and find good soil as far as they go, they really do not want mulching, save on very hot soils. Mulching of various kinds or loosening the surface of the ground is much easier to carry out in the kitchen and fruit gardens or orchard than in the flower garden, all the surface of which should be covered with living things during the fine season. This, the prettiest way and not difficult to carry out, we often see in cottage gardens, and in nature itself where the health of the forest and other fertile lands depends to a certain extent on the ground being covered with vegetation, which of itself prevents direct evaporation. Taking a hint from this, I am very fond of covering the surface with dwarf living plants of fragile nature, which do not much exhaust the soil, and which in very hot weather may help to keep it moist. This is done in the case of Roses and other plants which, being rather small and bare at first, want some help to cover the ground, and a number of very pretty plants may be used for this purpose, which will give us bloom in spring and good colour on the ground. One result of it is that we may have a beautiful spring garden in addition to the summer garden—that is to say, if our garden is planted for summer and autumn with Roses and the like, by the use of Tufted Pansies and other dwarf plants in the beds we get pretty effects early in the year, and through this living carpet may come up many pretty bulbs. Thus we may have in the same beds with a little care and thought, two or three different types of flower life.

The plants that may be used in this way are numerous, and mostly rock and mountain plants of Europe and cold countries, evergreen, often bearing pretty flowers and good in colour at all seasons, spreading into pretty carpets easily, and quite hardy, taking often a deeper green in winter, so that used over permanent beds they help to adorn the

flower-beds in winter. Through them in the dawn of spring the early
Crocus, Scilla, and Windflower come up to find themselves in green
turf of Thyme, Rockfoil, Stonecrop, varying these according to soil,
altitude or position; the cooler north favouring many mountain plants,
though some face the ardours of the warmer sun.

A grievous source of wasted effort in gardens is monotony arising
from everybody growing what his neighbour grows. Thus it comes that
the poor nurseryman who attempts to grow new or rare trees or shrubs
very often finds them left on his hands, so that many country nurseries
only grow a few stereotyped things, and we see public gardens and
squares in London given over to the common Privet, the common
Lilac let to run as a weed, and the common Elder, as in Lincoln's
Inn Fields.

Every lover of the garden could do something to check this fatal
monotony by taking up some plant, or family of plants, for himself,
which perhaps he is unable to find in the nursery gardens near at
hand. There are not only many beautiful species of plant which are
excluded from the ordinary nurseries, but even special nurseries, as
those for Roses, often exclude good kinds from their collections. It is
not only the introduction of new plants or species we have to think of,
but the raising of new forms (hybrids or varieties), the fine cultivation
of neglected groups, as the beautiful forms of our native Primrose, the
making more artistic use of old and well-known plants, the skilful
adaptation of plants and trees to the soil so as to get the highest
beauty of which it is capable without excessive care, and without
the deaths visible in many places after hard winters. Those who seek
to break the monotony of gardens must be prepared to face some
trouble, and must not take the least notice of what is thought right
in the neighbourhood, or of what can be obtained from the nearest
nursery garden. The further afield they look, probably the better in
the end it will be for them if they would escape from the trammels
of monotony.

Perhaps the most miserable of all garden-work is that of nailing the
shoots of trees to walls, on cold days, and the value of climbing plants
now in our gardens is so great, that the best mode of attaching them to
walls is a question which, though it may seem a small one from some
points of view, is important, and by no means settled for the best. In
our self-styled scientific age—the age also of the galvanised iron church
and the ironmonger's fence, which is no fence—our gardens have been
invaded by galvanised wire, which is put up at great expense on garden

and house walls, and is thought to be an essential improvement in all new work. The question does not merely concern walls for climbers round the house, but also walls in the fruit garden. In our cold country we cannot ripen the Peach or the choicer fruits without the aid of walls; galvanised wire is used in many gardens, but many growers discover that its effect on the trees is not good. There is a foundation of fact in these complaints, and they are common to French and English gardeners. In France, where the cultivation of wall fruit to supply the market with Peaches and fine winter Pears is carried out well the best growers are against the use of galvanised wire, and think it much better to have the wooden lattice only against the wall; so they keep to the older and prettier way of trellising the wall. For those who care about effect this is well, for whatever harm, the wire may do to the tree, of its ugliness there can be no doubt. The old French and English way of fixing branches to walls with trellis-work made of Oak in about 1-inch strips was a very good one. One advantage of such woodwork is that it looks well on the walls even before we get our plants up, and there is the great facility of being able to tie where we wish, thus avoiding the use of nails and the other miseries of training against walls.

There remains the question of fixing our lattice-work of Oak, Chestnut, Pine, or Bamboo. In old walls holdfasts must be driven; in new ones pieces of iron with strong eyes should be laid along here and there in the courses of brick or stone as the work goes on.

It is a great thing to be relieved from the ugliness and injury of the galvanised wire. We would like to go a little further and keep to old ways of tying things on walls. Those who look through their bills may perhaps come upon items, and not small ones, for tarred twine and other means of tying. In old times the shoots of the Yellow Willow did the work of tying fruit trees to walls better than any tarred twine as far as the main branches were concerned. To say that it is impracticable now is nonsense, as in some great nurseries where millions of plants are sent out every year, every lot is tied with Willow. The French way of using a Rush for tying, instead of twine or matting, is an excellent one. It is a Rush which is harvested and dried carefully, and it is the simplest thing in the world to tie with so as to allow for the free growth of the branch, and yet keep the shoot quite secure.

Whether staking trees and shrubs or wind-waving is the worst evil is doubtful, but much harm is done by staking. It is costly and troublesome, especially so for those large trees that are seen in pleasure grounds, surrounded by a kind of crinoline of galvanise wire. The evil of staking arises largely from planting trees too big as "specimens." To plant these is tempting to many, but generally we get a much better result from small trees that want no staking. Planting ornamental trees of considerable size is so common that staking is frequently done, and very often the trees are injured by the stakes, not only at the root, but also much in the stem, which sometimes leads to canker. It is known that canker (as in the Larch) enters the trees more readily where the wounds are ready to receive the spores, and we often see fruit-trees badly cankered through staking.

The wire-roping business for trees is a nuisance, as the ropes cut in if in the least neglected, and the tree often snaps there, and when the ropes are finally removed the trees often go down in gales. The best cure for the waste and dangers of staking is to plant small trees, but often where this is not done for any reason we may do good by cutting in the side shoots close to the stem. This leaves the tree with little for the wind to act upon, and the need of staking is avoided without injury to the tree. Transplanting trees involves so much injury to the roots that somewhat reducing the tops does good in all ways.

At Kew, when a large tree is transplanted, it is guyed up with three lengths of soft cord (commonly called "gaskin") if it appears likely to become loose. This is better than a stake, cheaper, and less likely to injure the stem by abrasion. A tree with branches low enough can be stayed by driving into the ground three stout stakes at equal distances round the tree, nearly at the circumference of the branches, and tying a branch to each of the stakes.

The picturesque grouping of trees and shrubs is a gain in the avoidance of the trouble and danger of staking. The pinetum, as seen in many country seats, is a scheme in which trees are isolated and dotted so as to encourage them as "specimens," which is the wrong way and the ugly way. In Nature these trees are almost always massed and grouped close, so that they shelter each other, and if in planting them we plant as a wood, closely, thinning them very carefully, we find them make trees and give better effects than in the common way they are generally placed, as the trees protect and comfort each other, and shade the ground.

Among the evils of the "bedding" and "carpet system" is the need of costly glass-houses in which to keep the plants all the winter, not one in ten of these plants being as pretty as flowers that are as hardy as the grass in the field—like Roses, Carnations, and Delphiniums.
 is absurd to grow Alternantheras in costly hothouses, and not to

give a place to flowers that endure cold as well as Lilies-of-the-Valley. Glass-houses are useful helps for many purposes, but we may have noble flower gardens without them. To bloom the Rose and Carnation in midwinter, to ripen fruits that will not mature in our climate, to enable us to see many fair flowers of the tropics—for these purposes glass-houses are a precious gain; but for a beautiful flower garden they are almost needless, and the numerous glass-houses in our gardens may be turned to better use.

For those who think of beauty in our gardens and home landscapes, the placing of a glass-house in the flower garden or pleasure ground is a serious matter, and some of the most interesting places in the country are defaced in that way. In the various dividing lines about a country house there can be no difficulty in finding a site for glass-houses where they cannot injure the views. There is no reason for placing the glass-house in front of a beautiful old house, where its colour mars the prospect. Often, in looking across the land towards an old house, we see first the glare of an ugly glass shed. If this were the case only in the gardens of people lately emerged from the towns to the suburbs of our great cities, it would not be so notable; but many large country places are disfigured in this way. And, apart from fine old houses and the landscape being defaced by the hard lines and colour of the glass-house, there is the result on the flower garden itself; efforts to get plants into harmonious and beautiful relations are much increased if we have a horror in the way of glass sheds staring at us. Apart from the heavy cost of coal or coke, the smoke-defilement of many a pretty garden by the ugly vomit of these needless chimneys and the effect on young gardeners in leading them to despise the far more healthy and profitable labours of the open garden have to be considered in relation to the cost, care, and ugliness of the glass nursery as an annual preparation for plants for the flower garden, these plants being with few exceptions far less precious in every way for flower garden or for room than those that are quite hardy.

Next to moving heaven, the heaviest undertaking is that of moving earth, and there are no labours of gardening men that lead to more wasted effort, where care and experience are not brought to bear on the work. Labour in many parts of the country has become dearer, and the question of moving earth without needless waste of energy is a serious one for all who have much groundwork to do. As instances of misuse of labour we see the soil from foundations carted far, and then put deep over the roots of old trees, to their death or injury. A man of resource would place this soil in some well-chosen spot near, and having first removed the surface soil and, resurfaced with it, plant it with a handsome group of beautiful shrubs or trees, so that the surface would in no ugly way differ from the general lie of the ground near. Carts and horses very often lead to waste of labour in removing earth when barrows and a few planks would do the work better.

In necessary groundwork there is inevitably much moving of earth in getting levels, carrying roads and paths across hollows, and for various other reasons. We should make a rule of getting the soil in all such cases as near at hand as possible. Mistakes in levelling ground are frequent, and often lead to twice moving of soil. The best man for groundwork is often a good navvy; many such men know how to make heavy groundwork changes without putting a barrowful of soil in the wrong place. Very often spare soil has to be removed, and in this necessary work ugly mounds are made, when, by a little care in choosing the place well and never leaving any ugly angles, and making the ground take the natural gradation of the adjacent earth, it could be well planted. Hardy trees take well to such banks if the good soil is kept on the top, as it should always be.

The same remarks may serve for the moving of turf, gravel, stones, and soil, save that to get good soil for the formation of beds, we must go where the good soil is; whereas for the bottoms of roads and paths, the support of banks, base of terraces or mounds, much saving may be effected by getting what we want in the nearest possible place, never fearing to make a hollow if need be, as that can be so easily planted with some free-growing tree or shrub; the hardy Pines, like Scotch, Corsican, and Silver Firs, being excellent for this, as they thrive in almost any earth, and often on surfaces from which the whole bed of fertile soil has been removed.

Apart from essential groundwork, there is the diversifying of ground artificially, as may be seen in our parks, owing to the false idea that you cannot make level ground picturesque with planting. Proof that this is not impossible may be seen in many a level country planted by Nature, as in the forest plain and in many a park and pleasure ground in Germany, France, and Britain. Trees are given to us to get this very variety of broken surface, and the idea that to make a place picturesque we must imitate—and usually badly imitate—naturally diversified ground is most inartistic. No doubt broken ground has many charms, but so has the fertile plain, and the best way is to accept and enhance the beauty of each variety of surface. To do so is the planter's true work. In cities and suburbs there is often occasion to conceal ugly objects, and earth if to spare may be used well and wisely in raising at once the base of a plantation of young trees; but an enormous amount of labour given to making artificial mounds might be saved without any loss, and with much gain to garden design.

The mania for foolish groundwork may be often seen, one of its results being the burial of the tree base, surrounded, perhaps, with a brick-lined pit-hole, as in St James's Park. Shooting earth and rubbish to fill up the hollows on such a precious space as Hampstead Heath is common, and as the surrounding district is busy in building, these attempts are, we fear, often the occasion of finding a shoot for earth and rubbish. The bringing in of such rubbish should be absolutely forbidden, as the only effect of this filling up of hollow places is to destroy the incidents of the ground, usually far prettier in form than the results of smug levelling up, or, worse still, the formation of such artificial mounds as we see examples of in the parks. Even the squares in our level Thames valley are not exempt from outrage of this kind, of which, perhaps, the most hideous example is that of Euston Square. A high and ugly earth-bank has been put all around the Square, so steep that even the cheap nursery rubbish of the London squares—Privet and Elder—refuses to grow upon it, and so in the summer days, instead of the grass and tree-stems and cool shadows, a bank of dusty rubbish meets the eye!

Another serious source of waste of the inexperienced in groundwork is burying the top surface, the most precious, and in many cases the result of ages of decay of turf and plants. In alluvial land and light friable hill soils this mistake does not so much matter, but in heavy land where there is a clay subsoil it is fatal. The first thing in all groundwork is to save the top soil with the greatest care, for the sake of using it again in its proper place; and how to save it, so that it may be available at the end of the work, is one of the most essential things the good ground-worker has to think of.

Trenches for the reception of pipes, drains, and foundations should not be opened until the materials are at hand, as in wet weather doing so often leads to the sides falling in and much needless labour. The direction of walks, roads, or designs for beds, borders, or gardens, should be carefully marked out and looked at from every point of view before carrying them out, having regard to their use and their relation to all things about them, and not merely to any plan on paper. Attention to this will often save much labour in groundwork.

A cause of much waste of labour in moving soil is the usual way of treating mud after the cleansing of artificial ponds—often a poor inheritance to leave to one's children. The silting up with mud goes on for ever, and while the mere expense of getting this out of the pond bed in any way is usually great, the cost is often increased through the idea that the stuff is of manurial value. This leads people frequently to heap it up on the banks to dry, then to liming it, and eventually to moving it on to the land, these various labours adding to the disfigurement of the foreground of beautiful ground often for a long time. Pond mud has very little manurial value generally, though it will differ to some extent according to the sort of soil the supply comes from. Usually, however, it has very slight value, and any labour bestowed upon it from that point of view is nearly always wasted. The best and simplest way is to put it direct on to some poor pasture near, or on to any ground where it may be got rid of with least labour to man or horse. Where the pond is ugly in outline and not essential either for its beauty in the home landscape or for its uses for fish or water store, it may often be worth considering whether the best way would not be to let the water off and turn the mud bed into a handsome grove of Willows and Dogwoods, and an excellent covert at the same time. I know nothing among trees quite so good in effect in the landscape, winter and summer, as the white, red, and yellow Willows, with an undergrowth of the red Dogwoods.

Where possible it is best to do without labels, except where we grow many kinds of things that differ by slight shades, as Carnations and Roses. The contents of a garden are usually in a state of change; we are continually adding to and taking from them; new plants are introduced; a severe winter kills a number of shrubs, which we determine not to replant. Fashion changes the garden vegetation too, and then the permanent labels, cast and burnt into hardware and cemented in cast iron, are thrown aside. I prefer a label which can be used again, such as a cast-iron label of "T shape" or, in other words, a slip of cast iron with an oblong head slightly thrown back. These are cast very cheaply in the iron districts. We have to paint them and write the names of the trees on them when they come to hand; but that can be readily done by a handy painter in winter. In a large garden, where much naming is required, the best way is to train a youth who is likely to remain in the place, by placing a copy of the desired kind of letters before him. It is an advantage to give the label a coat of copal varnish when the letters are dry, and generally to use white letters on a black or dark ground, and give three coats of black over one of red lead. These are the best labels for the shrubs and choice young trees of a pleasure ground or flower garden. The painting will last for twenty years, and if we cease to cultivate the plants to which they belong, the labels may be repainted.

With big trees it is always a mistake to use a ground label. The best labels for large trees are made of pieces of tin about 4½ inches by 3½ inches. About half an inch of the upper edge should be bent at a right angle so as to form a little coping for the label, two holes should be made just beneath the little angle, through which a strong copper wire should be put and firmly nailed to the tree. Place it so as to be easily read, at about 5½ feet from the ground. Paint it dark brown or black with white letters, and it will last for many years. All labels inserted in the grass in pleasure grounds are liable to be pulled up by mowers or others, and in this way to get lost, while the labels on the stems are safe from such mishaps.

For low trees and bushes to which copper wire may be fixed with ease, the simplest and most enduring labels are those that are made of cast metal galvanised, and as they are very enduring they are best for hardy trees and shrubs. The words on them should be as few as may be, and all needless ones omitted. Thus in fruit-tree labels it is needless to use the word Pear or Apple, but simply the variety, as "Ribstone." This plan makes these labels more legible than when they are crowded with letters. For half-hardy plants, annuals, and plants of a season only, wooden labels are often the most convenient. In most gardens it is the practice to write the name at the part that goes in the ground, and to go on from thence to the top—a bad way, for the label always begins to decay at the base, and thus the beginning of the name is lost, while the end of it may be quite legible. After a little practice it becomes as easy to write from the top as from the other end, and, in writing the names, always begin as near the top as possible.

The use of the wooden label should be given up in favour of labels with raised or incised letters. The main reason is that the endurance of the wooden label is too slight; moreover, some kinds of good stamped-metal label are less conspicuous in the garden than the wooden label, and any kind of conspicuous label is bad. At Kew they now use a lead label of their own stamping, so that should many labels get out of use, as is the case in large collections, it is easy to melt them down and use the metal again for trees and enduring plants of all kinds.

CHAPTER XXXVI

My Flower Garden

The Editor of *Country Life* took a fancy to have a plan of my garden, and I willingly agreed, but now I desire to say a few words about plans and the harm they have done. Plans should be made on the ground to fit the place, and not the place made to suit some plan out of a book. Infinite harm has been done to the good art of gardening by the copying of old plans by designers without sympathy or knowledge of the art itself. Books are full of these plans, and any clerk can copy them and suggest them for all sorts of unfitting situations. In this case I thought of nothing but the ground itself, its relation to the house, and what I wanted to grow in it.

When I had a garden of my own to make, I meant it to contain the greatest number of favourite plants in the simplest way. I threw the ground into simple beds, suiting the space for convenience of working and planting, not losing an inch more than was necessary for walks. I did what, so far as we have any evidence to tell us, the Assyrian king and the mediæval chatelaine did—that is to say, I cut my limited garden space into simple beds. No plan of any kind was used nor any suggestion sought from any garden, the question being decided in relation to the space. Any talk about styles in relation to such a thing is absurd. Having made my garden, one day a young lady who had been reading one of those mystifying books about formalities and informalities came in, and, instead of warming her eyes at my Roses and Carnations, said, "Oh, you, too, have a formal garden!" Just imagine what Nebuchadnezzar or the mediæval Lady in their small patches of gardens would think of any silly person who made such a remark instead of looking at the flowers!

Having cut the space up into the simple plan shown, the next question was to make the walks. For these we used Croydon gravel, but the best we could get here was unsatisfactory. In a real flower garden there must be work to do at midsummer as well as in January, and therefore the gravel walk is a serious hindrance if one has gardening to do all the year round. I made up my mind, therefore, to pave the walks as shown in the plan, using old half-worn London York stone pavings for this purpose, which at that time were often used in making the bottoms of roads, and not of much value. With these, work all the year round is pleasant, as sand, manure, plants or anything else may be spread about on the walks without adding to the labour or causing any unpleasantness. Where the whole flower garden is set out in a week as in bedding-out this would not matter so much; but a real flower garden, which is a thing of varied life, cannot be done in that way. The stones, when in irregular pieces, are sometimes set at random, and they are set in sand only, no cement or mortar being used.

Then came the question of edgings. These in most gardens are a nuisance, and a serious and constant source of labour which can be very often ill spared. Imagine the labour of keeping up a large garden with Box or other live edgings, harbouring insects and doing other harm. So we had stone edgings made from the same old London flagstones, broken up into handy pieces about 10 inches deep. These look well at all seasons and make a lasting edging, so that the gardeners have time to think of getting beautiful results instead of being bothered with needless labours. Otherwise the plan speaks for itself. In planting we not only seek to get variety, but also some difference in the height of things, and thereby obtain a varied surface and not a flat, hard one such as is commonly sought.

Another point gained was that we could devote the beds to permanent planting; we have not to tear up the beds every autumn to plant spring flowers, as is commonly done in the gardens about London and Paris. The spring flowers abound so much in our lawns and woods, and beyond a few pretty edgings of Aubrietia, nothing else was done to disturb the beds meant for summer flowers. We can leave our Tea Roses and Carnations alone all the winter, and prepare for the summer garden only. Many fine things in the flower garden will not bear an annual or biennial disturbance, and therefore it is essential to have beds that we can plant with some degree of permanence. When the beds get tired of their contents, we have only to change the plants, but it is a great comfort to have beds which one can leave alone for several years, instead of having the useless labour of disturbing the ground twice a year.

It will be seen that these two flower gardens on slightly different levels are in intimate relation to the house. The old hall door opens into the smaller garden, and the west garden door into the larger. The garden is, in fact, as it should always be—a larger living-room. The varieties of situation are so many that it is not always possible to secure this; but it is by far the best way to have the real flower garden, where all our precious flowers are, in close relation to the house, so that we can enjoy and see and gather our flowers in the most direct way. The stone paths enable us to do this in all weathers; going for half a mile to get to the flower garden is not the right way. The wild garden is right in that way, but for the choice flowers that need attention and that charm us most, the flower garden should be within easy reach and in the best and sunniest spot.

THE POSITION OF THE FLOWER GARDEN IN RELATION TO THE HOUSE

In olden times, so far as any evidence remains to us from pictures, prints, tapestry, etc., the place for the flower garden was quite near the house; and that is the place for it now. In the best conditions, it should be like an extension of the house—a larger flower room. The Scottish way of going half a mile to the kitchen garden to find the flower garden there, is not the best. There is no reason why there should not be mixed borders in the kitchen garden, but the real flower garden, varied and beautiful as it ought to be, should be within easy access of the sitting-rooms. In all artistic things formulas are dangerous, and the best way is to study the site, and, in a wide sense, the more varied the better, even as regards position. Always the south and warm sides of the house should be taken advantage of, and the cold side reserved for the entrance, and usually it should be cut off from the warmer, or garden, sides.

Sometimes the discovery of a vein of fine soil away from the house may justify the making of a garden there, in the same way as the late Sir Henry Yorke made a wood garden in Buckinghamshire. Having found a fine deposit of good peat, he made a very beautiful shrub and flower garden in it. We are in a time of doubt about this question, many people, tired of bedding-out, have turfed up their gardens, so that we often see what ought to be a flower garden turfed over. It is the ugliness, cost, and wholly inartistic result of bedding-out that tired people of it, and in many cases it would be well to go back to the old idea of the flower garden near the house.

A great mistake has been made in the past in placing the Rose garden away from the house. This was often done and told in every book. The coming of the China Roses of longer bloom, has altered the conditions as regards the Rose garden, and the best Roses should be in the flower garden, not by themselves only, but combined with all the other beautiful things that one cares for in a very choice flower garden. When we have to make our Rose and flower garden together, which is the right way, that demands more thought for the position and the shape and the formation of the ground. In old houses there are generally open and more or less square places round the house and near it, which offer good situations for the flower garden. The walls that surround such places do not prevent us from following the picturesque way of gardening. There is not the slightest foundation for this plea, because nothing can be more set in its surroundings than the cottage or the small town garden, which often surprises us with its picturesque and true effects.

Take the lawn-side, where the ground slopes gently away from the house, it may be, towards a river; one of the best of gardens is one on the lawn, with a background of trees and shrubs sometimes running in and out of the margins of the lawn.

Often people are found bold enough to put their houses in all sorts of situations—on bluffs, near rocks, and on river banks, which may limit their garden in a sense, but give other, and, perhaps, more delightful, opportunities.

Sometimes about country houses there happens a square garden made at first as a kitchen or front garden, which is occasionally turned into a flower garden, often with excellent effect. The walls and the shelter and the drapery of climbers help. I think I have had more pleasure from the little square garden at Warley, full of hardy flowers, both in beds and borders, than ever I had in any garden. In such situations one can get as far away from convention as one likes. Another very pretty site of a flower garden is an old orchard. The trees, the light and shade, and the form make it enchanting, as compared with the fully exposed garden. In some of these orchard gardens, the soil being very good and rich, the hardy flowers grow very finely indeed—I mean as regards the handsomer kinds of hardy flowers.

CHAPTER XXXVII

Design in Planting

Who is to help? I believe the best results can only be got by the owner who knows and loves his ground. The greatest evil is the stereotyped plan, the results of which are evident on all sides. But the man must love the work and know one tree from the other, and feel that his pictures can only come from constant thought as to the ground itself. Lessons? Yes, from Nature mainly. A few days in one of the side valleys in the Tyrol or any beautiful mountain land will tell us more than many books, also pictures of the great landscape painters like Corot, Daubigny, Constable, and R. Wilson. The breadth, air, forms, foreground, and values that interest painters, the atmosphere of Corot, skies of Diaz, water of Daubigny, and Nature's trees, landscape, and atmosphere should teach us much. It is ours to make such use of them as will give us better pictures than ever were painted.

The lie of the ground must be studied in the way of the good leader of soldiers, and there is also the quality of the soil to be thought of, as soil useless for rich cultivation may give us fine trees. With hardy trees in the landscape, views, air, and distances also must be studied, not only in the place but from it to the neighbourhood.

But how are we to know a landscape gardener? By this sign among others—that he will study the ground first and bring no plan in his pocket. Office plans are poor substitutes for the thing itself, but the custom of plans on paper is so fixed that it is not easy to get this truth accepted. There can be no true work in landscape save by one who knows trees by heart, and there is no royal road to that knowledge save by life study.

The relationships of nurserymen to garden design is a delicate one. A nurseryman's business is a wholly different one, and an honourable one, and if he does his own work well he has not the time to act as a designer of gardens. And in his case where is the control which should be exercised in all expensive work?

The garden designer should be free to go anywhere for his trees and plants. No one nursery has half the plants or trees he may require. He should not accept a fee from any tradesman and should be paid only by his employer, whilst free to reject all goods supplied which he does not think as specified, just as the trustworthy architect rejects all inferior building material. Professional control is as essential in this as in any other work, and happy is the owner who himself takes a living interest in trees and landscape views, as he will save himself from stereotyped designs and bad planting. Some trees have historical associations, form and habits, likes and dislikes, which should be known to one hoping to get from their use any artistic result.

The most evident mistake made in design of landscape work is the want of repose or breadth seen in so many parks and pleasure grounds. In the Home Counties one can scarcely see a piece of modern park land without the trees being in rings and in dots here and there, spoiling all the breadth and simplicity of the scene. Such planting spoils landscape effect, does no good to the trees, and the dots are too small for shelter. The best way by far is to keep such green spaces open and plant ground that is no good for Arable. Sometimes a single Pine spoils the middle of a lawn or an oak tree the middle of a ploughed field. The lawn-like beauty of park or garden is the most precious thing we have for giving us air, sky, and space, and grouping and massing is the right way.

The planting without thought of evergreens is a common evil in British gardens. Evergreens are often planted where people do not see what they may become after years of growth. Important views are shut out by coarse evergreens, and even the house itself may be hidden by their growth.

In France it has been a practice to mar any grace of public squares and gardens by a display of the efforts of the sculptor; but the French begin to see this mistake, and to cry out against it. It is now proposed to remove these statues into one great statue cemetery, where those who admire them might worship.

Close to Hyde Park Corner there is a sort of fountain out of place, which spoils a little lawn. Large memorial confectionery groups ought not to be allowed to break up the spaces in the parks. Lately, I am told, the fantastic idea of a playwright has been embodied in stone in Kensington Gardens. If each succeeding decade is to see outrages of that sort committed, what will eventually become of the repose and quiet grace of parks?

An effective way of destroying repose in a public garden is the caging of animals there. This leads to ugly shanties and pathways or cleaning, feeding, and various purposes that need not be named.

In the garden itself certain malformed trees are used by designers of architectural turn to give points—the Irish Yew, close-growing Juniper, and various hideous "sports" of the Western Arbor-Vitæ. These are often used from the fatuous idea that they are old and right in the old English garden—the fact being that they are all modern deformities.

It should be borne in mind that the garden is but a patch in many a country place. It is only when we leave it we begin to see the real opportunity for landscape pictures in field, park, or woodland. There never was so much teaching of art in academic schools in every big town or city and professors and books in abundance, and yet there never was so much bad art. This is the common opinion of good judges in Paris and London. In Lord Redesdale's book there is a passage which has a bearing on this:—

> "I remember how once, when a lady consulted Lord Leighton about her boy, who showed a great talent for painting, his answer was: 'Let him have the education of a gentleman in the first place; then, if he should still have an inclination for art, let him specialise.'"

There is evidence to show that the way advised by Lord Leighton is not the right way. Excellence in art is not to be had without early devotion to the work, and the education in colleges until a man is well over twenty precludes any full early training in art.

If we look at the history of our own great landscape painters we find that David Cox was the son of a blacksmith, and he was an artist with a true eye for the beautiful in nature. Constable was a miller's son, and began his studies with a painter and glazier friend in the fields—a much better place to study art than any academy. Turner was the son of a barber, but even in Maiden-lane a genius arose. Old Crome began life as a doctor's errand boy. Carolus Duran, whose portrait of Pasteur—a masterpiece—was seen in London some years ago, told me he was at work in the Academy at Lille at eight years of age.

By far the best landscape art in England arose from conditions different from those laid down by Lord Leighton, whose own work does not justify his teaching. A picture by one of the old Dutch painters, who, as boys, were apprenticed to their craft, was worth all he ever did.

This may seem apart from garden design, but it really is not so, because the problems that confront the landscape planter are the same as those which the landscape painter has to deal with, viz., beauty, repose, breadth, and air. The man who uses trees instead of pigments has a noble task.

CHAPTER XXXVIII

The Architect in the Garden

There is no reason why a student of the noblest and most essential of the arts, architecture, should trouble his head as to the hundred and one things a good gardener has to think of.

Architects as such have no knowledge of our garden flora, and for ages gardens were disfigured owing to their endeavours to conform trees to the lines of buildings.

We see something of the work of the architect as a gardener in front of Buckingham Palace; in first of all meaningless stone piers and then a flower garden out of place, planted with one flower—the scarlet Pelargonium. The spot was wholly unfit for a flower garden. There are many flower gardens in the near parks. It was planned to cut up the little park near by and make a spectacular display of architecture out of place, but, fortunately, some men in the "House" heard of it and knocked the scheme on the head.

The worst outrage on Nature and on Art is the destruction of the forms of our noblest trees. The old gardens, many of which still exist, were in the hands of architects who clearly did not know a tree from a shrub, and who planted forest trees in positions where their beauty and stature could not develop, and this led to their distortion through ceaseless clipping. In Vienna may be seen men perched on ladders 50 feet high endeavouring to clip Hornbeam and Beech into hideous shapes. Many English and Scottish gardens are disfigured by our finest evergreen native tree, the Yew, being carved into ugly shapes. With our present wealth of trees and shrubs there is not the slightest reason for putting a forest tree into the flower garden, but every reason against the practice.

It would be easy to fill a comic journal with the ugly monstrosities of the "Topiarist." Northiam and Levens are among the many gardens disfigured by these distortions of misplaced forest trees. Topiary work, from beginning to end, is inherited from the Italians and the practice of clipping trees to conform to the lines of building. Many places are spoilt for the artist by the hard black lines of Yew, and not a naturally grown Yew to be seen. It is easy to get good dividing lines without disfiguring trees; lines that call for clipping mean the destruction of all form and grace. The labour and time spent in deforming trees are sad to think of and a waste to make the earth hideous. We may see examples of it on all sides here, as well as in the Royal gardens of the great cities of Europe.

Statues of value as works of art should in our country be under cover. The figures of animals, too, are out of place in the garden. Redundant ornaments of any kind, such as vases, often spoil it. In a recent book on garden ornament I see a milestone figuring as an ornament in a garden in Ireland. The use of marble is objectionable for another reason. Sir A. Geikie, in a letter to *The Times*, 11th June 1919, wrote:—

"On no account should white statuary marble be employed in any structure in the open air. Even the purest air of the country contains carbonic acid, which, dissolved in falling rain, acts on the stone as a solvent. In our rainy climate only a few years suffice to remove the polish from the surface, which gradually becomes rough and granular, so that one can wipe off the crumbling powder with the hand. In the air of large towns other acids, produced from the burning of coal, are added to the atmosphere and increase the solvent action of the rain."

Excessive use of other stone is also a mistake, as we may see at Drayton Manor, Witley Court, and many other British gardens, also abroad, as at Potsdam, and in the Italian gardens, where statues of inferior merit mar any good effect that one might look for in a true garden.

The terrace is in place only when it is need of the ground. To make holes in the earth is to spoil the ground and a wasteful error. I remember once in Ireland, near a beautiful bay, seeing a huge formless mound of some thousands of tons of earth, and learnt that it was the earth that had been dug up to make a terrace which was quite needless in the situation. Many a fine foreground has been spoiled by the terrace. If terracing is really needed, the stone-work should certainly be left to the architect.

Water should reflect light and have some relation to natural conditions, as the lie of ground, but very often in gardens it is seen in petty stone basins near the house. One in Surrey is cut up by a little canal 18 inches wide. Trivial fountain basins are a mistake, and bring the mosquito. The recent addition to the garden flora of many noble hardy Water Lilies is some need for water; but for various good reasons artificial water is best as far away from the house as the ground will allow.

After the disfigurement of trees the next most fatal defect in modern gardens is the stereotyped flower garden. There was a time when the architect, impatient of the gardener's labours, attempted by means of coloured gravel, clipped trees, and various contrivances, to get a settled and permanent effect. That meant death in the flower garden, as may be seen in many old books where gardens were traceries made like panels in the house. There was no pleasure in this sort of garden, and people eventually tired of it and often put down grass instead as we may see about some of our finest old houses. In a book lately published on garden ornament, we may see a number of such pattern gardens with as much thought of life as in designs for wall-papers or carpets. One might as well attempt to stereotype the clouds of heaven as get a stamped arrangement of the flower garden. The flower garden should abound in life and beauty of form all through the summer and be the scene of the labours of men every fine day in the winter and spring. How stupid then to attempt to stamp all life and change out of a garden!

Another reason for architects keeping to their own essential work is the fact that the building art is in a state of decadence in our day. A much-trusted architect deplored to me the state of building in all parts of the country, saying that as the years go on the work becomes steadily worse. And this in spite of the number of journals and professors, just as in the art of painting, there never was so much teaching and so much bad painting. One may go along miles of road and never see a well-built cottage; but, instead, every variety of bizarre colour and flimsy structure. London is hideous with brick, and all the beautiful garden land of the home counties is bespattered with villas (not Italian) ugly in wall and roof.

EVIL EFFECT OF BOOKS
ON ITALIAN GARDENS

Heavy clay-loaded books on Italian gardens are now often issued; the photograph and the clayed paper of our day make these easier to print than in old days. When we look into them we find nothing about gardens—much stone-work out of place, extravagance in decoration; the parterre gardens not the best for gardeners to plant. The old Italians, content with these things, had no ideas of a true garden—but on the contrary, left Nature out of the scene. About their beautiful Northern lakes, the idea of the garden as a place for statues and stone-work out of place has given way before the garden flora of the northern world, and we may see these gardens full of life and beauty. In English gardens, where any copy of the Italian idea was attempted, the result was disastrous. Any lover of gardens who comes under the influence of such books had better see the meaning of planting in our islands by studying examples of the natural and artistic ways. Also of good landscape painting—not common, but in the work of the great masters, English or French, full of instruction. It may be well to see examples of the sham Italian garden, and the misuse of sculpture with our gardens. In France the sculptors had gone so far in destroying the charm and repose of the paths that the critics began to cry out in their journals and so stopped the outrage; but how get rid of the harm done? What may be learned in Italy is the beautiful landscape—a lovely mountain flora, thick in vast pastures on their flanks and summits even; a lovely Alpine flora; valleys flowing down from the Alps; everywhere many beautiful scenes; the cultivated fields, olive gardens; vineyards.

Great cities, rich in museums, telling us of the ancient life of the land, old, mediæval and modern, of the most fascinating of countries.

Cities like Paris and London offer so many worthy sites for statues of value in and around public buildings, open squares, and boulevards that there was no excuse for them in the parks. But there has been signs of their presence so much that art critics in the Paris *Figaro* rightly denounced the practice. In the Park Monceau, a charming retreat in Paris, it was too evident, and among them a monument to Maupassant, the dirtiest writer who ever soiled the literature of France.

In Hyde Park an outrage in the name of sculpture is perpetrated by a Mr Epstein. Of it the Hon. John Collier, a distinguished artist of our day, said at a dinner of the Artists' Club:—

"Here you have a female figure purporting to represent an exquisitely beautiful girl. What do we get? I have no hesitation in calling it a bestial figure, horribly misshapen, with enormous claw-like hands and withered pendulous breasts, an enormous and distorted pelvis, and head and face of a micro-cephalous idiot. Nearly all the critics, and high-brows who are not critics, go into ecstasies over the monstrous perversion of the female form.

"What distressed him most about the business was that Mr Bernard Shaw had expressed his approval of the monstrosity. Mr Bernard Shaw was compelled by his nature to contradict any opinion which was held by the public, though this opinion might be quite right."

As to private gardens, where one seeks the quiet of the garden of which Marvell speaks so well, one sees cement showing its ugly face. In one home county there may be seen an avenue of grotesque life-size figures, certainly not the work of any garden artist, and in another a maze with the figures of the natives of our isles—English, Scottish, Welsh and Irish—done in mean metal and as garden ornaments.

CHAPTER XXXIX

Topiarian Follies

In recent years an attempt has been made to make more popular and harmful this outrage on natural form. I read the following in best type in the staid columns of the *Observer* under the heading "Tree-Sculpture":—

> One may see trees—mostly Yew and Box—whose foliage ascends in spirals round their stems, like garlands twisted round so many Maypoles; trees cut into the shape of pillars and surmounted with leafy balls one on top of the other; trees in the forms of birds standing, sitting, and flying; trees shaped like pyramids, and even trees representing jugs and basins.

False forms of tree here, but not a word of the Yew in its natural form, so good that it deserves the name of our native Cedar. This true form may not be seen in many gardens, owing to the misuse of the tree usually clipped. To see the tree in its true beauty we must seek it along the North Downs by the Pilgrims' Way or in a country graveyard. Then in the *Times*:—

> Birds, without base, take about ten or twelve years to grow, and dogs from twelve to twenty years, while other subjects, requiring anything from ten to ninety years, include peacocks, serpents, and serpentine columns, tables, armchairs, sitting hens, geese and ducks, dogs (with and without kennels), ships, horses, and pigs. One man in the North had his crest, a pelican feeding her young, grown in Yew.

The fact is, a Dutch nurseryman possessing a stock of these distortions gave a dinner to the reporters of the daily and other journals; these took the man at his own estimate, and so we get many Press puffs of the most impudent outrage ever perpetrated on natural beauty in our gardens. The infliction has come to our gardens from Dutch William mainly. From his day date most of the examples of tree spoliation in our land. Not only does it mean the ruin of tree form, but injury to the gardens too. Ask the gardener at Northiam, Elvaston, Levens, or in any place where this parody of an art is carried out what they think of its effect on the growth of flower and shrub and you may hear the truth that it is very difficult to grow flower or shrub near the misplaced trees.

Ignoble labour, too, to the men who have to carry it out. The work of disfiguring was bad at all times, now deplorable when the flowering trees and shrubs from China and Japan are coming to us. Good taste is a more likely comrade of humility, and goes with a childlike reverence for the work of the Creator, as shown to us in the clouds, the mountains, the waves, the forests, the flowers, and in the flight of birds.

Much topiary work is inherited from the practice of clipping trees to conform to the lines of buildings. Many places are spoilt for the artist by the hard lines of clipped Yew, and not a naturally grown Yew to be seen. It is easy to get good dividing lines without disfiguring trees; lines that call for clipping mean the destruction of all form.

Topiarian effects appeal only to those blind to the grace and movement of the free, natural form. To artists of all lands we may, if need be, appeal. France, in its home landscapes, has for ages been disgraced by the Topiarian practice, and here is what one of her gifted writers, Theophile Gautier, says:—

> Les arbres du parc de Versailles portent des boucles et des frisures comme les courtisans; les poèmes sont tracés au cordeau comme les allées. Partout la régularité froide est substituée au charmant désordre de la vie; et qui produit une impression à peu près pareille à celle que vous donnent les jardins de Le Nôtre ou de la Quintinie; partout du marbre, du bronze, des Neptunes, des tritons, des nymphes, des rocailles, des bassins, des grottes, des colonnades, des ifs en quenouille, des buis en pot-au-feu.

In much of Northern Europe the evergreen trees that grace our land in winter are not to be seen save in a tub in a hall or glass-house. Holly, Ivy, true Laurel are killed before the winter frost. The true Laurel of the Greeks is, in our southern counties and near our coast, as happy in the open air as by a stream in Greece. To supply the need in the frozen

North a large business with evergreens in tubs has arisen in Holland and Belgium. The trees are grown in tubs; miles of them may be seen in nurseries.

A great danger in our isles arises from the constant practice of planting the Yew in gardens and by approaches, and it is sad to read this note in a daily paper:—

> More than fifty sheep out of a large flock pastured in West Lothian died from the effects of eating leaves of Yew trees.

The tree is deadly for stock in all states, and if a record could be made of its destructiveness it would amaze. The deaths of many animals are wrongly attributed to other causes. Worse still, the ignorance of the pretended landscape gardeners, who scatter the Yew liberally about, even near the approaches to the house, where the horses can scarcely miss it.

> I must write to tell you of our sad experience of the fatal effects of Yew clippings. About the beginning of the year some Yew trees had to be cut and some (not a large quantity) of the clippings were thrown on a rubbish heap in what we call the park. No one seems to have known the danger. A few weeks after, our tenant turned seven bullocks into the park, and four of the seven died. We have had to pay compensation for the act of our servant. The man did not know, and even a nursery gardener whom I had to see in connection with the matter was ignorant of the danger. You cannot emphasise too strongly the necessity of keeping Yew, alive or dead, out of the reach of stock and of horses which I am told are even more easily killed.—A. F. KIRKPATRICK, Deanery, Ely.

Even the arrival court to a country house is often bordered by a line of Yew near for any straying animal to poison itself. In many cases where the hard line of the Yew hedge is used it is to get a less artistic result than could be got in other ways by low walls, fences, and evergreens like Holly and Box, guileless of poisoning.

Anything more inartistic or wrong as to planting, than the clipping of trees, could not be conceived; all the more so when practised upon shrubs like the Holly, the beauty of which depends on the growth being free. The graceful toss and growth, and the play of light and shade, and, last of all, the finest effect of our winters, the berries of the Holly. Unhappily, when people see this clipping practised in public gardens they are very apt to imitate it in their own gardens, and thus acres of beautiful evergreens in the suburbs of London and every city in Britain are disfigured in the same way. The common idea that the hard line of clipped Yew hedge is the best background for garden effects is wrong, and may well be got out of the heads of designers of gardens.

BEAUTY AND SHELTER FROM EVERGREEN FOREST TREES

The following from the *Field*, 13th August 1925, tells of my effort here to soften the winter aspect of our woods, by planting the evergreen forest trees of the Northern world, many of which are as hardy as our native trees and thrive as well in our clime as on the mountains of California, N.W. America, and also of the mountains of Europe and North Africa.

"Few are aware of the wealth of beauty to be obtained from the planting of some of the noble evergreen forest trees of the north temperate regions. Not only is there beauty of form in the individual trees, but when they are boldly massed they give a warmth and shelter during the bleak winter months that one looks for in vain in a summer-leafing forest. Perhaps one of the best examples to show how to make a beautiful evergreen forest in the course of thirty years is to be seen near East Grinstead, at Gravetye, a little more than 30 miles from London. When he first went to Gravetye there were no noble North American evergreen forest trees on the estate, nor planted in the forest way. Nor was there any advantage taken of such trees for their value as shelter belts, or for their great natural beauty. The iron-bound clumps that occur in so many parks were no protection to man or beast, and the dotting about here and there of a few specimens were of little landscape value. Due north of the old Elizabethan mansion were some acres of open land bearing crops of oats that were not worth cutting; so in their place were planted Pine trees of approved hardiness. Only the wild or natural species were used; all fancy and variegated forms were excluded, as these never make good forest trees.

"The little trees were two to three years of age from seed, once transplanted. There was no trenching or other preparation of the ground, and it would have been a great mistake to have used older plants for the purpose. The little trees soon got their heads well up, and being closely planted in the forest way, they soon smothered the weeds and grass. For 'nurses' were used young Larch: also the common Furze or Gorse, sown when the trees were young, was a gain in nourishing one plantation of Corsican Pines to such an extent that the young Pines soon got the mastery of the Furze.

"There was only one failure among the Pines, and that was the white Pine of N.E. America (Pinus strobus), which could not endure in the cold clay. It was not the climate that was at fault, as this tree does as well on the shaly hills of Wales as it does in its own country. The finest Pine of Europe is the Corsican (P. Laricio). It leads the way for rapid and erect growth. Many of the Californian conifers have also done well at Gravetye, and the Sitka Spruce (Picea sitchensis) has been a great success, and now forms a vigorous grove. The Riga Fir, a good form of the Scots Fir, and the giant Thuya plicata are amongst the most vigorous; while the western Hemlock (Tsuga Albertiana) has grown into lovely and stately trees, making a fine shelter on the higher ground. The Algerian silver Fir (Abies numidica), which is found among the Cedars on Mount Babor, grows well; and the Himalayan blue Pine (P. excelsa) has been happy for thirty years on a bank of sandstone rock. The Swiss or Arolla Pine (P. cembra), although a slow grower, thrives on the cooler soils, and is at all seasons a good and effective shelter. For poor land and a northern aspect the white Spruce (Picea alba) thrives apace and makes a good shelter tree. The Austrian Pine does much better massed in the forest way than dotted on grass. It is also a valuable soil improver, as it sheds its leaves or "needles" in great profusion. The Colorado Fir (Abies concolor) grows well when put in the soil without preparation: while the valley Spruce (Abies grandis) from the same region charms by its grace and vigour in the poor soil of the wood.

"Our native Yew was sparse in the woods. It has been cut out in hedgerows and carefully trimmed up above the reach of any straying horse or cow. Any young Yew trees found in the place were put together in a group by themselves in a wood, and were carefully trimmed up out of harm's way, the trimmings being burnt on the spot. In its natural form the Yew is a beautiful tree and makes a fine shelter for game.

"Single trees are not alluded to in these notes, but only trees planted in large numbers to enable one to judge of their value for the forest or woodland. In all, over 70 acres of evergreen forest trees have proved their merit during the past thirty years, and what were at one time bare in winter are now a forest land filled with Pines, Firs and Spruces, which have flourished without the aid of trenching, digging or manuring. The planter rightly held that if the trees could not live and thrive in the natural soil they would not be of general use. Besides which a tree that would flourish without help, was the tree most suitable for the district.

"The results of the planting is that fine shelters have been made against prevailing winds. To go into a grove of Corsican Pines in a wild 'north-easter' is now like going into another clime, so noticeable are the warmth and shelter. In addition, one must consider the improvement in the landscape effect by the masses of evergreen forest trees, increasing by contrast the beauty of our native Oaks, Ashes or Beeches.

"To protect the Lebanon Cedar from rabbits, the way was found to bind a big faggot around the base of each tree, and this kept it safe for years. In regard to the Cedar of Lebanon, the planter thinks that it would be much better grouped, so that it might enjoy shelter and nourishment from all the rain that falls, and that Larch makes a good nurse until such time as the young Cedars become established. Grown singly, the Cedar gets no shelter from its fellows, and often little water, as the grass keeps this for its own needs."

CHAPTER XL

The Pergola

This is almost a need of the South of France and of Italy, often made in rough materials, but even then a useful thing for the farmer and vinegrower, who uses it to grow grapes. I said: now this is a beautiful idea if we could only get the climbing plants we have in England on such a structure; so I went to work to make myself a pergola beginning with one from the front garden to the kitchen—a route to follow. After several failures of the ordinary underwood trees of the place to make a pergola, I tried another experiment and got in one of those Sussex woodmen that William Cobbett praised so much, who knew the woods. We put our heads together and thought of the many stubs in the woods. Much of the land has always been woodland, as far as we know, and so we thought of the stubs, very strong ones, which had been cut for many generations. We found them and brought them in and put them at set intervals along the path, hoping that an oak staff in them would do all we wanted; but after twelve years' patient waiting we saw it was a vain thing and had to be given up. Then, at last, I saw the best way in that position was a 9-inch stockbrick pillar. This turned out the best, impervious to water, and, given this, it was easy to put the oak trellis over the rails, not touching the earth in any part. We lime-whited over the bricks, and the effect was very good in the summer and never failed us. This was our smallest pergola and was the best.

Then came the question of support for the many Clematis we had in vigorous health in the garden, and to support these the oak inserted in the ground did not last; was, in fact, a failure, so we thought the best way was to raise the oak trellis on an iron base. We used strong iron fencing, fixed our oak battens on this about a foot from the earth, and thus we had plenty of room to put our seasoned oak battens in the best and most enduring conditions. The effect of this has been quite satisfactory. For many years, on fine summer and autumn days, we had the Clematis in fine health on these.

Then came a wish to have a pergola on the west and north sides of the flower garden, but raised a few feet above its level. In that case we used plenty of seasoned oak but omitted to put a stone base under the wood, and so decay began. To get the effect right we had to insert brick or stone bases to the pillars and so free the oak from decay. This was not so simple as if we had thought of the right plan to base the pillars on stone or brick in the beginning; but once done, this turned out very satisfactory and was easily covered with Clematis, Vine, and Roses; and as the effect was on three sides we covered it all with creepers, vine and the best climbers, and never found a better way to get a good effect of these plants.

To get from the flower garden to the playground meant a considerable rise of the ground, and on hot days was not pleasant, so we made a stout, airy pergola, built with pillars of 14-inch stockbrick. This turned out very well and has carried any number of the climbing plants of the north.

Then came the necessity, after several failures, to get a good pergola to enable the carts to clear the hay. This we dug with great care at first, so as to have the pillars all set in stone. We had so many Wistarias near that it was easy to bring them over the pergola, and you never saw such a good effect as we thus obtained from these plants. This was one of the various ways in which we trained this beautiful climber, and it has turned out well in every case.

APPENDIX

This volume is basically the main section of the Fifteenth edition of Robinson's book, published in January 1933. It was reprinted in November 1934, a few months before the author's death, and that reprint has been used for this edition in the belief that it represents the author's latest views of his subject. It was the last edition of the book as such because the Sixteenth edition, issued 22 years later was "completely revised and edited by Roy Hay and reset with new material." Hay, a noted gardening journalist of the period, wrote a Foreword in which he said:

> The book which follows cannot please the devotees of William Robinson [because] . . . I have tried to make it fit the needs of a new generation . . . [I have had] to seek the help of specialists [particularly] M.A.T. Johnson. On him, rightly, should fall the mantle of William Robinson.

Hay added "Robinson had a hatred of Latin names . . . but for the sake of easy reference the Latin equivalent will always be found in the index [here]". Hay's Sixteenth edition can therefore be taken to be a quite different book from Robinson's, published because of the popularity of its model. However the publishers, Murrays, never re-issued Robinson's book again.

The notes which follow give a résumé of the various editions of Robinson's book, all published by Murray.

1883 First edition. This contained several pieces which were not reprinted in the later editions e.g. an essay on railway bank terraces.

1889 Second edition. The Preface claims that "many changes have been made, though it would probably be a better book if anyone who wrote [such] a book with a useful aim were compelled by law to keep to it and mend [amend] it all his life." The many changes included an end section called *Wasted Effort* which covered such subjects as "the endless shaving of lawns", "needless walks" plus, of course, "the evils of the bedding system".

It is interesting to note that from this Second edition onwards, Robinson was writing from his estate in Sussex, having bought Gravetye in 1883 after selling some of his city properties. However, he travelled to London daily, catching the 7am train from Three Bridges.

1893 Third edition. In this version Robinson explains that the old type has been broken up and the opportunity taken to add many flowering shrubs and trees to the second section though "the need of keeping the book to the handbook [style] precludes any considerable enlargement . . . I shall however never give up hope of making it better . . . I regret the book has long been out of print, and hope to prevent this in the future."

1895 Fourth edition. Amongst new material, Robinson wrote on Art in Relation to Flower-Garden and Garden Design.

1896 Fifth ("New") edition, reprinted 1897. Robinson listed about 100 contributors from his journal *The Garden* whose writings were published here.

1898 Sixth edition, reprinted same year. This is dedicated to W.T. Thistleton-Dyer of Kew.

1899 Seventh edition. Dedicated to the very Rev. Reynolds Hole. It has 3 additional chapters: XXXII; Flower Gardens, Pleasure Gardens, Bridges, Seats; XXXIII; "The Orchard Beautiful". XXXIV; "Labours for Good or Evil" Soils; Water Draining; Weeds and Rubbish Heaps; Monotony; Staking; Glass; Wasted Labour in Moving Earth; Trellising Best".

1900 Eighth edition, reprinted 4 times to 1903. Dedicated to M.B. Latour-Martin, the expert on water liles.

1905 Ninth edition. Contains one new Chapter II "Garden Design and Recent Writing upon it".

1906 Tenth edition, reprinted 1907.

1909 Eleventh edition, reprinted 1911.

1913 Twelfth edition, reprinted 1914. Contains an additional Chapter XXXVI "My Flower Garden".

1921 Thirteenth edition. Contains many new chapters, including "Topiarian Follies", reprinted from *The Times* 24 July 1915.

1926 Fourteenth edition. This contains the "New Preface" reprinted in the Fifteenth edition as "Preface to the New Edition". Also a new Chapter I "Landscape Mistakes near the Country House" followed by "Some Evils of Bedding and Carpet Gardening" and "Misuse of the Yew". Next an example of a "Hardy Flower Garden which was Gravetye in 1922".

INDEX